WITCH HUNT

The Persecution of Witches in England

David & Andrew Pickering

AMBERLEY

David Pickering provided the original pen and ink illustrations for this book

This edition first published 2013

Amberley Publishing
The Hill, Stroud
Gloucestershire, GL5 4EP

www.amberley-books.com

British Library Cataloguing in Publication Data.
A catalogue record for this book is available from the British Library.

ISBN 978 1 4456 0861 7

Typesetting and Origination by Amberley Publishing.
Printed in the UK.

CONTENTS

ABOUT THE AUTHORS

David Pickering graduated in English from St Peter's College, Oxford. An experienced writer, editor, and illustrator, he has compiled or contributed to nearly 250 reference books, mostly in the areas of the arts, English language, history, folklore, entertainment, and popular interest. As author, these have included a *Dictionary of Superstitions* (1995), a *Dictionary of Witchcraft* (1996), a *Dictionary of Folklore* (1999), a *Dictionary of Proverbs* (2001), a *Dictionary of Saints* (2004), *Pirates* (2006), *Ancient Rome* (2007), and a *Dictionary of Allusions* (2008). He has also broadcast many times on a variety of subjects on radio and television and lives in Buckingham with his wife, Jan, and two sons.

David's younger brother, Andrew Pickering, is a graduate in Medieval and Modern History from the University of Birmingham, and he also has Master's degrees in Victorian Studies from the University of Keele and in Archaeology and Heritage Management from the University of Leicester. He is a Senior Lecturer at Strode College in Somerset and Programme Manager of a University of Plymouth degree in History, Heritage and Archaeology. He has written several textbooks for A level students including *Lancastrians to Tudors* (2000), *Race and American Society* (2009), and *Different Interpretations of Witch-hunting in Early Modern Europe* (2009). He is presently working on a book concerning Britain's Iron Age slave trade. He lives in Bruton with his wife, Lisa, and two of their four children.

PREFACE

A great deal has been written about the witch-hunting phenomenon in early modern Europe over the last forty years. For students of the period the subject provides an ideal vehicle for exploring different historical approaches and modes of interpretation. For the academic historian, it is a battlefield of conflicting ideas. For the lay reader, it is a fascinating mystery and a shocking illustration of the capacity of individuals and communities to persecute.

Although witchcraft accusation accounts for a fraction of the punishments meted out by courts in the period, this crime has received the most attention both because of our enduring fascination with the supernatural, and also, when we see beyond the illusory magic, because of its apparent absurdity. Early commentators on the subject sought to find a rational explanation for witch-hunting by identifying a genuine cult of witches; more recently historians have tried to 'make sense' of it by providing a range of psychological, structural and functional explanations. Where their predecessors searched for links between pagan belief systems and the alleged behaviour of the witches of the Renaissance and Reformation eras, modern historians are more likely to take an anthropological approach by analysing what inspires witch-hunters in the modern world – for example, the horrific persecution of child 'witches' in parts of Nigeria.

This book aims to provide an overview of the subject, both in terms of its narrative and its historiography. This kind of information, of course, can be found in numerous sources, including books written by both of the present authors. What, hopefully, warrants a further book on the subject is the attempt here to organise witch-hunting episodes both chronologically *and* geographically – an approach that both promotes comparative study and helps the modern reader to engage with the subject by locating it in both time and place. As we have explained in the introduction to the gazetteer, the list is incomplete, partly because of authorial choice, but mainly because of the absence of evidence. Despite these shortcomings, as far as we are aware, this is the most comprehensive catalogue of English witch hunts that has been made readily available to the general reader since the publication of E. L'Estrange Ewen's pioneering works *Witch Hunting and Witch Trials* (1929) and *Witchcraft and Demonism* (1933). Where Ewen's lists were organised by Assize circuits, this gazetteer is organised by county and a detailed index of places enables the reader to identify witch-hunting episodes with modern towns and villages.

It is salutary to remember that, however remote the events described in these pages may seem, the victims and persecutors described in these pages were our ancestors. As an illustration of this truth, in our researches in the field of witchcraft we have come across a number of Pickerings; David, the family genealogist, has traced a likely ancestral link between our branch of the extended family and the seventeenth-century witchfinder Sir Gilbert Pickering of Titchmarsh. However, balancing things somewhat, quite a few Pickering women also appear as victims, and these too may well be distant relations. Since our mutual passion for all things historical was acquired from more recent Pickerings – our parents – we would like to dedicate this book to our mother, Valerie Pickering, and to the memory of our much missed father, Donald Pickering.

Andrew Pickering
Bruton, Somerset
February 2010

INTRODUCTION

The disgusting part of the whole story relates not so much to the acts of the witches, as to their ill-treatment by the public, the Church, the courts, the prison authorities, the witch-finders, and the body searchers, and to the final scene of a ghastly blot on Christianity, the exhibition by the hangman of his perquisite, the dead body.

E. L'Estrange Ewen (1933), *Witchcraft and Demonism*, p. 141

Starting in the early 1400s and more or less over by the 1770s, the great age of witch-hunting in western Europe was that of the sixteenth and seventeenth centuries. Historians' estimates of the total number of people executed for witchcraft presently fall within the range of 40,000-100,000 with, perhaps, something in the region of double that number facing charges.[1] These contested statistics reflect the difficulties that an incomplete historical record present to historians. All, however, agree with Norman Cohn (1975) that older estimates 'which put the figure [for executions] at some hundreds of thousands, are fantastic exaggerations'.[2] Of these, less than 1000, perhaps as few as 500, were English 'witches'.

Witch-hunts occurred in many parts of Europe, particularly in the central regions and in the far north. Most major hunts were carried out in German-speaking territories, although significant witch-hunting episodes can be identified in other places, however, including Sweden and the Basque region. Some historians have concluded that small autonomous or semi-independent principalities in the cultural 'borderlands' of Europe, such as Alsace-Lorraine and Luxembourg, were particularly susceptible. Other places however, such as southern Italy, were scarcely affected at all.

WITCH-HUNTING IN ENGLAND

For many centuries prior to 1500 attitudes towards witchcraft were relatively relaxed and it had no special legal significance. If criminal activity was proved, however, those guilty of sorcery risked severe punishment in much the same manner as any other transgressor.

In the medieval period, witchcraft was interpreted as a crime against man, rather than against God, and it was dealt with in a similar fashion as other offences: cases depended largely upon hard evidence of actual criminality, such as damage to crops or proven threat to life through poisons or spells. Witches were thus judged by their deeds, and proof of *maleficia* (evil acts) was necessary to obtain a conviction. Records exist of several suspected witches in medieval times being released by the courts or suffering only the mildest of punishments because no one could prove they had done any harm. As late as 1560, indeed, eight men who had actually confessed to conjuration and sorcery were released after a brief stay in the pillory and after promising not to practise witchcraft in the future.

In common with other suspected criminals in medieval times, witches could elect to undergo trial by ordeal. The first person to be charged with sorcery in England was Agnes, wife of Odo, who was arraigned in 1209 but acquitted after successfully undergoing the ordeal of grasping a red-hot iron. The ecclesiastical courts investigated alleged cases of sorcery and witchcraft until the fourteenth century, handing condemned persons over to the secular authorities for punishment. The first witchcraft trial to be heard in the secular courts took place in 1324, when twenty-seven people were charged in Coventry with consulting necromancers in a plot to kill the king.

The use of torture was not permitted in conventional English witchcraft trials and civil courts by tradition would not accept unsupported confessions as evidence and demanded fairly substantial proof of *maleficia*. Cases in which noblemen were implicated were taken rather more seriously by the civil courts, because they involved a risk of treason against the Crown, and defendants might be brought before the Privy Council or arraigned before a court of Bishops.

Witchcraft trials were extremely rare until the first statute to deal specifically with witchcraft was passed in 1542, during the reign of Henry VIII. This formalising of old assumptions could be seen as an element in the the so-called 'Tudor revolution in government' and the secularisation of offences that previously might have been considered Church affairs. It is probably no coincidence that this legislation was passed in the aftermath of the the Henrician Reformation that united Church and State under the King. The Act made no reference to pacts with the Devil, although it did comment on 'the conjuration of Spirits'. It demanded harsh penalties for alchemists and witches who aimed to perform *maleficia* through black magic, including the use of waxen images ('poppets'). Witchcraft itself, however, was still no grounds for a

Example of a witch's poppet, pierced in the eye, preserved in the Witchcraft Museum, Boscastle, Cornwall.

case and, as things turned out, only one suspect (later pardoned) was arrested under the Act before it was repealed by Edward VI in 1547. A new Act was prepared in 1559 but failed to become law and, for a few years, there was no statute prohibiting witchcraft in English law.

The climate changed significantly in 1563 when new legislation designed to control witches was issued under Elizabeth I. The Queen herself had supposedly been the target of several witchcraft plots, and she evidently appreciated that allegations by fortune-telling sorcerers that the monarch had little time to live could easily provoke a rebellion led by those looking to the succession. Several of Elizabeth's Protestant bishops had been influenced by witch burnings that they had witnessed in other countries, and pressed repeatedly for sterner measures to be taken at home. Bishop John Jewel, preaching before the Queen at Oxford around 1560, broke from his prepared text to deliver an alarmist warning about the activities of witches throughout the realm, claiming that because of witches 'Your Grace's subjects pine away even unto death, their colour fadeth, their flesh rotteth, their speech is benumbed, their senses are bereft.'

The 1563 Act was rooted in the key concept that witchcraft involved the 'conjurations of evil and wicked spirits' and that it was 'contrary to the laws of Almighty God'. Murder by witchcraft was punishable by death, and for those found guilty of using witchcraft to cause the 'wasting', 'laming', or 'consuming' of a person, or equivalent damage to his goods and chattels, the statute imposed a year's imprisonment and life for re-offenders and the death penalty if convicted on the same charges a second time. The method of execution was hanging 'by the neck until he or she be dead'.

A year's imprisonment was stipulated for any attempt to injure, kill, provoke a person 'to unlawful love', or to use witchcraft to find lost or hidden objects. A second offence of this kind was punishable by life imprisonment and the confiscation by the Crown of the individual's property. During the year of imprisonment the convicted

Hanging was the normal mode of execution for convicted witches in sixteenth and seventeenth century England.

The 1563 Witchcraft Act stipulated imprisonment and appearances in the pillory for certain offences.

witch was to be pilloried in a public place in the local market town for the duration of six hours, once in each quarter of the year. Any substantial length of time in a squalid Tudor prison was likely to be fatal for those so punished.

The reasons for the re-identification of witchcraft as a crime at the start of Elizabeth's reign are subject to debate. Historians in their explanations have paid particular attention to the context in which the legislation was passed, which included the passing of the throne from the overtly Roman Catholic Queen, Mary I, to her Protestant sister, Elizabeth. Some have also highlighted the significance of developments on the Continent in this period, including the enthusiasm for witch-hunting abroad in an age of confessional conflict. English Protestant theologians at the start of Elizabeth I's reign, some of whom had been exiled to continental Europe during Mary I's counter-Reformation, considered both witchcraft and Catholicism dangerous superstitions. It has long been thought that the phrase 'Hocus Pocus', used to mimic a magic incantation, is derived from the sacred words *'hoc est corpus'* ('Here is the body') as stated by Catholic priests in the Eucharist ceremony, the sacred Holy Communion that focused on the miracle of transubstantiation: the transformation of bread to flesh and wine to blood. Real and imagined Catholic plots in Elizabeth's reign, and also at the start of James I's, may have contributed to the stiffening of witchcraft legislation and helped to stimulate the anxieties that encouraged persecution of supposed 'deviants'.

Among the first major witchcraft trials to be based on the 1563 Act were those of the Chelmsford witches in 1566 and of the St Osyth witches in 1582, both in the county of Essex, followed by that of the Warboys witches in Huntingdon in 1593. Essex, a centre of Protestant dissent in the first half of the sixteenth century, came to be considered a hotbed of witchcraft activity and the majority of cases based on

Elizabeth's Act arose in the south-eastern counties, although subsequent decades saw concentrations of cases in Lancashire and Somerset among other areas. Another Act, in 1581, tightened up the prohibition against fortune-tellers and witches in general, and in all 535 indictments on charges of witchcraft were issued during the Queen's reign. Eighty-two of the witches tried were put to death, the first being sixty-three-year-old Agnes Waterhouse, who was hanged in Chelmsford in 1566. This was not to say, however, that the courts were entirely incapable of rejecting accusations based on dubious evidence: several celebrated cases resulted in the exposure of hoaxes (as, for instance, in the matters of the Burton Boy in 1597 and the Bilson Boy in 1622).

James I had developed a keen interest in the persecution of witches while reigning as James VI of Scotland. Shortly after he became king of England, a new Act of Parliament (1604) made the law even less tolerant by introducing the death penalty for every instance of causing injury by witchcraft. Conviction for intent to use witchcraft provided for the same punishment as the Elizabethan statute for first-time offenders but death for repeat offenders. Death by hanging now became mandatory even for first offences if *maleficia* were proved, and it did not matter whether the victim had actually died or not – it was more than sufficient if he or she had, by magic, been 'killed, destroyed, wasted, consumed, pined, or lamed in his or her body, or any part thereof'. Furthermore, the new legislation, unlike that of 1563, emphasised the diabolical dimension of witchcraft activity by making it a capital offence to consort with evil spirits or to remove body parts from graves for maleficent purposes.

In exceptional cases, in which heresy, poisoning, or treason was the charge, death could be by burning. Mother Lakeland of Ipswich, for example, was burned to death in 1645 for bewitching her husband to death, a deed that constituted an act of treason. Making a pact with the Devil also became a felony, as did keeping or consorting with 'any evil and wicked spirit', digging up corpses to use in spells, preparing love potions and divining the whereabouts of hidden treasure. The 1604 Act remained on the statute book until 1736, and it was under this Act that many of the most important English witch trials were prosecuted, including those of the Pendle witches in 1612, when nine were hanged, and of the later generation of Chelmsford witches in 1645, which resulted in the biggest mass execution in England. In America the Act was cited as the basis for the prosecution of the Salem witches.

Unlike certain other parts of Europe, burning was rarely the means of execution of witches in early modern England.

The person accused of witchcraft could be convicted without the evidence needed for the prosecution of most other crimes. For example, having an alibi made little or no difference in a case where sorcery was involved since the effect of the magic and the doing of the magic could be far apart in terms of both time and place. The secrecy of the witch's activities reduced the likelihood of witnesses to the crime and thus led one influential legal adviser in England in 1618 to instruct 'half proofes are to be allowed, and are good causes for suspition'.[3] The difficulty of finding witnesses could result in the relaxing of rules regarding witness statements from the spouse or children of the accused.

Alan Macfarlane has summarised the types of evidence needed in England to secure a trial:

> notorious reputation as a witch; cursing followed by an injury to the person cursed; known malice followed by a misfortune to the object of the malice; a relationship by blood or friendship to a proven witch; the victim's recovery after the suspected witch had been scratched or some of her property had been burnt; failure of the suspect to sink when immersed in water; an implicit confession by the suspect ('you should have left me alone then', in answer to an accusation by a neighbour, is an example); over-diligent interest in a sick neighbour on the part of a suspected witch.[4]

Certain 'strong presumptions' might result in a conviction. These included accusation by a 'white witch' and a deathbed accusation by the supposed victim of witchcraft. Most damning of all were the 'sufficient proofs', which included 'accusation by another witch; an unnatural mark on the body supposedly caused by the Devil or a familiar; two witnesses who claimed to have seen the accused either make a pact with Satan or entertain her familiars'.[5] He concludes with a chilling reference to Richard Bernard's *A Guide to Grand Jury Men* (1627):

> The type of evidence required for conviction as a witch can be illustrated by one example: Bernard urged that if a woman gave a child an apple and the receiver became ill soon afterwards, as long as there was known malice between them, this was proof enough for the execution of the accused.[6]

The local elite did not usually have the jurisdiction to try a suspected witch but they could refer the case to a higher authority or request special authorisation to organise a local trial. Although witch-hunting has been construed by some commentators as male-orientated sexual sadism, the intimate examination of women in England was usually carried out by midwives and other women. This was the case, for example, in the searching of Deborah Naylor in Essex in 1650. On this occasion four women, Anne Stannes, Mary Leaper, Mary Cooke, and Margery Silvester, were appointed by the Justice of the Peace, Christopher Muschamp, to carry out the search, which revealed several curious marks and one 'like a teate in her private partes'.[7]

Given their diabolical powers, it is not surprising to discover that accused witches were sometimes held more securely than other prisoners during their pre-sentence imprisonment. At Northampton Gaol they were kept in chains. A pamphlet from 1612, for example, referred to the 'jangling of irons' that held Anne Barber. Of the elderly Ann Foster, incarcerated in 1674, it was recorded in *A Full and True Relation of the Tryal, Condemnation, and Execution of Ann Foster* (1674) that 'No sooner was she brought in, but the Keepers of the Gaol caused her to be chained to a Post that was in the Gaol.' This caused her great pain and she was subsequently unchained to quieten her. However, this had the unfortunate consequence of 'allowing her more liberty that the devil might come to fuck her, the which he usually did, coming constantly in the dead time of the Night in the likeness of a Rat, which at his coming made a most lamentable and hideous noise which affrighted the people that did belong to the Gaol.' Of course rats a-plenty were to be found in a seventeenth-century gaol and the 'lamentable and hideous noise' most likely emanated from the mouth of Ann herself in her pain, grief, and confusion.

English witchcraft trials were usually small-scale, rarely involving more than three alleged witches. Furthermore, unlike most other parts of Europe, witchcraft trials were the business of senior judges who usually held court in circuits where they were not resident. Thus, they were more likely to be culturally and emotionally distanced from the accused than the local, poorly-trained judges elsewhere, who were often ready to condemn their neighbours.

Although England suffered a major witch-hunt in the mid-1640s, compared to, say, Germany, witch-hunting in England was, in Levack's opinion, 'mild and restrained'.[8] The belief in a Devil-worshipping sect, which helped fuel the continental witch-crazes, found in England less fertile ground, not least because the revelation of communal rites, especially the sabbat, typically emerged under the duress of torture. Moreover, witch-hunting in England was not initiated by any form of state Inquisition. In place of inquisitorial procedures, English witch-hunting was entirely reliant upon trial by jury. Consequently, English 'witches' were usually tried for the first offence or offences with which they were charged whereas in many other parts of Europe, by the time the accused got to court, a catalogue of other crimes was likely to have superseded the original.

Of those accused, a high proportion evaded execution. By the end of the seventeenth century it is likely that many cases were thrown out of court by increasingly sceptical authorities without a hearing. However, between 1563 and 1634, forty-six per cent of those tried in Guernsey for whom the record survives (thirty-three out of seventy-eight) were executed. Of the 291 tried in Essex whose fates are known seventy-four (twenty-four per cent) were executed between 1560 and 1672.[9]

SOCIAL CONDITIONS AND POPULAR BELIEFS

In comparison with the country today, early modern England was sparsely populated. The population when the Tudor era began in 1485, for example, is thought to have been scarcely two million, although it had reached about five million by the time Matthew Hopkins launched his infamous Essex witch-hunt in the mid-1640s. This dramatic population growth, albeit from a relatively low base, was a cause of tension in many communities as the scale of unemployment and poverty escalated dramatically in the second half of the sixteenth century. The population doubled in the hundred years between 1530 and 1630. As population growth increased demand for food and other limited resources, this in turn led to unprecedented inflation. The price of bread in England rose around six times in the 150 years after 1500 as real wages fell and the supply of labour outpaced demand. Desperate measures were taken, with the introduction of Elizabeth I's Poor Law at the dawn of the seventeenth century to try to deal with widespread poverty and the threat of roaming bands of beggars. Standards of living continued to decline until the eighteenth century. As the poor increased, the ability and willingness of the better-off to provide for them diminished.

Diseases, including plague and smallpox, were feared by all. Starvation was a real possibility confronting the poorest members of the close-knit communities in which they lived. In England, around one in six harvests was likely to be a total failure. The historian Wolfgang Behringer has argued that adverse climatic conditions during a so-called 'Little Ice Age' was a significant factor in the rise of witch-hunting in early modern Europe.[10]

Medical knowledge was limited and trained doctors were beyond the financial reach of the vast majority of the population. Instead, the poor treated themselves or looked to their neighbours for a cure. The herbalist Nicholas Culpepper noted in 1649 how 'All the nation are already physicians. If you ail anything, every one you meet, whether a man or woman, will prescribe you a medicine for it.'[11] They relied on their own knowledge and that of their neighbours, including the local 'wise woman' or 'cunning man'. In the opinion of the contemporary philosopher Francis Bacon this was not such a bad thing, since 'empirics and old women [were] ... more happy many times in their cures than learned physicians'.[12] His fellow philosopher Thomas Hobbes was of the same opinion, preferring to 'take the advice or take physic from an experienced old woman that had been at many sick people's bedsides, than from the learnedst but unexperienced physician'.[13] A well-known seventeenth-century medical manual, *Severall Chirurgicall Treatises* (Richard Wiseman, 1676), was nicknamed 'Wiseman's Book of Martyrs'.

The belief in witchcraft was shared by members of all social groups. Witchcraft accusations were an occasional part of fifteenth- and sixteenth-century politics, as in the cases of the Duke of Gloucester's wife in the 1440s and Anne Boleyn in the 1530s. The leading academics of the day, such as Elizabeth I's astrologer John Dee, were as likely to dabble in the occult and alchemy as they were in mathematics and natural science.

Witch-hunters had a firm biblical precedent for their activities. In the book of Exodus (Chapter XXII, verse 18) they could read 'Thou shalt not suffer a witch to live'. Elsewhere it was stated that 'A man or woman that hath a familiar spirit, or that is a familiar spirit, or that is a wizard, shall surely be put to death: they shall stone them with stones' (Leviticus XXI, 9) and 'There shall not be found among you anyone ... that useth divination or an enchanter or a witch or a charmer ar a consuler with familiar spirits or a necromancer' (Deuteronomy XVIII, 11).

Ironically, the first major British text on the subject was Reginald Scot's sceptical *Discoverie of Witchcraft* (1584) which refuted the claims of continental works

James I, author of *Daemonologie* (1597).

including the influential *Malleus Maleficarum*. However, in 1597, this was itself refuted by James VI of Scotland's influential *Daemonologie*. The King seems to have picked up his knowledge of continental witchcraft beliefs, including the all-important concept of the diabolic pact, while visiting Denmark to meet his prospective bride. When he returned to Scotland he took a deep interest in the trial of accused witches from North Berwick (1590-92).

When James became King of England in 1603 he had all copies of Scot's book destroyed by royal command, and English law concerning witchcraft was toughened up with the Act of 1604. His ideas concerning covens of potion-brewing witches conspiring in political assassination, key elements in the North Berwick case, clearly inspired Shakespeare's three weird sisters – the witches in 'the Scottish play', *Macbeth* (1605-06). The Pendle affair, England's first major hunt, was partly fuelled by these now contemporary beliefs in England, and the case is a very unusual one in English history in that participation at a sabbat meeting became a main charge and the one that turned it into a 'chain reaction' hunt. But for the English prohibition of the more severe forms of torture, this could have marked the beginning of witch-hunting on a Germanic 'witchcraze' scale.

John Cotta (1575-1650), a Northamptonshire doctor and demonologist, published *The Triall of Witch-craft shewing the true and right method of the Discovery: with a Confutation of erroneous wayes* in 1616. In an earlier book, *Ignorant Practisers of Physicke* (1612), he had exposed the fraudulent practices of 'quack' doctors. In *The Triall of Witch-craft* he is revealed as being fully convinced of the reality of witchcraft while, at the same time, having a keen sense of the medical explanations, revealed through experiment, for certain conditions that might otherwise be blamed on acts of *maleficia*. As Marion Gibson has observed, 'Cotta's book is an excellent illustration of the epistemological confusion surrounding witchcraft, and the way that belief in it was ingrained so that despite possessing a methodology that would eventually undermine belief in witches, early English Renaissance people were largely unable to use it.'[14] Taking a moderate position in the debate that was already raging by the early

Macbeth and the three witches.

THE
INFALLIBLE
TRVE AND ASSV-
RED VVITCH:

O R,

THE SECOND EDITION,
OF THE TRYALL OF
WITCH-CRAFT.

SHEVVING THE RIGHT
AND TRVE METHODE OF
THE DISCOVERIE:

WITH A CONFVTATION OF
ERRONEOVS WAIES, CARE-
FVLLY REVIEWED AND
more fully cleared and
Augmented

By IOHN COTTA, Doctor in Physicke.

LONDON,
Printed by *I. L.* for *R. H.* and are to be sold at the signe of
the *Grey-hound* in *Pauls* Church-yard.
1 6 2 5.

John Cotta, *The Tryall of Witchcraft*, 1616

seventeenth century, Cotta declared of witchcraft: 'Some judge no witches at all, others more then too many, others too few by many, in so opposite extremes, so extremely opposite...'. By tackling the subject of witchcraft he knew his readers might consider he was moving 'out of his supposed precincts' as a physician, demonology primarily being the business of clergymen.

As a doctor, Cotta was routinely confronted with conditions for which he could provide no rational or scientific explanation. Despite observing that 'it is a hard and difficult matter to detect Witch-craft' in such cases, he was not a sceptic in the Reginald Scot mould. He had no doubt that demons and witches were at work in the world. So long as the accuser was 'prudent, judicious, and able to discerne' and had 'reasonable proofe, or at least, likely and faire presumption' he was willing to accept an explanation of witchcraft for the otherwise inexplicable. Consequently, Cotta's book can be regarded as evidence for the theory that the subsequent decline of witch-hunting had at least something to do with expanding scientific knowledge.

Cotta's book was sufficiently influential for early settlers in America to nickname the natives living beside the Demariscotta River in Maine, 'John Cotta' because of their belief in witchcraft.

As more of the elite received university educations and entered the professions, so the demand for a growing range of cheap printed philosophical and religious texts that were rich in tales of magic and witchcraft grew. Lower down the social ladder, local practitioners of magical practices were recognised in most communities. 'Cunning men' and 'wise women' were well established in village life well before the coming of the witch-hunts of the late sixteenth and seventeenth centuries. These practitioners of 'good' magic and other services remained important in their communities throughout the witch-hunting era. Alan Macfarlane concluded that in Elizabethan times 'nowhere in Essex was there a village more than ten miles from a known cunning man/wise woman. The county was covered by a network of magical practitioners.'[15] They had a range of occupations and included among their number schoolmasters, medical practitioners, and yeomen farmers. In his list of sixty-three cunning folk, forty-four are men – an interesting contrast to the preponderance of women (around ninety per cent) charged with witchcraft in seventeenth-century Essex.

In some communities, the victim of witchcraft was likely to fight magic with magic by seeking assistance from the local 'white witch' – a wise woman, an astrologer, or a cunning man. Such a person would deploy their secret knowledge in determining whether the individual was in fact bewitched and identify who had carried out the *maleficium*. According to Thomas, such people played a key role:

> There certainly were cunning men who planted suspicions of witchcraft where none had previously grown, and denounced persons who would not otherwise have been suspected.[16]

One example is that of William Walford of Cold Norton, Essex, of whom it was said:

> his order is, when he comes to visit any sick neighbour, to persuade them that they are bewitched, and tells them withal [that] except they will be of that belief they can very hardly be holpen of their disease and sickness.[17]

Writers such as Keith Thomas and Robin Briggs have identified a symbiotic relationship between witches and 'witch-doctors' like William Walford: 'wherever one is found, there too will the other be'.[18] Of course, the white witch occupied a very dangerous position since he/she was prone to charges of using black magic. For this reason perhaps, some became what Briggs categorises as 'travelling specialists'. He concludes such people played a very important part in the witch-hunt phenomenon:

> It would clearly be wrong to imagine that every witchcraft case involved cunning folk, yet it is hard to think that either belief or persecution could have been so intense without the reinforcement they provided ... What can be said is that across the whole continent there is abundant evidence for the ubiquity of the cunning folk and for their propensity to identify witchcraft as the source of illness or misfortune.[19]

At the heart of popular cosmology, was the principle of order, that everything had its place. In Europe, intellectuals defined their universe in binary terms and the balance between polarised concepts such as night and day, hot and cold, male and female, good and evil. Maintaining the natural balance of the four humours was the focus of western medieval medicine. Malevolent magic that aimed to upset the balance of things needed to be protected against through official sacred religious rites and traditional folk customs. Under such circumstances, as Briggs has concluded, 'there was a tremendous scope for a do-it-yourself magical religion'.[20] Inevitably, when things went wrong, people would be likely to look out for anyone with the magic both to upset or re-order the balance.

It was often assumed that witches kept 'familiars': pet 'imps' that helped them in their *maleficia* and through which the witch was bound to the Devil. Accused women were likely to be searched for special teats by which the familiar could suckle her

Cunning folk, John and Alice West: the king and queen of the fairies, placed in the stocks in 1613.

An early seventeenth-century English witch
and her familiars.

blood. For example, Elizabeth Francis of Hatfield, one of the first witches to be tried
in England in the period, confessed in 1566 to having a demonic cat familiar called
'Satan'. In some cases, the familiar *was* the Devil who could change his appearance
into that of an animal as easily as he could into a tall, dark, handsome man. As the
tradition developed it came to be widely believed that the witch herself was capable
of such shape-shifting.

Although belief in the diabolical pact is now recognised as an important element
in English witch-hunting, the sabbat rarely featured in England's witch trials. Unlike
many continental witches, those in England, typically, were not accused of the more
dramatic crimes such as raising storms and sinking ships. Instead, their *maleficia*,
as indicated in the table below, were likely to be personal and directed at a specific
victim.

Table: Victims of witchcraft in Essex Assize indictments 1560-1680

	NUMBER OF CASES

Humans
    illness
    death
	
	108
	233

total	341
Animals	80
Other property	6

Source: Macfarlane, p. 153

The brewing of potions and weather magic, common elements in continental European cases, were rarely features of English witchcraft accusation.

WITCHES AND NEIGHBOURS

Witches were found most commonly, though not exclusively, in the small rural communities in which most people lived. In these intimate environments there was none of the anonymity that could be found in urban settings. Everyone knew each other's business and life history. Affection and enmity among neighbours could build up over long periods of time. Here, too, the conservative, illiterate peasantry held fast to old beliefs and suspicions, including, perhaps, a belief in witchcraft.

Typically victims of witch-hunts – although there were plenty of exceptions – were elderly, perhaps confused, peasant women, resented by their neighbours and feared because of their solitary and sometimes antisocial ways. All too often the cases against them depended upon hearsay or on highly unreliable testimony obtained from young children, encouraged in their denunciations by witch-hating fanatics, ill-intentioned relatives and neighbours, or gullible priests and judges.

For the last forty years historians of witch-hunting have shared one assumption in this most controversial of subjects – that monocausal explanations for such a complex subject are inadmissible. In his monumental work *Religion and the Decline of Magic*, first published in 1971 and still regarded as essential reading for students of the subject, Keith Thomas identified three elements in the forming of witchcraft accusations: intellectual factors, psychological factors, and sociological factors.[21] Where, traditionally, commentators were led in their thinking by the first of these – intellectual factors such as the influence of contemporary demonological texts – Thomas and his contemporaries were equally concerned with psychological and sociological conditioning. Thomas is closely associated with another great witch-hunt historian, Alan Macfarlane, who, with his *Witchcraft in Tudor and Stuart England* (1970), pioneered the direct application of anthropological models to witch-

The surviving evidence of witch-hunting in England strongly supports the popular stereotype of the witch as elderly, impoverished, and female.

accusation cases. Macfarlane, through his detailed regional study of witch-hunting in Essex, arrived at similar conclusions to Thomas in his more general work.

The so-called 'Thomas-Macfarlane paradigm' encompasses an apparently common framework for witch-accusation, which has been dubbed the 'charity-refused model'. As poverty and capitalism expanded, charitable gestures became more problematic. A combination of economic and cultural issues created situations where charity was denied by necessity or choice. Consequently, the individual who failed to behave in a charitable fashion was subject to the twin perils of the witch's curse and his own guilt complex. These could induce an accusation. Christina Larner has provided some interesting examples:

Take the accusation of Frances Rustat in 1659 in Hertfordshire: she claimed that after refusing payment to Goody Free for some eggs, on the grounds that she had no small change, she had never been well. She was now 'strangely handled with great pain' and claimed that 'if she died of that distemper Goody Free was the cause of her death'. Similarly in a 1570 case, a man failed to invite the accused witch to a sheep-shearing, which he should have done 'she being his neighbour', and she thereupon bewitched two of his sheep. In Scotland the sources of accusations and the close relationships between the accuser and accused were the same. In Dumfriesshire in 1671 Elspeth Thomson's sister-in-law failed to invite her to the christening of her child. Her milk failed, the child died, and Elspeth was held responsible.[22]

The accused and the accuser in English cases usually knew each other – they were the 'Witches and Neighbours' in the title of Robin Briggs' important study (1996, 2002). Quite likely the victim had identified the witch even before the harm had been done. For example, Mary Dingley warned Margery Singleton in 1573: 'I have a suspicion in thee and if any in my house should miscarry thou shalt answer for it.'[23]

Some interesting observations have been made regarding the percentage of single women targeted by witch-hunts. It has been calculated for Essex in 1645 that sixty-seven per cent of the women accused were widowed or unmarried. Elderly widowed women were particularly reliant on charity; if the marginally better-off women the widow turned to for support refused to help, the beggar in turn might be accused of sorcery in the event of any misfortune falling on someone who failed to provide. The beggar might be considered likely to resort to witchcraft for a number of obvious reasons: to make money from the sale of potions and spells; to make a pact with Satan in the hope of financial reward; to punish the community that would not help them.

Although the age of the accused is often missing from the available records of witch trials, where it does survive it suggests the majority of those accused were elderly. In Essex in 1645, of fifteen witches of known age, eighty-seven per cent were over the age of fifty; of these, three were in their fifties, seven in their seventies, and three in their eighties. The remaining two were aged between forty and forty-nine.[24] One enlightened English writer, in 1656, directly linked poverty in old age with the witch phenomenon:

> When overtaken by disaster, thought Thomas Ady, we should not ask ourselves, 'What old man or woman was last at my door that I may hang him or her for a witch?' ... We should rather say, 'Because I did not relieve such a poor body that was lately at my door, but gave him harsh and bitter words, therefore God hath laid this affliction upon me.'[25]

The impoverished 'witch' might sometimes have created her own myth. A pauper's reputation for witchcraft could be her lifeline: 'a very noble-man's request may be denied more safely than her petitions for small beer' one writer commented in 1615.[26] One Anne Ellis of Flintshire in the middle of the seventeenth century was routinely overpaid for the woollen stockings she hawked from door to door because of her reputation.[27]

Although their behaviour and social position was the main reason why people were accused of witchcraft, they might also have been those people that for other reasons were considered suspect. This included people with physical abnormalities. *The Compost of Ptolomeus* (1638) warned 'beware of all persons that have default of members naturally, as of foot, hand, eye, or other member; one that is crippled; and especially of a man that hath not a beard.'[28] The first victim of Matthew Hopkins' witch-hunt in Essex in the 1640s was one-legged. However, the absence of particular reference to appearances in most trial records and accounts suggests the personality or actions of the accused were as, or more, significant.

When James VI of Scotland (James I of England) declared that there were twenty female witches to every male witch he was probably close to the mark, if the records of the accusations are to be relied upon. Of the 303 people accused of witchcraft in Essex between 1560 and 1675 just twenty-three were male.

Conventional views of why so many alleged witches were women can be found in a tract by an English clergyman, dating from 1616:

> First, they are by nature credulous, wanting [i.e., lacking] experience, and therefore more easily deceived.

> Secondly, they harbour in their breast a curious and inquisitive desire to know such things as be not fitting...

> Thirdly, their complexion [i.e., psychological condition] is softer, and from hence more easily receive the impressions offered by the Devil...

THE
Compoſt of Ptolomeus,
Prince of Aſtronomie.

Very neceſſary and profitable for all
ſuch as deſire the knowledge of the
famous Art of *Aſtronomie*.

Corrected and amended, with new Additions.

K · Ptholomeus.

The Compost of Ptolomeus, 1638.

Fourthly, in them is a greater facility to fall, and therefore the Devil at the first took advantage, and set upon Eve in Adam's absence...

Fifthly, this sex, when it conceives wrath or hatred against any, is implacable, possessed with insatiable desire of revenge...

Sixthly, they are of a slippery tongue, and full of words: and therefore if they know any such wicked practices, are not able to hold them, but communicate the same with their husbands, children, consorts...[29]

The association of women with the domestic sphere, and witchcraft with the inexplicable illnesses of infants, is amply illustrated by this extract from the 1664 trial that resulted in the execution of Amy Duny:

As concerning William Durent, being an infant, his mother Dorothy Durent sworn and examined, deposed in open court, that about the tenth of March, *nono Caroli Secundi* [i.e., 1658], she having a special occasion to go from home, and having none in her house to take care of her child (it then sucking) desired Amy Duny her neighbour, to look to her child during her absence, for which she promised her to give her a penny: but the said Dorothy Durent desired the said Amy not to suckle her child, and laid a great charge upon her not to do it. Upon which it was asked by the court, why she did give that direction, being an old woman and not capable of giving suck? It was answered by the said Dorothy Durent, that she very well knew that she did not give suck, but that for some years before, she had gone under the reputation of a witch, which was one cause made her give her the caution: another was, that it was customary with old women, that if they did look after a sucking child, and nothing would please it but the breast, they did use to please the child, to give it the breast, and it did please the child, but it sucked nothing but wind, which did the child hurt. Nevertheless after the departure of this deponent, the said Amy did suckle the child: and after the return of the said Dorothy, the said Amy did acquaint her, that she had given suck to the child, contrary to her command. Whereupon the deponent was very angry with the said Amy for the same; at which the said Amy was much discontented, and used many high expressions and threatening speeches towards her, telling her that she had as good to have done otherwise than to have found fault with her, and so departed out of her house. And that very night her son fell into strange fits of swounding, and was held in such terrible manner, that she was much affrighted therewith, and so continued for divers weeks.[30]

Where, in an earlier period, the wisdom that comes with age might have added to a person's value to a community, in early modern times their supposed knowledge, their 'cunning', was sometimes enough to condemn them. William Perkins, in 1608, argued that 'good' witches were as culpable as bad since all such 'cunning folk' derived their power from the same satanic place:

The healing and harmless witch must die by this law, though he kill not ... For this must always be remembered, as a conclusion, that by witches we understand not those only which kill and torment; but all diviners, charmers, jugglers, all wizards, commonly called wise men and wise women ... because they deny God, and are confederates with Satan ... Men do commonly hate and spit at the damifying sorcerer, as unworthy to live among them; whereas the other is so dear to them, that they hold themselves and their country blessed that have him among them, they fly unto him in necessity, they depend upon him as their god ... Death therefore is the just and deserved portion of the good witch.[31]

WITCHFINDERS

The most notorious of the English witch-hunters was Matthew Hopkins, the self-styled Witchfinder General who instigated a reign of terror in the Puritan counties of eastern England in the years 1645–46, when witch-hunting re-emerged in England 'as an unforeseeable consequence'[32] of the outbreak of the English Civil War in 1642. His activities were centred on East Anglia and he and fellow witchfinder John Stearne condemned at least 100 witches to hang. Their activities have been variously attributed to financial greed, Puritan zeal, an obsession with witchcraft, and self-importance. Hopkins' most recent biographer, Malcolm Gaskill, has found in these two minor gentlemen a resemblance to 'the provincial nobodies of the twentieth century who engaged in genocide, demonstrating to the world the banality of evil.'[33] The English Civil War was a disaster on the grandest scale and it has been estimated that it killed around 3.7 per cent of the population – 'a greater proportion than during the First World War'.[34] In this context, in an era of barbarism and bloodshed, Hopkins was 'no more ruthless than his contemporaries'.[35]

Hopkins was born around 1621, the son of a minister in Essex, although Briggs claims he 'showed little sign of particular religious concern'.[36] He may have studied law and worked, without great financial reward, as an Ipswich lawyer, before turning witch-hunter in the Essex parish of Manningtree and Mistley in 1645. The work was paid – he charged forty shillings for each investigation – but, according to Briggs, this was 'no more than was necessary to meet their costs and provide a very marginal living'.[37]

Because of the law's reluctance to accept unsupported confessions and insistence upon proof of guilt, much emphasis was placed by Hopkins and his confederates on the business of obtaining confessions and searching suspected witches for the teats with which they fed their familiars. When such pieces of supporting evidence were secured, they were presented as substantial and undeniable proofs of a person having made a covenant with the Devil. Descriptions of the imps kept by accused witches were particularly shocking to the general population. These attendant demons, often taking the form of domestic animals such as cats and dogs, were a peculiarity of the

Although it only lasted around eighteen months, the witch-hunt conducted by Matthew Hopkins and his associates spread terror through East Anglia and beyond in 1645-46.

Swimming a witch.

Matthew Hopkins with two of
his victims and various familiars.

English witchcraft tradition – relatively few witches arrested elsewhere in Europe ever admitted employing demonic creatures to commit evil deeds on their behalf.

Witchfinders became adept at extracting testimony by such means as sleep deprivation (a process known as 'watching and waking'), enforced walking ('walking a witch'), and restricting suspects to a diet of bread and water. Another favourite witch test was 'swimming' (throwing a suspect bound thumbs to toes into water to see if he or she floated or sank), until this was banned in 1645.

Most of Hopkins' and Stearne's victims seem to have conformed to the poor, probably elderly, female stereotype. However, one victim, John Lowes, was an eighty-year-old clergyman with known Royalist sympathies in a Parliamentarian county. More typically, clergymen stood as witnesses in the Hopkins trials.

In his later defence of his activities, *The Discovery of Witches* (1647), Hopkins was insistent that he was not the instigator of hunts but that he was invited to look for witches by responsible civic leaders in the worst affected localities. In Alan Macfarlane's opinion, it would be 'naive to isolate these two as black-hearted villains leading on an innocent populace, as some have done...'[38] Gaskill has concluded that 'Hopkins and Stearne were not commanders-in-chief of the witch-hunt: they were the catalysts who gave the accusers confidence by confirming their suspicions and beliefs.'[39]

In some cases, the victims themselves sought out their persecutors, as Hopkins himself reported:

...[some] have come 10 or 12 miles to be searched [for the witch's mark] of their own accord, and hanged for their labour, (as one Meggs, a Baker did, who lived within 7 miles of Norwich and was hanged at Norwich Assizes for witchcraft)...[40]

THE DECLINE OF WITCH-HUNTING

Witchcraft prosecution declined, as elsewhere in Europe, in the latter half of the seventeenth century, not least through the enlightened attitude taken by such judges as Sir John Holt, who as Chief Justice stubbornly acquitted every witch brought before him. The 1604 statute under which most of the trials had been conducted was finally repealed in 1736, during the reign of George II, and the last hanging on a charge of witchcraft was that of Alice Molland in Exeter in 1685. The last person to be convicted on charges of witchcraft was Jane Wenham, who was tried in Hertford in 1712 and later pardoned. The last serious attempt to have someone tried on charges of witchcraft was made at Leicester in 1717, when Jane Clarke and her son and daughter, all from Great Wigston, were accused of various offences by no fewer than twenty-five of their neighbours: having undergone the ordeals of swimming and scoring above the breath (being scratched above the mouth and nose until they bled) they were allowed to go free after the jury threw out the indictments against them.

The population explosion of the early modern period ended around the middle of the seventeenth century and, as a consequence, according to the principles of supply and demand, inflation slowed and real wages improved. Improvements in agriculture, such as the introduction of water-meadows, increased the food supply. England became more or less self-sufficient in corn by the later seventeenth century. Rural poverty in the second half of the seventeenth century was being addressed in many regions by a more systematic form of communal provision.[41] With such improvements, social tensions between neighbours are likely to have lessened. Plague was also in decline, the last major epidemic occurring in England in 1665.

As for the experience of such factors as other forms of disease and infant mortality, it is very hard to explain the waxing and waning of the witch-hunt phenomenon

Witches and demons – images illustrating popular witchcraft beliefs by the time of the rapid demise of witch-hunting in England in the late seventeenth century.

in relation to these factors. As Alan Macfarlane has pointed out, 'it would be very difficult to show that disease and loss increased in mid-sixteenth century Essex or declined in that county after about 1650'.[42] Likewise, the witch-hunts predated the nineteenth-century medical revolution that, presumably, put paid to many folkloric beliefs regarding health issues. Nevertheless, in England at least, according to Keith Thomas, 'In several important respects the material conditions of life took a turn for the better during the later seventeenth century' and this 'must have done something to increase human self-confidence'.[43] It follows that reliance upon, even belief in, magic may have declined as a consequence. However, the extent to which changing social and economic conditions had an impact on witch-hunting cannot be quantified. Trial records sometimes highlighted social and economic issues that prompted accusations, but no such evidence exists for measuring the decline of witch-hunting.

The dissemination of new ideas and the changing of 'traditional' lifestyles are likely to have made some kind of contribution to this decline of witch-hunting. In England, printed news-sheets first appeared in the early years of the seventeeth century. One hundred and thirty provincial newspapers appeared between 1701 and 1760. By the third quarter of the seventeenth century it has been estimated that possibly forty per cent of the adult male population could read.[44] Industrial and mercantile progress probably increased social mobility. According to Thomas, the implications of all this should not be underestimated: 'The general effect of all these trends was to keep the provinces more closely in touch with the metropolis, to break down local isolation and to disseminate sophisticated opinion.'[45]

Furthermore, through such things as insurance schemes and new technology, people had more protection against misfortune wrought by, for example, fire, which, in the past, had sometimes been blamed on maleficent witches. In the same period, mathematicians began to formulate theories of probability that were widely discussed among England's scientific and philosophical community by the end of the seventeenth century. As Thomas has put it, 'It was this nascent statistical sense, or awareness of patterns in apparently random behaviour, which was to supersede much previous speculation about the causes of good or bad fortune.'[46]

Long after courts ceased persecuting witches, the lynch mob continued the work of the witchfinder. In 1751, Ruth Osborne and her husband, long suspected by locals at Long Marston in Hertfordshire of being witches, were dragged through a pond by an angry mob of several thousand people. Ruth Osborne drowned and the ringleader of the mob was hanged for her murder. Despite official disapproval, belief in the reality of witchcraft persisted in many rural communities into the nineteenth century, and as late as 1879 a man named William Bulwer, of Etling Green in Norfolk, was brought to trial for assaulting an eighteen-year-old neighbour called Christiana Martins and her mother, both of whom he had accused of being witches. When the magistrates tried to get to the bottom of the quarrel, Bulwer made no bones about his doubts concerning the Martins:

> Mrs Martins is an old witch, gentlemen, that's what she is, and she charmed me, and I got no sleep for her for three nights, and one night at half-past eleven o'clock, I got up because I could not sleep, and went out and found a walking-toad under a clod that had been dug with a three-pronged fork. This is why I could not rest; she is a bad old woman, and her daughter is just as bad, gentlemen. She would bewitch anyone; she charmed me and I got no rest day and night for her, till I found this walking-toad under the turf.

Isolated cases of witchcraft belief have continued to surface into modern times, with the occasional ritual killing, the discovery of disturbed graves and so forth. The twentieth century also saw a revival in interest in witchcraft as an occult science

William Hogarth's *Credulity, Superstition, and Fanaticism.*

The power of the witch to transform into other animal forms, such as that of the toad, was a major part of English witchcraft folklore.

speculatively descended (though the link is highly tenuous) from pre-Christian cults. The old witchcraft laws were invoked during the Second World War in order to prosecute mediums suspected of revealing classified information in the course of their séances and it was not until 1951 that the last references to witchcraft were finally removed from the statute books by the British Parliament.

THE HISTORIOGRAPHY OF WITCH-HUNTING IN ENGLAND

The earliest scholarly writing in modern times about witch-hunting emerged in the middle of the nineteenth century. The first significant British commentators on the subject, Margaret Murray and Montague Summers, both publishing in the 1920s, popularised the now redundant claim that the existence of a genuine and widespread cult of pagan worshippers explains the determination of the Christian authorities to search for witches in the early modern period. This myth, at least for the history of England, was exploded with the publication in 1929 of Cecil L'Estrange Ewen's *Witch Hunting and Witch Trials* – the first systematic and rigorous analysis of surviving witchcraft trial records. This ground-breaking work was based on the records of 1373 assizes held for the Home Circuit between 1559 and 1736. Using these, he was able to correct several misconceptions, including the notions that comparatively few people were executed for witchcraft in the later Tudor period and that witch-hunting was more intensive in the seventeenth century: 'So far as can be estimated from existing records, there were more trials in forty-two years of the reign of Elizabeth than during the entire [seventeenth] century'.[47] When he was writing, the late Victorian and Edwardian passion for psychic exploration was still very much in vogue. In undertaking this major work he took the stance of the rationalist, challenging the more excessive claims of his contemporaries:

To be honest, we of the present generation can offer little adverse criticism of the witchcraft believers. In the future among a more enlightened people, with more exact scientific observation and inference and knowledge of fundamental factors, no doubt the ancient witch-mania will be classed with the present spiritualistic phantasmagoria and charlatancy and religious rites and mumbo-jumbo, as the products of an exceedingly ignorant, gullible and superstitious age.[48]

Although modern 'enlightened' commentators do not belittle deeply considered early modern belief systems with the simple, patronising explanation that our early modern predecessors were 'ignorant' and 'gullible', they too face the challenge of the myths and 'mumbo jumbo' concerning the subject that have persisted to the present day.

Ewen's *Witch Hunts and Witch Trials* was followed in 1933 by his equally important *Witchcraft and Demonism*, a further analysis of court records covering other areas of England and Wales. Although the introductions to Ewen's books provide some attempt at explanation, his main purpose was not an interpretative one: 'In recording the evidence I have endeavoured to restrain myself from "writing up" the stories ... and each controversialist must pick out what suits his purpose or assists the grinding of his own particular axe.'[49] His pioneering work remains invaluable to all those endeavouring to explore the subject of English witch-hunting; in the words of one the most eminent writers in the field today, James Sharpe, 'all subsequent researchers have been vastly in his debt'.[50]

In 1937, the anthropologist E. E. Evans-Pritchard published *Witchcraft, Oracles and Magic among the Azande*. Subsequently, various commentators on witch-hunting in early modern Europe have applied the evidence of such anthropological studies. Some historians, notably Hugh Trevor-Roper in his 1967 essay 'The European witch-craze of the 16th and 17th centuries', searched for parallels between the fear and persecution of witches in the early modern period and that of Jews in more recent times. It is notable that C. L'Estrange Ewen, ten years before the outbreak of the Second World War, described the persecution of 'witches' by Matthew Hopkins and others in 1645 as a 'holocaust'.[51] The major works associated with the anthropological approach are Keith Thomas' *Religion and the Decline of Magic* (1971) and Alan Macfarlane's *Witchcraft in Tudor and Stuart England* (1970), both of which cite Evans-Pritchard's work. Recent historians, however, are less convinced of the effectiveness of such an approach: '...[in] comparing tribal societies studied by anthropologists in the first half of the twentieth century like is not being compared with like.'[52]

Keith Thomas and Alan Macfarlane found that, in England, witch-hunting was almost always the consequence of tension between neighbours, not the inspiration of people in clerical or judicial positions of authority. Such views have been substantiated by more recent historians, notably Robin Briggs, whose *Witches and Neighbours* (1996, 2002) explored thoroughly the psychological foundations of witchcraft beliefs and accusations. In so doing he was writing in the tradition of historians of mentalities and pioneering scholars such as G. Zilboorg who, back in 1935, had applied aspects of the new science of psychiatry to the subject.[53]

In the 1970s, a number of important texts written from a feminist point of view were published, raising questions regarding gender relations that remain a cause of controversy. These have been further addressed in recent times, with varying degrees of success, by such writers as Anne Barstow[54] and Diane Purkiss.[55] Other historians have focused on political and legal structures and the mechanics of witch-hunting; these include Gregory Durston's *Witchcraft and Witch Trials* (2000). However, whatever their approach, few historians now would challenge the observation of Brian Levack in 1985 that 'monocausal explanations' for this immensely complex subject 'have proved to be singularly unconvincing, if not demonstrably false'.[56]

SOURCES OF EVIDENCE FOR WITCH-HUNTING

The main sources of evidence for witch-hunting in early modern England are court and gaol records, pamphlets and ballad sheets detailing sensational cases, and the various tracts and treatises written about the subject during the period. In addition, there are accounts of otherwise undocumented witch-hunts and witchcraft cases to be found in other contemporary or near-contemporary personal writings such as letters, and also in early regional histories. What such sources do not usually record are those 'witch-hunts' that occured outside of court processes. Anthropological studies, and historical records that indicate a widespread belief in witchcraft in England long after the 1736 Act, suggest that the persecution of 'witches' on a local level, without recourse to the law, was endemic in close-knit village communities.

The vast majority of gaol records and indictments from the period have not survived. Where witchcraft cases have survived, they still present the historian with fundamental problems: do they represent the 'tip of an iceburg of latent accusations'[57] or are they the records of exceptional episodes? The records themselves are often hard to interpret and they do not always include the information the historian seeks when profiling the phenomenon. For example, gaol 'calendars' are of limited use since, often, they do not record the crime of the inmate.

The reaching of generalised conclusions on the basis of regional studies for those areas where the record is more complete is also a dangerous approach since, for example, the well-documented Home Circuit records provide plenty of examples, whereas an examination of over fifty files of legal records for the palatinate of Durham between 1471 and 1719 provides virtually nothing of significance in terms of witchcraft accusations and trials.[58] Arguably, the bigger mystery is not why some places suffered witchcraft accusations and trials but why most places, most of the time, did not.

Sometimes the historian has to rely heavily on second-hand accounts, such as that of

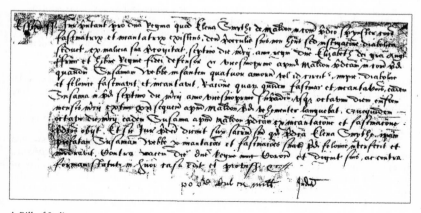

A Bill of Indictment.

A page from a Gaol Book.

Thomas Potts concerning the Pendle witch trials, which, on occasion, when alternative
records exist, have been found to be wildly inaccurate. The commercial literature is
especially problematic; Henry Goodcole claimed that his motive in writing the tale of
Elizabeth Sawyer, the witch of Edmonton, was:

> to defend the truth of the cause which, in some measure, hath received a wound
> already by most base and false ballads which were sung at the time of our returning
> from the witch's execution. In them I was ashamed to see and hear such ridiculous
> fictions of her bewitching corn on the ground, of a ferret and an owl daily sporting
> before her, of the bewitched woman braining herself, of the spirits attending in the
> prison; all of which I knew to be fitter for an ale-house bench than for a relation
> of proceeding in Court of Justice. And thereupon I wonder that such lewd ballad-
> mongers should be suffered to creep into the printers' presses and people's ears.[59]

Consequently, this most fascinating of historical topics is one that is riddled with
historical controversy in all of its aspects, including what sort of people were
persecuted, why and by whom, and why the official persecution of witchcraft went
into an abrupt decline in the closing years of the century, many years before the
passing of legislation that prevented it.

The learned writers of 'Devil literature' during the period could be as easily swayed
by the evidence of hearsay as some judges. The writer of *Saducismus Triumphatus*,
Joseph Glanvill, Fellow of the Royal Society, built his case regarding the reality of
witchcraft in Somerset on the word of Robert Hunt, the Justice of the Peace who
tried Jane Brooks of Shepton Mallet who was executed at Chard in 1658. Hunt was
convinced by his unnamed informers and this was good enough for Glanvill:

> This I think is good evidence of the being of witches; if the Sadducee be not satisfied

Glanvill's
*Saducismus
Triumphatus.*

with it, I would fain know what kind of proof he would expect. Here are testimonies of Sense, the oaths of several credible attestors, the nice and deliberate scrutiny of quick-sighted and judicious examiners, and the judgement of an assize upon the whole.[60]

GAZETTEER

Most of the cases recorded in this book involve women, not just as victims but also as persecutors. Witch-hunting, it seems, had at least as much to do with conflict between women as it did with a struggle between the sexes. In many instances the charge is one of causing the sickness and death of a child. This, perhaps, reflects the domestic sphere with which women were so much involved as mothers, midwives, wet-nurses, and servants. When things went wrong and foul play was suspected those women that moved within this intimate sphere were likely to be the first to receive the scrutiny of an anxious or bereaved parent. In many cases they are described as widows or spinsters, suggesting that their age or disadvantageous economic situation as single women made them more vulnerable to accusation. In most cases, where a record has survived, they would appear to be women of fairly humble labouring or 'husbandman' backgrounds, very likely reduced to a condition of poverty and begging to survive. The evidence clearly reveals that, although the heightened fear of witches may have been inspired from above, witchcraft accusation mostly concerned people, both accusers and accused, from the middle or lower orders of English society.

Although quite a few cases of the bewitching of livestock appear, the most common acts of *maleficium* recorded in these cases are the causing of, often fatal, human ailments. Usually this is some form of 'wasting' condition that might lead to death. In many accounts, those afflicted would suffer temporary episodes of collapse or paralysis. Although, theoretically, the witch could use magic to persecute others a long way away, it is striking that in the vast majority of cases the accusations appear to concern near neighbours. In his treatise *Daimonomageia* (c. 1637), one contemporary medical writer, William Drage, provided the following definition:

A Disease of Witchcraft is a Sickness that arises from strange and preternatural Causes, and from Diabolical Power in the use of strange and ridiculous Ceremonies by Witches or Necromancers, afflicting with strange and unaccustomed Symptoms, and commonly preternaturally violent, very seldom or not at all curable by Ordinary and Natural Remedies.

In the more spectacular cases the afflicted levitated or vomited curious objects such as bent pins. Rarely, it seems, would the witch's curse or sorcery lead to immediate death. Sometimes the conjuring of evil spirits is stated as the means by which these deeds were enacted, but references to a diabolical pact between the witch and the Devil are extremely rare.

Usually, it would appear, witches worked alone or, very occasionally, in twos or threes. Sometimes another family member might be accused of abetting the witch

A witch's familiar.

in her work. In some of the more detailed accounts a distinctly English emphasis is placed upon the role of 'familiars' – appearing as pet dogs, cats, moles, polecats, toads, and the like.

The concept of sabbat meetings, common in parts of continental Europe in the period, is rarely invoked in the sources. Cases involving several witches working in consort are exceptional and often they became the subject of the sensationalised pamphlet accounts that provide the most detailed, and some of the most problematic, evidence for episodes of witch-hunting. For obvious reasons these have received far more attention in books concerning witchcraft than the other more mundane cases listed. Consequently the popular impression of the witch-hunting phenomenon has been skewed by the disproportionate emphasis placed on the most famous accounts, such as that of the Pendle witch-hunt. However, the great number of short tracts and substantial books, some of which reappeared in several later editions, indicates the fascination of the age with the subject of witchcraft. It is reasonable to conclude that such literature, made widely available by the invention in the fifteenth century of the printing press, played a significant role in the escalation of witch-hunting.

The records clearly reveal the potentially fatal combination of popular belief in witchcraft and elite enthusiasm to crush anyone associated with non-conformist, disruptive behaviour. However, one of the striking facts presented by the records of witchcraft accusation is how rarely in the seventeenth century they led to a guilty verdict. Time and again the terms *'non cul'* (not guilty) or *'ignoramus'* (the bill was found to be untrue and thrown out) appear in the gaol delivery records. Many of these have been included in this selection but for the Home Counties, for which the record is much more abundant: these, for the most part, have been left out.

In his analysis of the Home Circuit records, C. L'Estrange Ewen concluded that '81 persons out of every 100' escaped execution and that, despite the unparalleled intensity of persecution in 1645 associated with Matthew Hopkins, the 'most dangerous period was the decade 1598-1607, being the last six years of the reign of Elizabeth and the first four years of James I'.[61] Significantly, perhaps, this was an epoch of change, distress and uncertainty. This *fin de siècle* also marked the end of a dynastic age, that of the Tudors, and the arrival of the first Stuart king, James I. Political and religious challenges manifested in the rebellion of the Earl of Essex in 1601 and the Gunpowder Plot of 1605. The 1590s were dominated by bad harvests, soaring food prices, dearth, and food riots. In the early years of the seventeenth century the records reveal a series of extreme weather events, such as severe flooding in 1606 and the bitter winters of 1607 and 1608, in which rivers froze for months on end and Londoners warmed themselves by fires lit on the ice of the Thames.[62]

By the late 1650s the continued hearing of witchcraft cases on charges brought by the near neighbours of the accused suggests that old popular assumptions concerning witchcraft remained strong but the absence of guilty verdicts would seem to indicate the emergence of more 'enlightened' sceptical judges and juries or, perhaps, more stringent legal standards regarding what constituted empirical evidence. Indeed, it is possible to detect this shift in some places as early as the 1630s. The witch-hunting enthusiasm of the mid-1640s seems to have been an anomaly in terms of the general pattern, and one that, probably, had much to do with the social and political upheavals of the first English Civil War (1642-46).

Although torture, officially, was an unacceptable means of gaining confessions, it is clear from these records that witch-hunters and those in authority deployed certain persuasive measures. For example, in sixteenth-century Great Yarmouth the pillory and imprisonment were suffered by Elizabeth Butcher, not as a punishment, but as methods for forcing a confession. The infamous Pendle witches spent weeks in prison before they were condemned, in foul conditions that probably hastened the death of one of their number and must have weakened their resolve. Matthew Hopkins, the notorious 'Witchfinder General', appears to have relied extensively on sleep deprivation and 'walking' the prisoner to encourage a confession. Sometimes references in the sources are made to the practice of employing 'searchers' to find evidence of teats for suckling imps or even the Devil's mark, by which a diabolical pact might have been sealed.

In the great majority of cases cited in this gazetteer the witchcraft accusation is linked to a specific person, time, and place. Where the record is vague and lacking detail, particularly if the location of the alleged witchcraft is not mentioned, it is likely to have been left out of this record. Most entries are drawn from first-hand accounts – records of assizes, gaol books, and near-contemporary tracts. The record is incomplete and problematic; the earlier period is less represented than the later and for some areas there is very little surviving evidence. The Gaol Book record for the Western Circuit, for example, does not begin until 1670 and thus scarcely anything is known of a supposed major persecution of witches in Cornwall in the mid-1660s.[63] Even for the most complete series of records – those for the Home Circuit (Essex, Hertfordshire, Kent, Surrey and Sussex) – a quarter of the files are missing for the period before 1645.[64] For those records that do survive it is now recognised that sometimes the details are likely to be incorrect. The common assumption of the clerks, retained in this gazetteer for convenience, that the place where the crime was committed was the place where the accused lived, is not necessarily always an accurate one. Despite these problems, the records do shed some light upon changes in the scale and nature of witchcraft accusations and punishments over time. They also help to reveal significant regional variations. Some counties, Wiltshire for example, hardly make an appearance, partly because of the absence of records but also because witchcraft accusations are rare in those records that do survive.

Though far from complete, this catalogue of indictments and punishments is testimony to the horror of the witch-hunting that occurred sporadically throughout

England in the hundred years after the passing of the Elizabethan witchcraft Act of 1663. Although, compared to other crimes, relatively few people were brought to trial on witchcraft charges it is, nevertheless, abundantly apparent that belief in witchcraft was a prominent feature of sixteenth- and seventeenth-century mentalities, and that the social and legal structures of the day both encouraged the persecution and enabled the prosecution of its alleged perpetrators.

Unless otherwise detailed, the evidence for these trials is in the surviving assize and gaol records, many of which were first published more or less *verbatim* by E. L'Estrange Ewen between 1929 and 1933. Some of these records, for example those for Essex, can now be accessed online via the National Archives website at http://www.nationalarchives.gov.uk. The records of the Guernsey Royal Court were transcribed and translated from the French by John Linwood Pitts and published in 1886. His work is now available as an Ebook on line at http://www.gutenberg.orq. Most of the extensive London-printed tracts and treatises referred to and used in the compiling of this gazetteer of witch-hunting are also available on the internet in facsimile and transcript form through *Early English Books Online* at http://eebo.chadwyck.com/home. Useful selections of this kind of material can be found in Marion Gibson (2000), *Witchcraft Cases in Contemporary Writings*, and Barabara Rosen (1991), *Witchcraft in England, 1558-1618*.

The world turned upside down – a representation of the 'distracted times' affecting England at the start of the English Civil War.

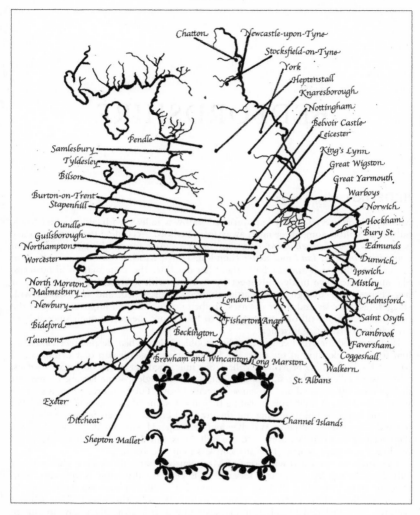

Chatton
Newcastle-upon-Tyne
Stocksfield-on-Tyne
York
Heptenstall
Knaresborough
Nottingham
Belvoir Castle
Leicester
King's Lynn
Great Wigston
Great Yarmouth
Warboys
Norwich
Hockham
Bury St. Edmunds
Dunwich
Ipswich
Mistley
Chelmsford
Saint Osyth
Cranbrook
Faversham
Coggeshall
Walkern
St. Albans
Channel Islands

Samlesbury
Tyldesley
Bilson
Pendle
Burton-on-Trent
Stapenhill
Oundle
Guilsborough
Northampton
Worcester
North Moreton
Malmesbury
Newbury
Bideford
Taunton
Beckington
Brewham and Wincanton
London
Fisherton Anger
Long Marston
Exeter
Ditcheat
Shepton Mallet

The location of major witch-hunting incidents in early modern England.

BEDFORDSHIRE

BEDFORD, 1613, c. 1637

Mother Sutton was an elderly impoverished widow who lived with her daughter, Mary Sutton, at Milton, some three miles away from Bedford. According to a contemporary account, *Witches Apprehended, Examined and Executed, for notable villanies by them committed both by land and water* (London, 1613), Mother Sutton was a witch in league with the Devil and she had taught her daughter the same diabolical business. She appears to have made ends meet by working with livestock as a 'hogsherd or hog-keeper', and 'though many cattle oftentimes miscarried, and were taken with staggerings, frenzies and other diseases, to their confusions and impoverishing of the owners, yet she not till of late suspected to be a cause thereof, though since it hath evident been proved against her.'

Undiscovered for over twenty years, her troubles began when, despite receiving from him food and clothing in the past, she fell out with 'a gentleman of worship called Master Enger dwelling at Milton Milles'. She unleashed her magic on Enger's horses, which were killed in their stables at night, 'some strangled, some having beaten out their brains, others dead and no cause perceived how.' Furthermore, when 'his swine were in the fields at their troughs eating their meat, some of them would suddenly fall mad, and violently fall to tearing out the guts and bowels of their fellows. Others by ten and twenty in a company, as if they had been carried with one desire, would leave their feeding and run headlong into the mill dams and drown themselves.' All in all Mr Enger lost £200 worth of livestock in less than two years.

The situation worsened when one of Mary Sutton's three illegitimate children was cuffed on the ear by an 'ancient servant' of Enger's for throwing 'stones, dirt, filth' into one of his master's mill dams, upsetting other children playing in the vicinity. In retaliation the Suttons worked their magic to unsettle both Mr Enger and his 'ancient servant'. This included the ploy of shape-shifting into a great black sow to agitate the servant's horses taking produce to market, with such effect that they bolted in different directions and wrecked the cart. When Enger's seven-year-old son called Mother Sutton a witch when he met her grinding corn at his father's mill, the boy became the focus of their malevolence, with tragic consequences:

> To effect their devilish purpose to the young child of Master Enger, they called up their two spirits, whom she called Dick and Jude: and having given them suck at their two teats which they had on their thighs (found out afterward by enquiry and search of women) they gave them charge to strike the little boy and to turn him to torment. Which was not long in performing, but the child being distract was put to

such bitter and insupportable misery as by his life his torments were augmented and by his death they were abridged. For his tender and unripe age was so enfeebled and made weak by that devilish infliction of extremity as in five days, not able longer to endure them, death gave end to his perplexities.

A friend of Mr Enger told him of the efficacy of the swimming test, whereby a witch's guilt could be proven, for, when bound and slung into a body of water, she would float. Having beaten her with a cudgel 'till she was scarce able to stir', when Enger had Mary Sutton tested she sank for a moment then floated as if on a plank. Enger then 'commanded her to be taken out, and had women ready that searched her and found under her left thigh a kind of teat, which after the bastard son confessed her spirits, in several shapes, as cats, moles, &c., used to suck her.'

After another swimming and a bout of interrogation (and, very likely, further cudgelling) Mary Sutton eventually 'confessed all; and acknowledged the Devil had now left her to that shame that is reward to such as follow him.' Mary and her mother were convicted at Bedford on Monday 30 March 1613 and executed on the Tuesday.

Another Bedford 'swimming' story dates to around 1637 and is told in *Daimonomageia* by W. Drage, printed in 1665. It involved 'Goodwife' Rose and is a classic charity-refused tale. Having begged a maid for some 'pease' (presumably pease pudding – the regular fare of labouring folk in the past) and been refused, she was accused of bewitching it and making it 'worm-eaten'. She was also suspected of making a man ill. Both she and the maid were subjected to the swimming test. Goodwife Rose would not sink but the maid did with such certainty that she nearly drowned and had to be resuscitated by the onlookers. Doubtless this would have confirmed Goodwife Rose's guilt but the outcome of the case, if real, is not known.

The swimming of Mary Sutton.

BERKSHIRE

WINDSOR, 1579

The details of this extraordinary case are preserved in a contemporary pamphlet entitled *A Rehearsall both straung and true, of hainous and horrible actes committed by Elizabeth Stile, alias Rockingham, Mother Dutten, Mother Deuell, Mother Margaret, Fower notorious Witches, apprehended at Winsore* (London, 1579).

In 1579, a sixty-five-year-old widow from Windsor named Elizabeth Stile (also known as Rockingham), exposed her coven of witches and confessed, at Reading gaol, to murder by witchcraft. The coven comprised a man called Rosimond (also known as Osborne) from Farnham and his daughter, Mother Devell, who lived near the pond in Windsor, Mother Dutten, Mother Margaret who, crippled, lived in Windsor's alms house, and Stile. Their former leader was an old woman by the name of Seidre who, until her recent death, had also been a resident of the alms house. Stile and her fellow witches had used sorcery to kill five people: Master Gallis, mayor of Windsor; a local farmer called Lanckforde and one of his maids; and two butchers, one by the name of Switcher, the other called Masclyn. The procedure involved 'pictures of red wax about a span long and three or four fingers broad' which were pierced with 'an hawthorne pricke'. Stile confessed to killing another man called Saddock just by clapping him on the shoulder. An ostler giving evidence in the trial claimed he was punished with aching limbs when Stile was angered by the paucity of the alms he offered her; only when he took the advice of the cunning man, Rosimond, and scratched the witch, drawing her blood, was he cured. In Stile's own confession she gave several accounts of how the witches sometimes undid each other's acts of *maleficia*. She and the other female witches also kept familiars which they fed with blood from various places on the right-hand side of their bodies. Dutten's familiar took the form of a toad, Devell's was a black cat called Gille, Mother Margaret had a kitten called Ginnie, and Elizabeth Stile herself kept a rat by the name of Philip. Rosimond specialised in shape-shifting, turning himself into the form of such creatures as a horse or an ape.

Stile, Dutten, Devell, and Mother Margaret were all found guilty and executed.

READING, 1634

In 1634, William and Edith Walles were accused of causing the sickness, by witchcraft, of a Reading servant named Edward Dynham. Dynham's symptoms comprised feverish episodes of sweating and shaking during which he would suffer the sensation

Woodcut showing witches and imps from *A Rehearsall both straung and true*, 1579.

of a mouse running up and down inside him. The cause of the dispute seems to have been a row between Edith Walles and Dynham's wife, Clement, whom Walles called a 'whore'. When Edith Walles was searched, various anomalies were discovered: 'under her armpit something like a nipple, but more soft and "flaggye", and the like on her hip, and in her privy parts something like a teat'. The searching of her husband revealed a 'blue spot', which bled when pricked. Edith was gaoled and William Walles was released on bail.

NEWBURY, 1643

An unidentified woman was summarily executed at Newbury in 1643 after she was suspected of witchcraft.

The case arose when a group of Parliamentarian soldiers, passing through Newbury during the Civil War, happened to spy a woman apparently walking on the water of the River Kennet. When the woman reached the bank it was clear that she had crossed the river using a small board as a raft, but this plain piece of evidence was stubbornly ignored by the soldiers, who were convinced that they had caught a witch red-handed. When the women failed to answer their questions satisfactorily it was decided that she should be shot. One of the men then fired his weapon and the woman was hit in the chest, but the bullet allegedly rebounded and 'narrowly he missed it in his face that was the shooter'. As recounted in a contemporary five-page tract entitled *A most Certain Strange and True Discovery of a Witch, Being taken by some of the Parliament Forces, as she was standing on a small planck-board and sayling on it over the River of Newbury* (1643), the witch reacted with striking indifference when the soldiers fired at her: 'with a deriding and loud laughter at them, she caught their bullets in her hands and chewed them'.

It was then remembered by someone present that a witch's power could only be broken by drawing blood 'above the breath'. One of the soldiers slashed her across the forehead with his sword, thus destroying her immunity to their assaults. A pistol

A most Certain Strange and True Discovery of a Witch, 1643.

was discharged below the luckless woman's ear, 'at which she straight sunk down and died'.

The fact that the incident took place just after the battle of Newbury suggests that the story may have evolved as an elaboration of a rumour that a Royalist female spy had recently been identified and executed. According to the *Mercurius Civicus* of 21–28 September 1643 this spy had been sent to destroy the armoury of the Earl of Essex. The unnamed witch is said to have died with a prophecy foretelling Parliamentarian victory: 'And is it come to passe, that I must dye indeed? Why then his Excellency the Earle of Essex shall be fortunate and win the field.'

To some observers, the political aspect of the legend indicates that it may have had its roots in subconscious fears about threats to the patriarchal state and the natural order of things. Of the witch herself, the 1643 tract concludes: 'Her soul we ought not to judge of, though the evils of her wicked life and death can escape no censure.'

CAMBRIDGESHIRE

CAMBRIDGE, 1659

An extraordinary account of witchcraft and transformation in Cambridgeshire was published in a 1659 tract entitled *Strange and Terrible Newes from Cambridge*. In a tirade against Quakers, the tale tells of how Jane Philips lapsed for a few weeks into Quakerism by joining a group associated with Robert Dickson and Jane Cranaway before returning to the Church of England. Subsequently, she was transformed by the Quakers into a mare and made to carry them to an unnamed town near Cambridge for a Quaker meeting. Transforming back into human form, Jane Philips had Dickson and Cranaway arrested, having shown the constables bruises on her hands and feet and her smock torn and bloodied where her riders' spurs had struck her sides. The prisoners pleaded not guilty and were released.

Strange and terrible newes from Cambridge, 1659.

CHANNEL ISLANDS

GUERNSEY AND JERSEY, 1562-1736

The proximity of the Channel Islands to the coast of northern France meant that, although under English jurisdiction, their residents felt keenly the influence of French cultural attitudes. In particular, the attitude of the French towards witchcraft was much less relaxed than it was on the English mainland, and consequently witch-hunting took hold in the Channel Islands to a degree not experienced elsewhere in Britain.

Guernsey witnessed the worst of it, with fifty-eight women and twenty men being tried on charges of sorcery in the hundred or so years encompassing the reigns of Elizabeth I, James I and Charles I. Another sixty-six trials took place on the island of Jersey between 1562 and 1736. A notably higher percentage of trials held here culminated in convictions than they did in mainland England, where only one in five witches sent for trial was actually found guilty. Records suggest that nearly half of those accused in the Channel Islands were sentenced to death.

The means of execution also reflected Continental practice, with convicted witches often being burned instead of hanged (or burned after being hanged first). Others were banished, whipped, or had their ears cut off. Among the most grisly executions that took place was that of a pregnant witch who was burned alive in Jersey's Royal Square: as she died she gave birth, and the baby was tossed into the flames by those who had come to watch.

Cases usually rested on the discovery of the Devil's mark or on evidence of evil-doing (*maleficia*), which might be as trivial as a shirt being infested with lice or a cow failing to give milk. A law passed in Jersey in 1591 effectively eradicated the distinction between 'black' and 'white' witchcraft: henceforth, anyone who turned to a witch or diviner for assistance 'in their ills and afflictions' was rendered liable to a term of imprisonment. Again in imitation of French practice, the authorities in the Channel Islands had a more permissive attitude towards the use of torture in extracting confessions. Unusually, torture was often employed against suspects after the death sentence had been passed, rather than before, in order to learn the names of accomplices.

Among the most sensational cases heard by the authorities in the Channel Islands was that of Collette du Mont and two other women in Guernsey in 1617. Having been accused of various evil acts, which included harm to both livestock and various people, all three were convicted and sentenced to death. At this point, Collette du Mont, a widow, confessed her guilt and was at once consigned to the torturers. Under their hands, the condemned woman elaborated upon her confession, describing how

The burning of a
witch.

she flew to a witches' sabbat after smearing herself with flying ointment and how she
had allowed the Devil to have intercourse with her when he came to her in the form
of a black dog:

> That the Devil having come to fetch her that she might go to the Sabbath called for
> her without anyone perceiving it: and gave her a certain black ointment with which
> (after having stripped herself), she rubbed her back, belly and stomach: and then
> having again put on her clothes, she went out of her door, when she was immediately
> carried through the air at a great speed: and she found herself in an instant at the
> place of the Sabbath, which was sometimes near the parochial burial ground: at other
> times near the seashore in the neighbourhood of Rocquaine Castle: where, upon
> arrival, she met often fifteen or sixteen Wizards and Witches with the Devils who
> were there in the form of dogs, cats and hares; which Wizards and Witches she was
> unable to recognise, because they were all blackened and disfigured...

Somewhat tellingly, the 'dog' had stood on its hind legs and had a paw that felt just
like a human hand. Other witches tried in the Channel Islands similarly described
Satan appearing at sabbats in the form of a cat among other animal disguises.

Reason eventually prevailed towards the end of the seventeenth century, and
cases of alleged witchcraft became rarer, as noted by Philippe le Geyt (1635-1715),
Lieutenant Bailiff of Jersey:

> How many innocent people have perished in the flames on the asserted testimony of
> supernatural circumstances? I will not say there are no witches; but ever since the
> difficulty of convicting them has been recognised in the island, they all seem to have
> disappeared, as though the evidence of times gone by had been but an illusion.

CHESHIRE

ALLOSTOCK, 1590

Late in Elizabth I's reign, Anne Acson of Allostock, a blacksmith's wife, was accused of bewitching two black cows belonging to John Brome. She was found not guilty.

CHESTER, 1604-55

The records of the Chester Sessions for 1604 offer a glimpse into the world of the 'cunning folk', the local wise women and cunning men, who seem to have played a significant role in many people's lives in early modern England. On this occasion, three men, John Hickson, John Walker, and 'Gilden' John Walker (possibly father and son), were charged with making prophecies. A few years later, in 1611, Henry Awdcrofte appeared on charges of conjuring and sorcery. Other men facing witchcraft charges at the Chester Sessions in the seventeenth century included Jock Hockenhull, accused of buggery and sorcery, and his associate Robert Yonge, in 1628, and an alleged sorcerer and conjurer, William Rowe, in 1630. John Cheetham, a yeoman of Bredbury, was found not guilty of a sorcery charge in 1633. A Handley schoolmaster, John Haye, also fell foul of the law in 1655 for declaring himself a 'wiseman' with the ability to find by magical means lost or stolen goods.

Among the prisoners recorded in the Chester Castle gaol calendar for 1613 was Elizabeth Lightbound, a yeoman's wife from Christleton. She was charged with causing bodily harm to Richard Ryder, also of 'Crissilton', Richard Burrows, and Mary Cotgrave. Similar charges at Chester in 1611 were made against Alice Smith, while one Mary Preece of Broughton was accused of being a 'soothsayer and charmer attributing the title of blessing contrary to the law of God and that she hath used charming and blessing within the space of 2 years past'. Alice Smith was also charged with the same: evidence perhaps of two local 'wise women' who had fallen foul of their neighbours. Elizabeth Lightbound was found not guilty of 'witching' but, nevertheless, she appears to have been confined to gaol for many months. Alice Smith was released on bail. Women could be arraigned merely for practising sorcery, regardless of the outcome; this appears to have been the offence of Isabella Wade and Margery Macklin when their case was heard at the Chester Sessions in 1630.

WOODFORD, 1621

A married woman, Margery Taylor of (presumably) Woodford, was charged in April 1621 with causing the sickness and death of Thomas Lunt, a baby, by witchcraft. Her fate is unknown beyond the evidence that she was released from Chester gaol on bail later in the year.

NORTHENDEN, MANCHESTER, 1626

Elizabeth Reade, the wife of a Northenden yeoman, was charged in 1626 with causing harm to horses belonging to John Coppoke – a grey gelding and a black bay. Having supposedly bewitched the animals on 10 June 1626, they both died on 10 July. She was found not guilty and released.

ACTON, 1631

A widow, Sibil Marcer of Acton, was executed in 1631, having been found guilty of killing by witchcraft Hugh Bassenett. Unusually, in cases that typically speak of wasting sicknesses leading to death, the victim died on the day he was, allegedly, bewitched.

HIGH LEGH, 1633

A widow, Elizabeth Urmston of High Legh, was accused of causing the wasting sicknesses of four people: William Stelfox, Thomas Stelfox, Elizabeth Stelfox, and Elizabeth Poole. Her daughter was charged with abetting her in her witchcraft. They were found not guilty at the 1633 Chester Sessions.

WARBURTON, 1639

A Warburton blacksmith, Thomas Bosse, was accused in 1639 of causing the sickness by witchcraft of three of his Warburton neighbours – Thomas Warburton, a yeoman, Anne Coe, and another yeoman, John Rowlandson. Anne Coe and John Rowlandson are recorded as having died as a consequence. The final outcome of the trial is unknown.

NANTWICH, 1650, 1664

Katherine Davies of Nantwich was accused, in 1650, of bewitching to death a neighbour's black calf worth seven shillings. She was also charged with causing the deaths of several children but found not guilty at the Chester Sessions. In causing the sickness and death of an eight-year-old, Richard Bromhall, she was accused of working in consort with a Nantwich widow named Ellen Shufflebotham. Of this charge she was also found not guilty and acquitted.

The wife of a Nantwich collar-maker, Mary Briscoe, was charged at the Chester Sessions on several accounts: the bewitching to death of two Wico Malban neighbours, John Clowes and Anne Field, both of whom languished for some time before their deaths, of practising 'the devilish arts', and also of the bewitching of one Richard Wright. However, as in other recent cases, a more sceptical jury found her not guilty of all charges. Alice Bayley of Norley, a widow, was charged in 1669 of causing the sickness and death of two people, and she too was found not guilty. Similarly, in these seemingly changing times, Catherine Stubbs of Goostrey, also a widow, evaded prosecution in 1670, despite the determination of the Leadbeater family to have her punished for causing, by witchcraft, the wasting disease of one of their kin.

WARFORD, 1654

A group of three witches was accused on three charges of *maleficium* in 1653 in the vicinity of Knutsford, Cheshire. Ellen Stubbs, the wife of a Warford labourer, and her daughter Elizabeth Stubbs, were allegedly joined in their dark arts by Anne Stanley, the wife of a labourer from nearby Withington. Between them, with the aid of evil spirits, they were accused of causing the deaths of Anne Lowe and Elizabeth Furnivall, and also of Thomas Grastie's black cow. Found guilty of the death of Elizabeth Furnivall, though not of that of Anne Lowe, all three were hanged in October 1654, over a year after the opening of the proceedings against them.

RAINOW, 1656, 1659

Anne Osboston was the wife of a Rainow husbandman, James Osboston. She was accused of several acts of *maleficium*, several of which dated back to 1651. These included causing the sickness and death of a gentleman, Anthony Booth of nearby Macclesfield; of a Rainow neighbour, John Pott, and his wife, Barbara; of a Rainow husbandman, John Steenson; and of another Rainow woman, Elizabeth Cowper. In this last murderous act she was, allegedly, assisted by Ellen Beech, another married woman from Rainow. A third woman at the same hearings, Anne Thornton, a widow, was accused of the death of an infant, Ralph Fynchett of Eccleston, less than a week after his birth. All three of these unfortunate women were found guilty and hanged.

The wife of another Rainow husbandman, Elizabeth Johnson was charged in 1658 on charges of 'invocation and conjuration of evil and wicked spirits' to bewitch to death eight-year-old Elizabeth Haigh of Rainow. She appears to have spent the winter of 1658-59 in Chester gaol but was released when she was found not guilty in April 1659. Three other women suspected of similar crimes had charges against them examined at the 1658 Chester Sessions. Anne Vaudrey was accused of bewitching Amy Babbington's child to death, and Anne and Elizabeth Stockton of Malpas were accused of enchantment and sorcery. None was found guilty.

SUTTON, 1657

Katherine Stubbs was a widow from Sutton, near Macclesfield, who was accused on several witchcraft charges at the Chester Sessions of 1657. These included causing the wasting illness of Henry Lees, a Macclesfield yeoman, and his wife, Joan, and likewise of her Sutton neighbours, Ellen Worthington and John Tompson. She was found not guilty on all accounts.

WINCLE, 1675

A note in the margin of the record of the case of the case of Mary Baguley, a widow of Wibore Clough in Macclesfield Forest, Mary Baguley, indicates that she was almost certainly hanged for witchcraft in 1675. In these more lenient times this was an exceptional outcome. She was accused of bewitching Robert Hall at Wincle who, after a ten-day illness, died.

CORNWALL

PADSTOW, 1581

Anne Piers of Padstow was examined before Sir Richard Greynevile in 1581. Her son had recently been taken as a pirate at Studland and she, a suspected witch, was identified as the likely recipient of his stolen goods. Her fate is unknown.

ST TEATH, 1645

An interesting mid-seventeenth-century story of bewitchment by spirits and the acquisition of magical powers, with a distinctly Cornish twist, was recalled in a letter written by Moses Pitt to the Bishop of Gloucester in 1696.[65] In this letter Moses explained how a nineteen-year-old Pitt family servant, Anne Jefferies of St Teath, fell ill with convulsions after she was visited, while knitting in her master's garden, by six small fairies all dressed in green. When she recovered from her lengthy illness she discovered she was now endowed with the power to heal and she became well-known in the locality as a consequence. She was not paid for her magical work but she ceased to require provisions from the Pitt family and it was rumoured that the fairies now provided for her. Eventually she attracted the attention of the local clerical and secular authorities and she was brought before ministers and the magistrates for interrogation. For a time she was incarcerated in Bodmin Gaol before being discharged.

LOOE, 1671

A letter sent from Falmouth by Thomas Holden to Joseph Williamson[66] tells of a non-conformist woman who appears to have become the scapegoat for a range of issues of national importance:

> A woman about Looe is apprehended for a witch. I am informed she has discovered that she was in the fleet when the Duke of York was at sea, and hindered the prosecution of that victory against the Dutch, and that she has been the cause of the Queen's barrenness and several other things, and that she caused the bull to kill Col. Robinson, an MP And JP, because he prosecuted the Nonconformists, she being one herself, either a Presbyterian or 'baptize'. She was discovered by cats dancing in the air, and inviting one of her neighbours to the same craft. Some say she is maze and saith and confesseth anything, but letters that come thence say she hath several marks about her where the devil has sucked her. She is in gaol.

The fate of this probably deranged woman is not known.

A TRUE

ACCOUNT

OF A

Strange and Wonderful

RELATION

OF ONE

John Tonken,

OF

PENSANS in *CORNWALL,*

SAID

To be Bewitched by some Women; two of which on Suspition
are committed to Prison. He Vomiting up several *Pins,* pieces of *Walnut-shels,* an Ear of *Rye,* with a *Straw* to it half a
yard long and *Rushes* of the same Length; which are kept to
be shown at the next Assizes for the said County.

This may be Printed, R. P.

LONDON,

Printed by *George Croom,* at the *Blue-Ball,* in
Thames-street, near *Baynard's-Castle,* 1686.

*A True Account of a Strange and Wonderful Relation of one John Tonken of Pensans in
Cornwall, 1686.*

PENZANCE, 1686

The troubles of John Tonken were reported in a six-page pamphlet entitled *A True Account of a Strange and Wonderful Relation of one John Tonken of Pensans in Cornwall* (London, 1686).

John was fifteen or sixteen years old when, in the spring of 1686, he was 'strangely taken with sudden fits' during which he saw an old woman 'in a blue jerkin and red petticoat, with yellow and green patches' who told him that he would not be well again until he had vomited a quantity of nut shells, pins, and nails. No one else present either saw the apparition or heard her speak. Sure enough, shortly afterwards, in the midst of further fits, he began to throw up small numbers of walnut shells and pins, some of which were crooked. The mysterious woman reappeared, sometimes as before and sometimes in the form of a cat. He was heard shouting at his invisible foe and crying out that she intended to choke or poison him. Furthermore, he was observed springing from his sickbed 'three or four foot high, from between two men that usually sat on the bed by him'. In addition to the walnut shells and pins he also coughed up 'great quantities of straws and rushes, some of them being a yard long'. In total he threw up sixteen or seventeen pins 'and as many straws and rushes as would fill the pole of a man's hat', a piece of bramble, and 'several pieces of flat sticks'. On one occasion, while lying in bed, he suddenly cried out that 'he was prick'd in the Heel' and, sure enough, a nail was found embedded in his foot. Finally, after further persecution, the old woman and two other witches appeared before him and she 'bad him farewell, and said she would trouble him no more'. A couple of days later he was well enough to move about with the aid of crutches. Meanwhile, two old women, Jane Noal and Elizabeth ('Betty') Seeze, were arrested and incarcerated in Launceston Gaol. The pamphleteers – the Mayor of Penzance, Peter Jenken, and Justice of the Peace, John Geose – concluded their account hoping 'they will be found out at the next Assizes, and so receive a reward due to their merits'.

CUMBRIA

THURSBY, 1672

The accusations levelled against Elizabeth, the wife of John Howe of Thursby, and presented before Thomas Denton, J.P., in August 1672 provide a classic case of disputes between neighbours, exacerbated by the domestic disasters endemic in rural communities. When John Robinson's horse died in the plough he remembered Elizabeth's threats following a dispute two weeks earlier concerning a payment Robinson had requested having ploughed a piece of her land. When, subsequently, he bought a cow and calf she warned him that 'he would not get much good out of her' and, sure enough, the cow sickened and had to be killed, and the calf died. John Coultherd blamed her for the death of his cow a couple of weeks after she had milked her without authorisation. Joseph Williamson fell sick with convulsions just hours after Elizabeth Howe had run her fingers through the corn he was endeavouring to sell at Carlisle. Similarly Grace Clemetson, four years earlier, was convinced that her son was a victim of Elizabeth's *maleficium* when he named her as the cause of his severe illness. It was only after the witch was presented before him so that he could scratch her and draw her blood that he began to recover. The same course of action was taken by another family of Howes, probably related, when, according to the testimony of her husband Edward, Anne Howe 'blooded her' and was promptly relieved of a very serious sickness. He declared that, in his opinion, if she 'had not gotten blood of her she could not have lived above four and twenty hours longer'.

However, fortunately for Elizabeth Howe, times had changed and a sceptical court acquitted her of the charges brought against her.

AINSTABLE (1685)

Thomasin Thompson was gaoled in 1685 on suspicion of bewitching to death the valuable livestock of her Ainstable neighbours. These included a black steer and two black heifers. Eleven witnesses gave evidence at her hearing, which culminated in a not guilty verdict.

DERBYSHIRE

ILKESTON, 1650

Although the outcome of her trial is not known, the case of Anne Wagg provides interesting evidence for who motivated witch-hunts and why. Of the six people testifying against Anne, two were male and four female. Five of the six are named as residents of Ilkeston, and the sixth almost certainly was as well. These neighbours of Anne Wagg were ordinary working people in a small agricultural market town; the occupations of the men only are recorded: Francis Torratt was a baker, and William Smith is described as a husbandman. Anne Wagg clearly was living in reduced circumstances and in two of the testimonies her argument with her neighbours was to do with begging and charity refused – John Elliott would not give her milk, and Elizabeth Gothard refused to give her some whey or to sell her, presumably at a reduced rate, butter. In all six cases Anne was accused of causing the sickness of livestock and people; John Elliot's healthy calf died the morning after he had refused Anne milk, Elizabeth Gothard's child suddenly fell ill after she had refused Anne whey, and the same child had a relapse and died following the butter incident. Of the six people the examinates claimed to have been the victims of Wagg's witchcraft, three were children, all of whom died as a consequence of their illness, and three were adults, at least one of whom died, naming Anne Wagg as her tormenter on her deathbed. As for Anne herself, it seems that her reputation as a witch was developed over a period of at least three years.

DEVON

DARTMOUTH, 1601

A series of depositions concerning the activities of Michael and Alice Trevisard of Hardness, Dartmouth, and their son, Peter, was presented before Sir Thomas Ridgway, J.P., in 1601. It transpired that Michael Trevisard, a fisherman, and his wife had long been suspected of witchcraft by their neighbours. Alice Butler explained how Michael Trevisard had foreseen the death of her child and how her servant, Alice Beere, had died after refusing Trevisard the use of a hatchet. Apparently he had responded with the ominous words 'Shall I not have it? I will do thee a good turn ere twelve-month be at an end.' Within eleven weeks Alice Beere was dead.

Meanwhile, Joan Baddaford claimed that, following a disagreement, Alice Trevisard's curse drove her husband mad. Furthermore, after she had given evidence against the Trevisards, Alice warned Joan 'Thou or thine may be burned before long be.' Three days later Joan's small child fell into the fireplace in her home. Despite the fact that the fire was not yet alight the child's neck was 'burned to the bone' and it died three weeks later.

A sailor from Dartmouth, William Tompson, recalled how he had met Alice Trevisard around midnight, remarking that she was dressed in a 'long grayish cape down to her foot'. When he happened to stumble and fell to the ground she laughed and so he struck her in the face with his musket rod. In response she declared 'Thou shalt be better thou hadst never met with me!' Sure enough, William soon suffered a number of personal disasters – his ship caught fire and, although he was rescued, he was taken to Spain and imprisoned for a year. When he got back to Devon he again met with the witch, who warned him he would be imprisoned again within a year and soon after he was captured a second time by the Spanish.

Further examinates had tales to tell of the Trevisards' activities. A thirteen-year-old, Christopher Honeywell, claimed that he and a friend had seen Michael Trevisard bewitch his father's boat so that it transported itself, to a place predetermined by Trevisard, of its own accord. Others who quarrelled with the Trevisards blamed them for various misfortunes including further accidental burnings of small children, the death of cattle, and a gun exploding in George Davye's face when he was shooting for pleasure. Susan Tooker fell ill with a sickness that lasted seven weeks after refusing Peter Trevisard a drink and then being threatened by him with the remark 'that it had been better to have delivered him drink'. John Galsworthie, a Hardness husbandman, declared that four years earlier he was crippled for twelve months soon after his wife had requested Alice Trevisard to settle a debt and received in reply the retort 'I pray God that thou never prosper in body nor goods.' Galsworthie's wife also fell ill and died within about three years of her unfortunate encounter with the witch.

In all, eleven of the Trevisards' neighbours and acquaintances testified against them. Their fate, however, is unknown.

EXETER, 1672, 1685, 1696

At Exeter, in 1672, Phelipa Gewen was accused of 'laming' three people by witchcraft and killing another. She was found not guilty.

Although not the last person to die in England as a result of being implicated in witchcraft, as several more victims lost their lives as a result of mob lynching or being subjected to such informal tests as scoring above the breath or swimming, Alice Molland is usually reckoned to have been the last person to have been legally executed for witchcraft in England. Having been found guilty at Exeter Assizes in March 1685 of the murder through witchcraft of Joan Snow, Wilmot Snow, and Agnes Furze, she was sentenced to death by Sir Creswell Levins. If the sketchy records of the case are to be relied upon, she was hanged at Heavitree in Exeter on 20 March 1685. A plaque commemorating her execution and that of the three witches executed there three years earlier has been placed in the wall of the ruined Rougemont Castle in the city, near the site of the court house in which the trials took place.

The claim of Alice Molland to be the last legally executed witch in England is sometimes contested on the strength of two probably fictitious pamphlets that attempted to grant this 'honour' to two women hanged at Northampton in 1705 or else to a woman and a child hanged in Huntingdon in 1716. Both cases are otherwise unrecorded.

It was fortunate for Elizabeth ('Bett') Horner, also known as Turner, that by the end of the seventeenth century witch accusations that made it to court were likely to be heard by sceptical judges and juries. According to an account of the trial preserved in a letter written by Archdeacon Blackburne,[67] who witnessed the proceedings, Bett Horner was accused in 1696 of persecuting the daughters of Thomas and Elizabeth Bovet. Thomas Bovet testified that the youngest, Alice, had died suddenly and mysteriously at about four years of age. The physicians could find no natural cause of her death. Alice's older sister Mary, about ten years old, suffered from a curious condition that crippled her for a period of about seven weeks. During her illness her distorted, twisted legs would lead her, eyes closed in a trance, towards the open fire. On such occasions she declared that Bett Horner made her do it. Meanwhile, another daughter, Sarah, when she was in bed, was scratched by a cat that she knew to be the shape-shifting witch. When questioned, she was able to describe perfectly the witch's present costume despite having not set eyes on her for half a year.

Consequently Bett Horner was arrested and imprisoned. During this time the two surviving daughters were assailed by some invisible foe that left bruises and bite marks on the arms and faces of the children. Equally incredibly, they vomited quantities of stones and pins. Sarah urinated two crooked pins and another emerged from her body through the skin of her middle finger. Her mother, Elizabeth Bovet, testified to having seen her daughter walk vertically up and down the nine-foot high wall of her room, and that Sarah told her Bett made her do it. In her distress Sarah denounced Bett Horner as the murderer of Alice; ten-year-old Mary testified before the court that she had seen the witch suckle a toad through a teat on her left shoulder. However, when Bett was requested to expose her shoulder before the court, all that was found was one innocuous mole.

Four more witnesses made allegations against Bett Horner. These included John Fursey, who described his horror at seeing the witch at night on three occasions materialise out of the ground before him. Other allegations concerned the mysterious disappearance of the contents of a barrel of her recently-brewed beer after Alice Osborn had a row with Bett, and Margaret Armiger's surprise encounter with her twenty miles away from the prison in which she was being held. However, although she faltered a little over 'Forgive us our trespasses' when commanded to recite the Lord's Prayer, the judge and jury found no evidence sufficient to convict her and she was released.

BIDEFORD, 1682

One of the last major witchcraft trials to be staged in England was that of Susanna Edwards, Temperance Lloyd, and Mary Trembles at Exeter in 1682. These three destitutes from the Devon port of Bideford were tried for witchcraft after they became suspected of being members of a coven. Temperance Lloyd, queen of the alleged coven, had already been tried twice on charges of witchcraft, while Susanna Edwards was said to have been recruited by the Devil himself. Mary Trembles had been invited to join the coven by Edwards. Their story was recorded in dramatic detail in a pamphlet entitled *A True and Impartial Relation of the Informations against Three Witches* (1682). By the time of their trial a fully-fledged 'continental' version of the diabolical pact, with the Devil appearing in the form of a dark young man and suckling blood through designated teats, informed the proceedings.

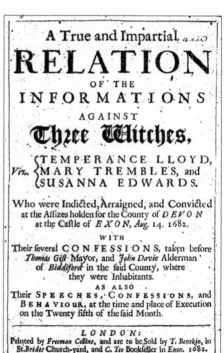

A True and Impartial Relation of the Informations against Three Witches, 1682.

After she was arrested, Susanna Edwards gave her gaoler a long glare: when he was immediately seized by a fit, accusations that she had the power of the evil eye were voiced. Edwards' account of her meeting with the Devil in the guise of a black-dressed gentleman crossing Parsonage Close caused a sensation and the three women's voluntary confessions, imaginative and shocking, left little room for doubt concerning their culpability in the eyes of the public.

Nonetheless, some of the evidence brought against the Bideford women was tenuous in the extreme. One 'witness' gave as the sum total of his testimony the fact that he had seen a cat jump in at the window of one of the accused. According to one contemporary account of the trial, 'This informant saith he saw a cat leap in at her window, when it was twilight; and this informant further saith, that he verily believeth the said cat to be the devil, and more saith not.'

The judge, who was described as a 'mild, passive man', was inclined to take pity on the three impoverished and clearly confused and frightened old women, but the whole of Exeter seemed to be of a different opinion:

> The women were very old, decrepit and impotent, and were brought to the assizes with as much noise and fury of the rabble against them as could be shewed on any occasion. The stories of their acts were in everyone's mouth ... all which the country believed, and accordingly persecuted the wretched old creatures.

Worries surfaced that there would be a riot if the three women were acquitted, and in the end the judge capitulated. Susanna Edwards, Temperance Lloyd, and Mary Trembles were sentenced to death and all three were hanged on 25 August 1682. It was reported that Susanna Edwards and Mary Trembles wept on their way to the gallows, while Temperance Lloyd chewed nonchalantly on a piece of bread.

Plaque on the wall of Rougemont Castle, Exeter, commemorating the last executions carried out in England on charges of witchcraft.

DORSET

NETHERBURY, 1566

John Walsh of Netherbury was interrogated before the Bishop of Exeter in 1566 on charges of dabbling in witchcraft. A fourteen-page pamphlet account of the proceedings, *The Examination of John Walsh*, was published in London in the same year (a copy is preserved in the Devon Record Office). Although the 1563 Act was in place, he evaded capital punishment because he was not accused of, or found guilty of, any act of *maleficium* that harmed or killed animals or people, and he had the good fortune to be tried in a Church court at a time when the secular courts were likely to impose more severe sentences for witchcraft. Although the outcome of the hearing is unknown, it is probable that, at worst, he would have been sentenced to some form of penance for his sins. It is likely that Walsh's association with a Catholic priest helped make him suspect in the eyes of the Anglican authorities.

Walsh's case provides fascinating insights into contemporary Elizabethan beliefs. One clear assumption of his questioners was that he had familiars to help him engage in his magical activities. Although at first he denied having a familiar, it is clear that his interrogators did not believe him and, under pressure, he seems to have made a full confession. The elaborate means by which he raised his familiar, learned in part from the fairies, involved a 'book of circles' given to him by his former employer, a deceased Catholic priest called Robert Drayton. From Drayton he had, apparently, learned his 'physic' and 'surgery', which he had practised for the past seven years. The ritual involved placing two candles of 'virgin wax', joined together to form the shape of a cross, upon one of the great circles in the book. The familiar he conjured up sometimes took the shape of a pigeon, sometimes a dog, and sometimes it appeared in the form of a man with cloven feet. With this familiar he conducted his (white) magic with the further use of candles and 'a little hallowed frankincense'. Although his interrogators suggested that a cunning man with magical power to do good might also use the same magic to cause harm, he denied categorically using any of his knowledge to cause 'hurt either in body or goods'. With this denial the record of the interview ends.

WAREHAM, 1638

It was claimed, in 1638, that two hours after Mary Sheapeard of Wareham had removed one of Jane Coward's stockings Jane lost the use of her hands and feet. She did not recover until, on the advice of the mayor, she shook Mary Sheapeard by the hand. Another woman, Ann Crew, claimed she had witnessed Edward Gill falling sick

❧ The Exami=
nation of John Walsh, before
Maister Thomas Williams, Com=
missary to the Reuerend father in God
William bishop of Excester, vpon
certayne Interrogatories tou=
chyng Wytchcrafte and
Sorcerye, in the pre=
sence of diuers gē=
tlemen and o=
thers.
¶ The. xx. of August.
1566.
(∴)

¶ Imprynted at
London by John Awdely,
Dwelling in litle Britain streete
wythout Aldersgate. 1566.
The. xxiij. of De=
cember.
(∴)

The Examination of John Walsh, 1566.

and lame after she had seen Mary Sheapeard helping him on with one of his leggings. The outcome of the case is not known.

LYME REGIS, 1687

The case of Deanes Grimmerton, a married woman of Lyme Regis, was heard before the justices Sir Robert Wright and Sir John Powell at the summer sessions in Dorchester in 1687. Richard Storch accused her of bewitching his eighteen-year-old son, Nathaniel, and of causing his severe fits. During these he had visions of Deanes. When Nathaniel pointed out the place where the apparition manifested, his overseers struck at it in the hope of injuring the witch. Nathaniel, however, pleaded with them to stop as the blows they struck caused him pain instead. When his body was inspected, a nail and a number of pins were discovered embedded in his skin. Nathaniel's own testimony provided a fascinating description of the costume of a seventeenth-century 'witch': 'clothed with a long-crowned hat, a long red whittle, a red coat, a green apron, and a white cloak about her neck under her whittle'. Deanes appears to have been a pipe smoker: Nathaniel believed his bewitchment began with the occasion when, working as a tailor in a local woman's house, Deanes came in with a pipe of tobacco which she shared with him and others present. Mary Tillman's daughter, Elizabeth, also eighteen years old, suffered similar torments to those of Nathaniel, including fits and piercings with brass pins. She also saw apparitions of Deanes Grimmerton, sitting on her bed or holding her down in her chair, during her illness. When Elizabeth died, her mother was convinced that Deanes Grimmerton had killed her. However, the jury at Dorchester, presented with such insubstantial evidence, found Grimmerton not guilty and she was released.

ESSEX

DANBURY, 1560

John Samond of Danbury was accused of causing the disease and death by witchcraft of two of his Danbury neighbours: John Graunte and Bridget Peacock. He pleaded not guilty; his fate is not known. At the same Sessions Joan Haddon of Witham was accused of bewitching Joan Bowltell and acquiring money by deceitful means.

GREAT WALTHAM, 1564

Elizabeth Lowys of Great Waltham was charged with several counts of *maleficium* in 1564. These included bewitching to death John Wodley and Robert Wodley of Chelmsford, and a three-year-old boy named John Canell of Great Waltham. She was found guilty but made a plea of pregnancy, which, if upheld, might have delayed her execution.

CHELMSFORD, 1566, 1579, 1589, 1610, 1645

The market town of Chelmsford in Essex was the scene of repeated episodes of witch-hunting.

In 1566, Agnes Waterhouse, a sixty-three-year-old widow from the village of Hatfield Peverel, became an early victim of the Witchcraft Act of 1563. Tried alongside Agnes Waterhouse were her daughter Joan and another elderly woman called Elizabeth Francis, both residents of Hatfield Peverel. Elizabeth Francis was the first to go to trial, charged with causing illness in the infant son of one William Auger, among other crimes. Francis was imprisoned and committed to appearances in the pillory.

Elizabeth Francis confessed to having been taught the rudiments of the black arts by her grandmother when she was a child of twelve. From this long-deceased woman, called Mother Eve, Elizabeth Francis had inherited a white spotted cat-familiar called Sathan. Through Sathan, Francis had acquired a flock of eighteen sheep (which none the less 'did all wear away, she knew not how') and had nearly ensnared a rich husband by the name of Andrew Byles. When Byles eventually refused to marry her she had instructed Sathan to destroy his wealth and then to bring about his death, which quickly followed. The cat went on to find her another husband, a yeoman called Christopher Francis, but the arrival of a baby proved unwelcome and Sathan obligingly killed it. Also at Elizabeth's request, the cat, turning itself into a toad, caused lameness in her husband by hiding in his shoe and touching his foot.

Agnes Waterhouse.

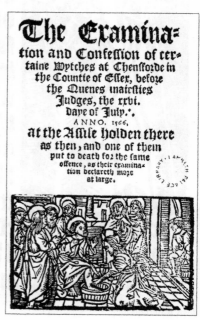

The Examination and Confession of Certain Witches at Chelmsford in the County of Essex, 1566.

⸿Ione Waterhouse, daughter to the
mother Waterhouse, beinge of the
age of. xviii. yeres, and exami／
ned, cōfeſſeth as foloweth.

Fyrſt, that her mo／ther this laſte wyn ter would haue lear ned her this arte, but ſhe lerned it not, nether yet the name of the thinge. She ſaith ſhe neuer ſaw it but once in her mothers hand, and that was in the like nes of a tode, and at that time comming in at a ſodeyn when her mother called it oute to worke ſome thynge withall, ſhe herde her to call it Sathan, for ſhee was not

Joan Waterhouse.

After many years of faithful service (given in exchange for drops of her blood), Elizabeth Francis passed the cat on to Agnes Waterhouse, as described in a contemporary chapbook entitled *The Examination and Confession of Certain Witches at Chelmsford in the County of Essex*, the first of many such accounts of witchcraft trials to be published in the years that followed:

> After all this, when she had kept this cat by the space of fifteen or sixteen years, and some say (though untruly) being weary of it, she came to one Mother Waterhouse, her neighbor (a poor woman), when she was going to the oven, and desired her to give her a cake, and she would give her a thing that she should be the better for so long as she lived. And this Mother Waterhouse gave her a cake, whereupon she brought her this cat in her apron, and taught her as she was instructed before by her grandmother Eve, telling her that she must call him Sathan, and give him of her blood and bread and milk as before.

Through Sathan, Agnes Waterhouse allegedly procured the death of her enemy, William Fynee, by causing him to contract a wasting disease. The cat also committed sundry other petty acts of malice at her command, largely against the livestock of people who had caused her offence.

When brought before the Attorney-General, Sir Gilbert Gerard, Agnes Waterhouse made a poor witness in her own defence and was condemned to hang, the first of many in the Chelmsford area. The fact that no less a figure than the Attorney-General had presided over the case established the trial as a precedent that many other later judges felt bound to follow. The admittance of unsupported confessions, spectral evidence (claims that the accused had been witnessed consorting with evil spirits), evidence from children, and the acceptance of the Devil's mark as proof of guilt set the pattern for decades to come. Waterhouse's confession that she said her prayers in Latin (the Catholic practice) did little to endear her to her Protestant judges.

Joan Waterhouse, aged eighteen, stood in the dock largely as a result of the depositions of a twelve-year-old girl, Agnes Brown, who blamed her for problems with her right arm and leg. The highlight of her evidence was her detailed description of a black dog, allegedly Sathan in disguise. Joan was, however, acquitted of the charge against her. Two other Hatfield Peverel women, Lora Winchester and Joan Osborne, were found not guilty of causing the deaths of livestock and of a six-year-old boy.

Another outbreak of witch-hunting fever swept Chelmsford in 1579 when Elizabeth Francis and three others appeared before two respected Justices of the Queen's Bench, John Southcote and Sir Thomas Gawdy. Their activities were published in a short pamphlet entitled *A detection of damnable driftes, practized by three witches arraigned at Chelmifforde in Essex* (1579). In the intervening years, Francis had been accused once more of using witchcraft, specifically of casting a spell over a woman named Mary Cocke and causing her to experience a marked decline in her health, but had escaped with a year in prison and four appearances in the pillory. There was to be no such leniency for Francis this time, however: she was found guilty of murdering one Alice Poole, a neighbour who had refused her request for 'some olde yest', by means of witchcraft and was duly sentenced to hang. The evidence again depended largely on the confessions of the accused. In this case, Elizabeth Francis' vivid description of how a demon in the guise of the dog appeared to aid her in her desire for revenge against Alice Poole served only to convince the judges of her guilt:

> Whereupon sodenly in the waie she hard a greate noise, and presently there appered unto her a Spirite of a white colour in seemyng like to a little rugged Dogge, standyng neere her uppon the grounde, who asked her whether she went? Shee aunswered for

A Detection
of damnable driftes, practi-
zed by *three VVitches arraigned at*
Chelmiffozde in Effex, at the
laſte Aſſiſes there holden, whiche
were executed in Apzill.
1 5 7 9.

Set fozthe to difcouer the Ambuſhementes of
Sathan, whereby he would ſurpzife vs
lulled in ſecuritie, and hardened
with contempte of Gods
vengeance thzeatened
foz our offences.

Imprinted at London for Edward White,
at the little North-dore of Paules.

A detection of damnable driftes,
practized by three witches arraigned at
Chelmifforde in Essex, 1579.

IOAN PRENTIS
& hir Bid

TACK
GILL

The Chelmsford witches; woodcut from
*The apprehension and confession of
three notorious witches,* 1589.

suche thinges as she wanted, and she tolde him therewith that she could gette no yeest of Pooles wife and therefore wished the same Spirite to goe to her and plague her, which the Spirite promised to doe...

Accompanying Francis on the gallows at the close of proceedings was Ellen Smith, who was found guilty of causing the death by witchcraft – through the agency of 'a thyng like to a blacke Dogge' – of a four-year-old girl, and Alice Nokes, who was condemned to death on similar charges. The fourth accused, Margery Stanton, was acquitted on charges of causing livestock to perish.

Three years later Chelmsford was the scene of the infamous trial of the St Osyth witches, which resulted in more deaths. Another mass trial followed in 1589, when nine women and one man were arraigned mostly on charges of murder by witchcraft. It was recorded in a sensational pamphlet entitled *The apprehension and confession of three notorious witches* (1589). The trial culminated in the execution of four of the accused, of whom three – Joan Prentice, Joan Cony, and Joan Upney – were hanged within two hours of the guilty verdict being reached. Perhaps in the hope of clemency at the last hour, the three women confessed their crimes on the scaffold. As in many of the previous cases, much damning evidence came from children and hinged on the procurement of murder through the agency of familiars. In Joan Cony's case, these were alleged to appear in the form of four black frogs, called Jack (who killed men), Iyll (who killed women), Nicholas (who killed horses), and Ned (who killed cattle). Joan Upney's familiars similarly appeared in the guise of toads and moles, while Joan Prentice had a familiar that took the form of 'a dunnish culloured Ferrit, having fiery eyes'.

Then, in 1610, Katherine Lawrett, from Wake Colne in Essex, was charged at Chelmsford with using witchcraft to cause the demise of a valuable horse belonging to a man called Francis Plaite.

The fact that Chelmsford had already been the scene of such notoriety did much to lend credibility to the allegations that Matthew Hopkins, the self-styled Witchfinder General, levelled at a number of local women in 1645, in what was fated to be remembered as the deadliest instance of witchcraft persecution of the seventeenth century.

This fourth mass trial of witches in the Chelmsford area began with the torture of a one-legged woman, Elizabeth Clarke of Manningtree, herself the daughter of a hanged witch, who confessed to keeping familiars and also to having intercourse with the Devil over some six or seven years. She went on to implicate five other women, who in turn identified others, and in all thirty-two women were brought before the county sessions on 29 July 1645.

Most of the accused were arraigned on the strength of confessions extracted by such means as swimming and sleep deprivation: on Hopkins' instructions, suspected witches were forced to sit cross-legged on a stool for hours without a break or were walked continuously back and forth until they were exhausted. Through the use of such methods, one suspect, Rebecca West, was 'persuaded' to admit to marrying the Devil and also accused her mother, Ann West (who had been imprisoned on charges of witchcraft once before), of being a witch. Others described outlandish imps resembling cats, mice, and squirrels. To add substance to the 'evidence' he had gathered by such means, Hopkins himself claimed to have lain in wait for Clarke's familiars and reported that he saw five of them materialise in the form of a cat called Holt, a legless spaniel called Jarmara, a greyhound called Vinegar Tom, a rabbit-like creature called Sack and Sugar, and a polecat called Newes.

Charged with causing death by witchcraft and/or entertaining spirits, the women had little chance against Hopkins and his detailed knowledge of the witchcraft laws.

They were tried under Robert Rich, Earl of Warwick, and Sir Harbottle Grimston, who proved highly susceptible to Hopkins' suggestions. Only one of the accused was acquitted of all charges; nineteen of the others, including Elizabeth Clarke, were hanged for their crimes.

GREAT DONMOW, 1567

In 1567, Alice Prestmarye of Great Donmow was found guilty of causing by witchcraft the life-threatening illness of Edward Parker, son of a local tanner. Her punishment is not known.

GREAT COGGELSHALL, 1567

In 1567, a widow of Great Coggelshall, Alice Atru, was found guilty of bewitching to death a valuable horse belonging to her Great Coggelshall neighbour Thomas Richolde and a white pig belonging to Edward Goodaye, also of Great Coggelshall. For this she would have faced the punishment of a year in prison and the humiliation of standing at the pillory in a public place for six hours at quarterly intervals during that year.

LITTLE BADDOW, 1569

Two women from Little Baddow were accused of witchcraft at the Essex Lent Sessions in 1569. Alice Bambricke was accused of causing the death of a baby in the village but was found not guilty. Alice Swallow, however, was found guilty of bewitching to death the daughter of a neighbouring yeoman as well as four horses, and of using witchcraft to cause the life-threatening illness of a Little Baddow husbandman named John Daggnett. She was punished accordingly, presumably by hanging.

THE ESSEX SESSIONS, 1572

In 1572, at the Essex Lent Sessions, William Skelton, a labourer from Little Wakering, was found guilty of bewitching to death the daughter of a neighbouring yeoman. At the same hearing, Margery Skelton, who seems to have been William's widowed mother and a person with a reputation as a 'wise woman', was found guilty of bewitching to death the daughter of another Little Wakering yeoman. Together they were also found guilty of using witchcraft to kill a sailor from Barling and also a Barling infant, Agnes Collen, aged one and a half. Meanwhile, Katherine Pullen, a spinster from Tollesbury, was found guilty of bewitching to death John Dennynge's wife, Joan, and Elizabeth Francis, a spinster of Hatfield, was found guilty of using witchcraft to murder a neighbouring miller's wife. It can be presumed that they were all executed.

Several more people were called before the court on witchcraft charges in the Summer Sessions of 1572. Some were found not guilty, but Agnes Francys, the wife of a weaver from Hatfield Peverel was found guilty of bewitching to death one Walter Wilmotte. In the hope of postponing her execution she pleaded pregnancy. A Halstead woman, Agnes Steademan, was found guilty of causing by witchcraft the fatal sickness of a neighbouring yeoman's wife, also of two counts of bewitching cattle. Presumably she was hanged.

MALDON, 1574

At the Essex Lent Sessions of 1574, Alice Chaundler of Maldon was found guilty of bewitching to death a neighbouring fletcher's eight-year-old daughter, and a Maldon weaver named Robert Briscooe, together with his two-year-old son and five-year-old daughter. It can be assumed Alice Chaundler was hanged as a witch.

BARKING, 1574

In the Essex Summer Sessions of 1574, Celia Glasenberye of Barking was found guilty of killing three of her Barking neighbours by witchcraft – a tanner, a glover, and the son of a yeoman. She was also found guilty of causing another yeoman to fall sick and to lose 'the use of his members', and of bewitching yet another yeoman's grey gelding. Almost certainly she was hanged for her supposed murderous activities.

THAXTED, 1574

In the Essex Summer Sessions of 1574, two Thaxted women were found guilty of acts of *maleficium*. Alice Hynckson, a widow, was found guilty of bewitching to death three cows and seven ewes belonging to a neighbouring husbandman. For this she received a one-year prison sentence and quarterly appearances in the pillory. Elizabeth Taylor, a labourer's wife, it can be presumed, was executed for bewitching to death in Thaxted the daughter of a London basket-maker, and also the daughter of a local carpenter.

HATFIELD PEVEREL, 1576

Witchcraft appears to have been particularly prevalent in Hatfield Peverel during this period. Agnes Waterhouse was condemned in 1566 and Agnes Francys followed her in 1572. In 1576 a third Hatfield 'Agnes', Agnes Bromley, was found guilty of bewitching to death sundry livestock and a local labourer named John Baker. Presumably she was hanged.

BRENTWOOD, 1576

In 1576, Joan Baker of Brentwood was found guilty of using witchcraft to cause the fatal sickness of Mary Noke, a glover's wife, and, together with another Brentwood spinster, Elizabeth Aylett, of causing the continuing sickness of Mary Noke's daughter, and killing outright a ten-year-old child named John Welles. All of their victims were Brentwood residents. It can be assumed they were hanged for their alleged crimes.

ST OSYTH, 1582

The village of St Osyth, near Brightlingsea in Essex, suffered more than most communities in Essex and East Anglia during the witchcraft panic that swept eastern England in the late sixteenth century and again in the mid-seventeenth century.

The first mass trial of witches from St Osyth took place at the Chelmsford county sessions in 1582. A surviving account of the trial, a substantial 1582 treatise entitled

¶A true and iuſt Recorde, of
the Information , Examination
and Confeſsion of all the Witches , taken at
S . Oſes *in the countie of* Eſſex : *whereof*
ſome were executed, and other ſome en-
treated according to the determination of lawe.

Wherein all men may ſee what a peſtilent
people Witches are, and how vnworthy to lyue
in a Chriſtian Common-
wealth.

Written orderly, as the ca-
ſes were tryed by euidence,
By W. W.

¶*Imprinted in London at the*
three Cranes in the Vinetree by
Thomas Dawſon
1582.

A true and just Recorde of the Information, Examination, and Confessions of all the Witches taken at St. Oses, indicates that some fourteen women from St Osyth were indicted on charges of witchcraft. Of these, ten were charged with 'bewitching to death', which carried the death penalty.

The trial, presided over by Judge Bryan Darcy, appears to have had its roots in a series of village vendettas that had escalated from trivial quarrels. At the heart of the affair was Ursula Kempe (otherwise called Grey), an impoverished local woman who offered her services as a midwife and nursemaid and who also had a reputation for 'unwitching' those who feared they were under the influence of malevolent magic.

Witnesses attested that Mother Kempe had cured a young boy, Davy Thorlowe, of illness by the use of incantations but had subsequently taken offence when the boy's mother, Grace Thorlowe, had declined to employ her as nursemaid to her infant daughter. When the baby girl fell out of her crib soon afterwards and broke her neck, suspicion immediately fell upon Kempe, although no accusations were made openly. Ignoring the rumours, Grace Thorlowe allowed Kempe to suggest a treatment for her arthritis. Kempe recommended a method that she had learned from an old 'wise woman', later described by Mrs Thorlowe in court, telling her to:

> Take hog's dung and charnel and put them together and hold them in her left hand, and to take in the other hand a knife, and to prick the medicine three times, and then to cast the same into the fire, and to take the said knife, and to make three pricks under a table, and to let the knife stick there. And after that to take three leaves of sage, and as much of herb John (alias herb grace) and put them into ale, and drink it last at night and first in the morning; and that she taking the same had ease of her lameness.

The patient refused, however, to pay Kempe's fee of twelve pence, upon which her condition worsened.

At this juncture, Grace Thorlowe decided to make a complaint to the authorities and it was agreed that the matter should be presented to the county sessions. At Ursula Kempe's ensuing trial Darcy persuaded the defendant's illegitimate eight-year-old son Thomas Rabbet to elaborate upon his mother's activities as a witch, and then offered the unfortunate woman the chance of clemency if she would admit her guilt, telling her: 'They which do confess the truth of their doings, they shall have much favor; but the other they shall be burned and hanged.' Mother Kempe seized the opportunity and, 'bursting out weeping', confirmed her son's account of her practices.

According to her own testimony, Ursula Kempe had kept four familiars, which manifested as two male cats (a grey one called Titty and a black one called Jacke), a black toad named Pigin and a white lamb she knew as Tyffin (in defiance of the tradition that familiar spirits were unable to manifest as lambs). These imps she fed on white bread or cake and beer; at night she also let them 'sucke blood of her upon her armes and other places of her body'. The black cat called Jacke had caused the death of Kempe's sister-in-law, while the lamb had rocked the infant Thorlowe from her crib.

The accused woman threw herself on the court's mercy, completing her confession by identifying a number of other St Osyth women as witches like herself. It should be noted that at no point did Kempe or anyone else suggest that these women had acted in confederation as an organised coven; Kempe knew of her neighbours' activities only by spying through windows and allegedly learning their secrets from her lamb-familiar. She had herself learned the art of witchcraft some ten years earlier from the now-deceased wife of a man named Cocke, of Weeley, whom she had approached for relief from 'lameness of the bones' – only to be told that the cause was a witch's spell.

When these women – Elizabeth Bennet, Alice Newman, Alice Hunt, and her sister Margery Sammon – were brought before Darcy they followed Kempe's example, not only giving full accounts of their familiars but also repeating the allegations against each other and naming yet more accomplices. Alice Hunt confirmed that her own sister was a witch and then implicated one Joan Pechey, while Margery Sammon returned the compliment against her sister and also named Pechey; Alice Newman, meanwhile, gave details of Bennet's guilt. Also implicated were Agnes Glascock and Cicely Celles, both accused of bewitching to death; Joan Turner, charged with employing the evil eye; Elizabeth Ewstace, who had caused harm to a neighbour's animals; Annis Herd (or Heard); and Alice Manfield and Margaret Grevell, who were both indicted on relatively minor charges.

By the time the accusations had died down fourteen women – mostly of deprived and disreputable backgrounds – stood in the dock. The charges against them ranged from damage to property and livestock to the bewitching to death of some twenty-four persons. Less serious complaints against them included accusations that they had prevented beer from brewing, butter from churning, and carts from moving. Virtually all were suspected of having kept familiars.

When the sensational proceedings of the court finally came to an end, two of the accused (including Margery Sammon) were not indicted, two were discharged but held in prison suspected of various felonies, four were acquitted, four (including Alice Newman, who was accused of murdering her husband and four others) were convicted but reprieved and two (Mother Kempe and Elizabeth Bennet) were sentenced to hang.

Bennet – who confessed to owning two familiars, a dog-like creature called Suckin and a creature 'like a lyon or a hare' called Lierd – was executed for killing a farmer named William Byet and his wife and two others. She was alleged to have murdered Byet after he had refused to sell her milk and had called her an 'old trot, old whore, and other lewd speeches'. Despite the court's guarantees, Kempe herself went to the gallows after confessing to causing three deaths by witchcraft between 1580 and 1582.

Among the luckier ones who were acquitted of witchcraft was Annis Herd, who was charged with causing the death of the wife of a parson called Richard Harrison. She was said to keep no less than twelve imps or spirits, which resembled rats and which she fed on straw or hay. As in several of the other cases the trouble stemmed from a trivial falling out, in this instance over some missing ducklings that Annis Herd was rumoured to have stolen. Harrison's wife, evidently a highly-strung character, railed against the suspected thief and subsequently decided that the original crime had been compounded by a spell cast upon herself. The parson's wife went into a gradual physical decline and, despite her husband threatening to break every bone in Annis Herd's body if she did not lift her spell, eventually she died. On her deathbed, the dying woman made it perfectly clear whom she blamed for her condition, lamenting as she died, 'Oh, Annis Herd, Annis Herd, she hath consumed me.'

Coming between the infamous trial of the Chelmsford witches in 1566 and that of the Warboys witches in 1593, the St Osyth trial marked a significant stage in the development of the witch-hunting mania that gripped eastern England for many years. The acceptance of some very dubious testimony, in particular that of several children well below the age at which statements were legally admissible, set an ominous precedent for many future trials (including that of the Salem witches a hundred years later). Wallace Notestein, in his *History of Witchcraft in England from 1558 to 1718* (1911), commented: 'The use of evidence in this trial would lead one to suppose that in England no rules of evidence were yet in existence. The testimony of children ranging in age from six to nine was eagerly received. No objection indeed was made to the testimony of a neighbour who professed to have overheard what he deemed an incriminating statement ... nothing was excluded.'

The shadow cast over St Osyth by the trial persisted for many years, and more alleged witches from the village were among the victims of the witch-hunts presided over by Matthew Hopkins in the 1640s. Another noteworthy byproduct of the trial was the publication in 1584 of Reginald Scot's *Discoverie of Witchcraft*, which did much to counter the spread of the witchcraft hysteria in England by exposing the flaws in such belief.

In 1921, a plough furrow exposed two female skeletons at St Osyth. The skeletons, which had been pierced at the knees and elbows with iron rivets in an apparent attempt to prevent the dead from rising, were tentatively identified as those of Ursula Kempe and Elizabeth Bennet (though they may been two of the witches killed during the Hopkins era). They were preserved for many years in the Boscastle Museum of Witchcraft, Cornwall, before being sold to the artist Robert Lenkiewicz in the late 1990s.

GREAT LEIGHS, 1584

In 1584, Elizabeth Brooke of Great Leighs was hanged for using witchcraft to kill a woman, as well as James Holmested's six cattle and four pigs, several sows belonging to George Fytch, Thomas Cornyshe's two cows and two horses, and the five cows and and four pigs owned by James Spylman.

UPMINSTER, 1616

In 1616, Susan Barker was found guilty and hanged for bewitching two men. She was also accused of unearthing a human skull from a grave to use in a spell to bewitch a woman.

HARWICH, 1634

For being found guilty of bewitching a woman to death at Harwich, Jane Prentice of Harwich should have been sentenced to death in 1634. However, she appears again

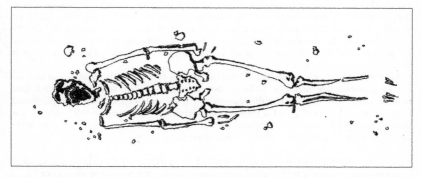

Skeleton of a supposed witch discovered in a cottage garden in St Osyth, Essex, in 1921.

in the Gaol Calendar of Colchester Castle, together with her daughter, Suzan Prentice, and an Elinor Witherill, charged with 'felony and witchcraft'. This time she was found guilty of causing the wasting sickness of another Harwich woman, Ruth Hatch. Jane Prentice's ultimate fate is unknown.

COLCHESTER, 1651

In 1651, a Colchester weaver and cunning man, John Lock, was sentenced to a year in prison with quarterly appearances at the pillory for using witchcraft to tell William Fayrcloth, another Colchester weaver, where he would find an amount of yarn that had been stolen from him.

NEVENDON, 1653

In 1653, Mary Hurst of Nevendon, was found guilty of bewitching a Nevendon neighbour, William Hodge, and causing him to suffer from some form of wasting disease. Her sentence is not recorded.

COGGESHALL, 1699

In 1699, old Widow Coman (or Comon) of Coggeshall, Essex, became the victim of one of the last English witch-hunts. Widow Coman had a long-standing local reputation as a witch but her fate was finally sealed when James Boys, the vicar of Coggeshall, became determined to make her confess her sins and admit to her use of magic.

Under pressure from the vicar, Widow Coman confessed to signing a pact with the Devil, under which she agreed not to enter a church for five years, to keeping a familiar (which she fed 'at her fundament'), and to sticking pins in waxen images. Further 'proof' of her guilt was obtained when she stumbled over the words of the Lord's Prayer and when she refused to renounce the Devil and his imps during a service of exorcism held by the vicar.

The Reverend Boys did nothing to intervene when, on 13 July 1699, a mob of villagers led by a certain James Haines seized the old woman and dragged her off to the local river. There, in front of a crowd of several hundred people, Widow Coman was subjected to the ordeal of swimming to determine whether she was guilty of witchcraft (if she floated she was a witch; if she sank she was innocent). When she bobbed repeatedly to the surface this was taken as confirmation of her guilt. To make doubly sure, the procedure was carried out twice more, on 19 and 24 July 1699, each time with the same result.

Though she was never brought to trial on charges of witchcraft, Widow Coman did not long survive her duckings. In December that year she died from a chill she is said to have contracted during her ill-treatment at the hands of the mob. The Reverend Boys subsequently instructed a midwife to search the deceased widow's corpse for witch's marks and two large supernumerary 'nipples' for the feeding of imps were allegedly found, as Boys himself later described in his diary:

> Upon her death I requested Becke the midwife to search her body in the presence of some sober women, which she did and assured me she never saw the like in her life that her fundament was open like a mouse-hole and that in it were two long bigges

out of which being pressed issued blood that they were neither piles nor emrods for she knew both but excrescencies like to biggs with nipples which seemed as if they had been frequently sucked.

Convinced of the justice of his actions, on 27 December 1699, the Reverend Boys saw to it that Widow Coman was buried without any of the rites that a dutiful Christian might expect.

GLOUCESTERSHIRE

TEWKESBURY, 1649

A report by a 'Person of Quality' of trial proceedings at Gloucester in 1649, published in 1693 as *A Collection of Modern Relations of Matter of Fact concerning Witches and Witchcraft upon the persons of People*, and attributed to Sir Matthew Hale, records the malefic activities of an unnamed young woman accused of harming livestock. Discovering that, although his sow seemed 'to have great store of milk', her young pigs were 'almost famished', a Tewkesbury man decided to keep a close eye on his animals. Subsequently he was surprised to see a curious creature that looked like a polecat in the vicinity of the pigs. Although he managed to pierce it with the prongs of a fork, the animal escaped. A maid was observed by neighbours leaving the vicinity of this incident and it was discovered that she was bleeding from injuries to her thigh, injuries that corresponded exactly to those that the polecat-like creature must have sustained. Consequently the maid was arrested and tried but no comment upon the outcome of her trial appears in the pamphlet.

CHIPPING CAMPDEN, 1660

'The Campden Wonder' is the ancient nickname for mysterious events that are reputed to have occurred in Chipping Campden in 1660. In 1661 Joan Perry, a suspected witch, was found guilty and hanged on Broadway Hill for murdering William Harrison, steward to the Viscountess Campden, even though his body had not been found. Her two sons, who, allegedly, she had bewitched, were hanged with her as her accomplices. Two years later, however, William Harrison turned up alive and well with a tale of abduction by pirates and a spell of slavery overseas. This extraordinary tale was recorded in 1676 by Thomas Overbury in *A True and perfect Account of the Examination, Confession, Tryal, Condemnation and Execution of Joan Perry and her two sons ... for the supposed murder of William Harrison, Gent.*

Broadway Hill.

HERTFORDSHIRE

HODDESDON, 1573

Thomas Heather of Hoddesdon 'being a common conjurer' was found guilty in 1573 of invoking evil spirits 'in a certain wood' to help make him rich. However, he appears to have been pardoned and acquitted.

ROYSTON, 1606

Two women, Alice Stokes and Christiana Stokes, who were hanged for witchcraft following their trial at Hertford in 1606, appear to have been a mother and daughter team. They were accused of various acts of *maleficium*, including the killing of their neighbours' cattle and causing severe sickness. After a young woman accidentally threw water over Christiana Stokes, her child died after falling out of its cradle. After the women had been arrested, a chest belonging to them was found to contain the paraphernalia of their profession, including sets of human bones, hair of all colours, and a curious parchment on which was drawn a coloured picture of what looked like a human heart and other diagrams resembling anatomical elements. Alice Stokes confessed to using these materials and two spirit helpers to cause pain and suffering to cattle and humans.

Interestingly, presumably prior to their arrest, one of their alleged victims was punished for scratching Alice Stokes and drawing blood. This person had been sick and, believing Alice to be the cause, he drew her blood in the belief that this would lift her spell. The man did recover but Alice sued him for his violent attack and he was fined five shillings, after which his illness returned.

A somewhat unreliable contemporary pamphlet comments on more Royston witches, including Joan Harrison and her daughter, both, allegedly, condemned to death and hanged at Hertford for witchcraft in the same year, 1606.

HERTFORD, 1635

A record survives of the pitiful death in Hertford Gaol in 1635 of Joan Meade, a woman of about seventy years of age who had been arrested on suspicion of using sorcery.

THE *n. 50*

MOST CRVELL
AND BLOODY MVR-
ther committed by an Inkeepers
Wife, called Annis Dell, *and*
her *Sonne* George Dell,

Foure yeeres *since*.

On the bodie of a Childe, called
Anthony Iames in Bishops Hatfield in
the Countie of Hartford, and now most miraculously
reuealed by the Sifter of the faid *Anthony*, who at the
time of the murther had her tongue cut out, and
foure yeeres remayned dumme and speechlesse,
and now perfectly speaketh, reuea-
ling the Murther, hauing
no tongue to be seen.

With the feuerall VVitch-crafts,
and moft damnable practifes of one *Iohane Harrison*
and her Daughter vpon feuerall perfons, men
and women at Royfton, *who were all execu-*
ted at Hartford *the 4 of August*
laft paft. 1606.

LONDON.
Printed for *William Firebrand* and *John Wright,*
and are to be fold at Chrifts Church
dore. 1606.

Pamphlet detailing the supposed crimes of Alice and Christiana Stokes.

THE
DIVELS DELVSIONS
OR

A faithfull relation of John Palmer *and*
Elizabeth Knott *two notorious* VVitches
lately condemned at the Sessions of Oyer
and Terminer *in* St. Albans.

Together with the Confession of the aforesaid
John Palmer *and* Elizabeth Knott, *executed* July 16.

Also their accusations of severall VVitches *in*
Hitchen, Norton, *and other places in the*
County *of* Hartford.

July 19 *LONDON*
Printed for Richard Williams Stationer at St. Albans,
Anno Dom. 1649.

*The Divel's Delusions; or A faithful relation of John Palmer and Elizabeth Knott, two
notorious Witches, 1649.*

CHESHUNT, 1647

In 1647, a glover's wife, Elizabeth Browne, was found guilty of bewitching to death a neighbouring Cheshunt woman, Mary Addams. Her sentence is not recorded but, presumably, she was hanged.

ST ALBANS, 1649

This case is especially noteworthy in the history of English witch-hunting since one of the two accused, unusual in English cases, was male. It is also important in revealing something of the extent to which belief in diabolical conspiracy had developed by the mid-seventeenth century. The activities of John Palmer and Elizabeth Knott, 'two notorious witches' from the parish of Norton in St Albans, were detailed in a short pamphlet that was printed in London in 1649, shortly after their trial and execution. It is entitled *The Divel's Delusions; or A faithful relation of John Palmer and Elizabeth Knott, two notorious Witches*. The pamphlet takes the form of an anonymous letter sent by someone from St Albans 'to a friend in the country'.

John Palmer, according to his own confession, had been a witch for sixty years. He had made a pact with the Devil and had a 'mark upon his side, which gave suck to two familiars, [one in the] form of a dog which he called George, the other in the likeness of a woman called Jezebel'. He 'seduced Elizabeth Knott his kinswoman, to consort with him in his villainy' and, using a clay image of their victim, they magically contrived the death of a neighbour and, presumably, landlady, Goodwife Pearls of Norton in revenge for 'hanging a lock upon his door for the not paying of his rent'. Palmer also confessed, among other things, to bewitching and killing the horse of a Mr Cleaver.

Others were implicated in Palmer's diabolical activities. In all he named eleven further associates in various localities: Mary Bichance and Widow Palmer of Hitchin; John Salmon senior, Joseph Salmon and his wife Judith, John Lamen senior and his wife Mary, and John Lamen junior of Norton; Mrs Mayes of Weston; and two local servants, Sarah Smith and Anne Smith. Therefore it may have been supposed that he was involved in a coven of thirteen, a number typical of those exposed in witch-hunts in continental Europe during the period. Furthermore, the writer of the pamphlet commented on a 'cunning man' called Marsh of nearby Dunstable who, despite his reputation for white magic, was, according to Palmer's confession, 'the head of the whole College of Witches'.

John Palmer and Elizabeth Knott were tried at St Albans in July 1649. The Assize records have not survived but, according to the pamphlet, both were hanged for their crimes.

LITTLE HADHAM, 1659

Alice Free of Little Hadham was accused in 1659 of causing the sickness and death by witchcraft of Frances Rustat, who had fallen ill after delaying payment for the eggs she had bought from 'Goody' Free. Alice Free was bound over 'to appear and answer such things objected against her for matter of witchcraft'. The outcome of the case is not known.

WARE, 1669

A pamphlet entitled *The Hartford-shire Wonder, or Strange News from Ware*, printed in 1669, tells the story of recent remarkable events at Ware. The troubles began when a wheelright, Thomas Stretton of Ware, crossed a local wizard. Subsequently the wizard's wife visited Stretton's house, where she met his twenty-year-old daughter and asked for a drink. Unaware of her father's quarrel, the daughter gave the wizard's wife what she required. Soon after, she fell sick with fits. A week later the woman returned, this time asking for a pin, which Stretton's daughter gave her. After this her fits grew worse, her body swelling 'like a bladder puft up with wind ready to burst'. For the next six months she stopped eating, she vomited eleven pins, flames issued from her mouth, and hair or flax sometimes appeared on her tongue. Apparently the witch was discovered after foam from her victim's mouth was burned, magically forcing the witch to betray herself. The pamphlet concluded that many former sceptics were converted to belief in witchcraft when they saw the afflicted girl. The story, though, is not substantiated by other, more reliable, records.

The Hartford-shire Wonder, or Strange News from Ware, 1669.

WALKERN, 1712

In 1712, an old woman called Jane Wenham appeared before the Hertford Assizes on charges of witchcraft; she is now remembered as the last person to be formally tried as a witch in England.

Nicknamed the 'Wise Woman of Walkern', Jane Wenham, of Walkern, near Stevenage, was seventy years old in 1712 and had long had a local reputation as a witch. Typical of the stories told about her was one that described how she bewitched a farm labourer called Matthew Gilson after he refused her a pennyworth of straw. As a result of her vengeful curse, Gilson ran down the road begging anyone he met for some straw and, when this was not forthcoming, thrusting handfuls of fresh manure inside his shirt. Jane Wenham, however, did not respond well to accusations that she was a witch and when Gilson's employer repeated the allegation she complained to the local magistrate, Sir Henry Chauncey. Chauncey passed the case to the local clergyman, who gave Jane Wenham a stern warning before fining the farmer one shilling for the insult, but this did not satisfy Wenham and she was heard to promise she would get justice 'some other way'. The farmer's daughter then fell ill and his livestock sickened.

More serious legal proceedings followed when Wenham was again accused of witchcraft practices, this time by Anne Thorn, the clergyman's sixteen-year-old servant-girl. The girl complained that Wenham had used magic to afflict her with fits and with hallucinations of cat-like demons, and had also caused her to vomit pins. On one occasion the girl had been forced by the witch's magic to run for half a mile, despite the fact that she had recently injured her leg in an accident, and then to gather sticks at Jane Wenham's command. The allegations were corroborated in part by a number of people, including one James Burville, who claimed ominously that he had seen numerous cats at Anne Thorn's door, one of them bearing a face just like Jane Wenham's.

An English engraving from *c.* 1700 showing witches, broomsticks and cat familiars.

On the strength of these accusations, backed up by her dark reputation, Jane Wenham was arrested and searched for the Devil's mark in the time-honoured fashion, pins being plunged deep into her arm numerous times to see if the blood flowed freely and to ascertain whether she felt any pain. No insensitive spots were located but the prisoner made a full confession, admitting that she was a witch just as everyone claimed she was, but protesting that she practised only harmless 'white' magic.

Notwithstanding the confession made by the old woman (who appears to have genuinely believed she had a witch's powers), it was decided that a charge of 'conversing familiarly with the Devil in the shape of a cat' would suffice. The sixteen witnesses assembled to give evidence against the accused included three clergymen. Further evidence was produced in court in the form of 'cakes' of feathers and a suspicious ointment that was found under the woman's pillow. According to the prosecution, the ointment was made of human fat, rendered down. When ordered to recite the Lord's Prayer, which no witch was supposed to be able to do without making a mistake, she stumbled over the words. The judge, Sir John Powell, was clearly unimpressed by the case and when told that the accused had been seen flying through the air merely observed that as far as he knew there was no law against flying. Despite this, the jury found Jane Wenham guilty, obliging the judge to condemn the defendant to death. Powell, however, obtained a reprieve for the defendant and subsequently secured a royal pardon for her – to the fury of many locals.

The case generated intense interest on a national scale and helped to polarise opinion about witchcraft: large numbers of tracts and pamphlets about the affair were published. After the verdict Jane Wenham found it impossible to return to her home village, such was the intensity of feeling towards her, but a local gentleman, the Whig William Cowper, First Earl Cowper, proved sympathetic to her plight and provided her with a small cottage at Hartingfordbury, where she lived quietly until her death in 1730. Anne Thorn, who had furnished the original charges against Wenham, was advised by her doctors to wash her hands and face twice a day and a young man was appointed to watch over her while she recovered from her hysteria. The treatment proved a success in more ways than one, Anne Thorn going on to marry the young man sent to watch her.

Some sources contend that there were trials on charges of witchcraft after 1712, but there is little documentary record of this. In Northamptonshire, for instance, it is sometimes claimed, on the strength of a contemporary pamphlet, that Mary Hickes and her nine-year-old daughter Elizabeth were tried as witches after being accused of taking off their stockings to raise a storm. They were allegedly condemned as witches and hanged at Huntingdon on 28 July 1716, but on closer examination it appears that the pamphlet on which this is based is simply a reworking of a Chelmsford trial that took place many years earlier.

LONG MARSTON, 1751

In 1751, sixteen years after the witchcraft statute of 1604 under which suspected witches were brought to trial was repealed, an elderly couple called John and Ruth Osborne fell victim to what is generally recognised to have been the last witch-hunt in English history.

The Osbornes were paupers who lived among more prosperous neighbours in the village of Long Marston, near Tring in Hertfordshire. Ruth Osborne was believed to be just short of her seventieth birthday, while John Osborne was said to be fifty-six. Their troubles had begun back in 1745, when the couple fell foul of a local dairyman-cum-publican by the name of John Butterfield (Bullerfield according to some sources) who resided in the nearby hamlet of Gubblecote. When Butterfield refused Ruth Osborne's pleas for a little buttermilk one day, she allegedly retaliated by muttering curses against him. Butterfield subsequently accused Ruth Osborne and her husband of bewitching his calves, causing them to fall ill, and also blamed them for fits that he suffered.

Butterfield got a sympathetic hearing from the neighbours who drank at his house in Gubblecote, and it was eventually agreed that the couple should be swum in order to test whether or not they were witches: if they floated they were witches, if they sank they were innocent. It appears that Butterfield believed that there existed a legal right to swim suspected witches, provided the test was first announced in public. Accordingly, Butterfield and his confederates had news of the planned swimming proclaimed by the town criers in three local towns, Hemel Hempstead, Leighton Buzzard, and Winslow. No one voiced opposition to the test, although efforts were made to protect the couple from the threat against them by removing them first to the workhouse in Tring and then, in the early hours of 22 April 1751, to the vestry of the church there.

Around mid-morning of 22 April an angry mob ransacked Tring workhouse in search of the Osbornes and threatened to burn the building down and to assault the master of the workhouse, John Tomkins, unless the couple were produced. Tomkins, fearing for his life, led the mob to the church, where the pair were seized from the vestry. The mob was now estimated to number around 4000 people, leaving the local constable powerless to intervene.

The mob beat the Osbornes with sticks and then hauled them up the road to Gubblecote. Here they entered Ten Acres field and dammed up a stream to form a

The Half Moon public house in Wilstone Green, where Ruth and John Osborne were taken before they were swum as witches in 1750. It was also here that Ruth's corpse was later brought and where the inquest into her death took place.

pool in which to carry out the swimming. A yeoman farmer called Nott (or Robert) Gregory, however, braved the mob's threats and dismantled the dam that had been made, obliging the crowd to transfer their prisoners to the Half Moon alehouse in nearby Wilstone Green while attempts were made to found a suitable pond elsewhere.

After three-quarters of an hour it was decided to take the Osbornes to a body of water known as Wilstone Wire (otherwise given as Ware, Wear, or Were). Although there are other possibilities for the location of this pool, local tradition places the site at a point on Watery Lane, between Wilstone Green and Long Marston, known as Dinah's Pond (Dinah being a name Ruth Osborne was formerly known by when working for a local family). It was filled in by a local farmer, who was unaware of its history, in 1971.

One witness of the swimming described how Ruth Osborne, clad only in a sheet, was bound at the wrists and feet and dragged through the water, which was five feet deep, to the opposite bank by means of a rope tied round her. Others recalled her being forced to the middle of the pond by two men, one of them identified as a chimney-sweep called Thomas Colley, who used a stick to push the struggling old woman repeatedly under the surface. The mob then dragged the old woman's lifeless body to the bank, as Edward Chapman of Wingrave told the subsequent inquiry held in Tring:

> One of the men dragged her across the pond to the bank where her husband lay and dragging her across the sheet came off and she was quite naked and when they had got her to the other side three or four of the mob took her up and carried her to a public house on Wilstone Green and the examinant also says he then saw her and believes she was dead, drowned in the manner aforesaid...

John Osborne was also dragged through the water, but somehow survived the ordeal. When all was over Thomas Colley went through the crowd 'collecting money for the pains he had taken in showing them sport'.

Details of the affair reached the ears of the authorities and in due course (and in spite of a general reluctance among the participants to name names) three of the mob's leaders – William Umbles, Charles Young (known as Redbeard), and Thomas Colley – were tried at the Hertford Assizes for the murder of Ruth Osborne.

On 24 August 1751, Colley was escorted by a force of 108 men and seven officers of the Oxford Blues (now the Royal Horse Guards) to a gibbet erected near Wilstone Green (according to local tradition, on Lukes Lane at Gubblecote Cross). Despite the show of force by the authorities, a large crowd gathered on the day of the execution, many of them voicing the opinion that it was unjust to kill a man for ridding the community of a known witch.

Colley himself had by now come to realise the folly of his actions and asked for the following address, which he had written the day before his execution, to be broadcast throughout Hertfordshire:

> Good people,
>
> I beseech you all to take warning by an unhappy man's suffering, that you be not deluded into so absurd and wicked a conceit as to believe that there are any such beings upon earth as witches.
>
> It was foolish and vain imagination, heightened and inflamed by the strength of liquor, which prompted me to be instrumental with others as mad as myself in the

horrid and barbarous murder of Ruth Osborne, the supposed witch, for which I am now so deservedly to suffer death.

I am fully convinced of my former error, and, with the sincerity of a dying man, declare that I do not believe there is such a thing in being as a witch; and pray God that none of you, through a contrary persuasion, may hereafter be induced to think that you have a right in any shape to persecute, much less endanger the life of a fellow-creature. I beg of you all to pray to God to forgive me, and to wash clean my polluted soul in the blood of Jesus Christ, my Saviour and Redeemer. So exhorteth you all, The dying Thomas Colley.

The execution was carried out and Colley's body was left to hang in chains as a warning to others who might consider taking similar action against suspected witches in the future. As for John Osborne, some accounts say he died soon afterwards as a result of his ordeal, while others say he never found employment again and ended his days in the workhouse.

HUNTINGDONSHIRE

WARBOYS, 1593

The trial of the 'Witches of Warboys' held at Huntingdon in 1593, as recorded in a substantial contemporary tract, *The most strange and admirable discoverie of the three Witches of Warboys* (1593), was one of the most widely reported witchcraft cases to take place in England prior to 1600 and proved highly influential, providing a model for many subsequent trials. One reason for the degree of interest shown in the case was the untypically high social standing of the victims of the alleged witches.

The three accused witches were the impoverished Alice, John, and Agnes Samuel, who were said to be responsible for bewitching the five daughters of a wealthy country squire, Robert Throckmorton, their neighbour in Warboys. They were also suspected of the murder by witchcraft of Lady Cromwell, grandmother of the man destined to govern England as Oliver Cromwell, Lord Protector.

At the heart of the case was the hysteria of the Throckmorton girls, which began with a series of fits (probably epileptic) suffered by ten-year-old Jane Throckmorton in 1589:

> Sometimes she would neese [sneeze] very loud and thick for the space of half an hour together, and presently as one in a great trance and swoon lay quietly as long. Soon after she would begin to swell and heave up her belly so as none was able to bend her, or keep her down. Sometime she would shake one leg and no other part of her, as if the palsy had been in it; sometimes the other. Presently she would shake one of her arms, and then the other, and soon after her head, as if she had been infected with the running palsy.

Being a close neighbour, seventy-six-year-old Alice Samuel felt it would be polite to call in at the house to inquire after the child's health. Unfortunately, she chose to visit while Jane was actually having a seizure, and the girl was quick to identify the old woman as the source of her suffering:

> Look where the old witch sitteth ... did you ever see (said the child) one more like a witch than she is? Take off her black thrumbed [fringed] cap, for I cannot abide to look on her.

Jane's claims were enthusiastically backed up by her four sisters, aged between nine and fifteen, who went on to exhibit similarly alarming symptoms.

Examination by two doctors brought in from Cambridge failed to reveal any medical cause for the girls' condition and the children's accusations of witchcraft became

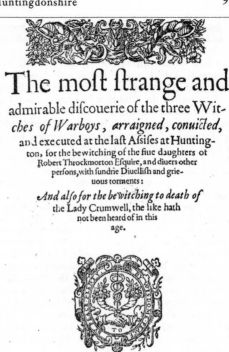

The moſt ſtrange and
admirable diſcouerie of the three Witches of *Warboys*, *arraigned*, *conuicted*,
and executed at the laſt Aſsiſes at Hunting-
ton, for the bewitching of the fiue daughters of
Robert Throckmorton Eſquire, and diuers other
perſons, with ſundrie Diuelliſh and grie-
uous torments:

And alſo for the bewitching to death of
the Lady Crumwell, the like hath
not been heard of in this
age.

LONDON
Printed by the Widdowe Orwin, for Thomas Man, and Iohn Win-
nington, and are to be ſolde in Pater noſter Rowe, at the
ſigne of the Talbot. 1593.

The most strange and admirable
discoverie of the three Witches of
Warboys, 1593

increasingly difficult for their parents to ignore. Sir Gilbert Pickering of Titchmarsh, brother of Robert Throckmorton's wife Elizabeth, heard of the affair and decided to investigate. At Sir Gilbert's insistence, Mother Samuel was brought before the girls, upon which they threw even more violent fits. They also scratched the old woman's hand, apparently in the belief that by drawing blood they could break the witch's power over them. Others in the Throckmorton household began to suffer seizures, among them seven of the servants and the children's aunt, Mrs John Pickering. Up to this point, the girls' fits had intensified whenever Mrs Samuels was close at hand; now, however, the reverse occurred, with the girls going into helpless spasms whenever the old woman was absent. To counter this, the hapless Alice Samuels was ordered to move into the Throckmorton household.

The children took every opportunity to heap further accusations on the unwilling house guest, as contemporary reports related:

Many times also as she sat talking with these children, being in their fits by the fire side, they would say unto her: Look you here, Mother Samuel, do you not see this thing that sitteth here by us? She would answer no, not she. Why, they would say

again, I marvell that you do not see it. Look how it leapeth, skippeth, and playeth up
and down, pointing at it with their fingers here and there as it leaped.

The next significant visitor to the stricken Throckmorton household was Lady
Cromwell, wife of the Throckmortons' landlord Sir Henry Cromwell, the richest
commoner in England. Lady Cromwell was clearly convinced by the girls' stories and
tried to destroy the hold that Mrs Samuel was reputed to have over them by cutting
off some of the woman's hair and ordering it to be burned to break any spell she had
cast. The attempt failed, however, and shortly afterwards Lady Cromwell was taken
ill following a nightmare in which she was tormented, she claimed, by Mrs Samuel
and her cat. In July 1592, when Lady Cromwell died after months of ill health, it
was recalled that, on the occasion of the great lady's visit to the Throckmortons, Mrs
Samuel had complained of her ill-treatment with the rather ominous words, 'Madam,
why do you use me thus? I never did you any harm as yet' – which in retrospect
sounded very like a threat.

Towards the end of 1592, in a desperate effort to stop the nonsense, Mrs Samuel
ordered the girls to desist from their fits, upon which the seizures immediately ceased.
Thoroughly confused, even Mrs Samuel began to doubt her innocence and, prompted
by the local parson, she made a public confession to the effect that she must indeed
be a witch. The girls' fits recommenced when Mrs Samuel retracted her confession the
following day, thus furnishing the authorities with further 'proof' that the woman did
indeed have magical influence over the Throckmorton children.

The case was presented to two local justices of the peace and Mrs Samuel was taken
before William Wickham, Bishop of Lincoln. Under pressure from these dignitaries,
she broke down once more and admitted her guilt. This time she gave more detail
of her activities as a witch, describing for good measure her three familiars, called
Pluck, Catch, and White (or Pluck, Smack, Hardname, Catch, and Blew, according to
a variant account), which manifested to her as chickens.

Alice Samuel, along with her husband John and daughter Agnes, was tried for the
murder of Lady Cromwell by witchcraft at the Assizes held before 500 people in the
Court Hall, Huntingdon, on 5 April 1593. As well as the Throckmorton girls, other
locals came forward to make further charges relating to illness and death caused to
their livestock by the Samuels. The trial culminated in all three defendants being found
guilty and in the abject Alice Samuel confessing to intercourse with the Devil. Agnes
Samuel refused to admit any guilt and also declined to plead pregnancy as a possible
way out of her dilemma, arguing resolutely: 'Nay, that I will not do: it shall never be
said that I was both a witch and a whore.'

All three condemned witches were hanged on Mill Common two days after the
trial ended and their property, worth some £40, was forfeited to Henry Cromwell,
who used it to set up a fund for an annual sermon against witchcraft to be preached
at Huntingdon. The last was given as late as 1814, although by then the preachers of
the sermon generally used the opportunity to attack belief in witchcraft rather than
to warn against it. The Throckmorton girls, finally released from their fits, apparently
returned to their normal lives.

The case remains one of the best-known witchcraft trials in English history and
amply demonstrates the degree to which the fear of witches had gripped the public
imagination by the year 1600. Many later authorities lamented the court's gullibility in
accepting the wild accusations of young girls, but to contemporaries their allegations
only confirmed their innermost fears, preparing the way for the 1604 Witchcraft Act,
which imposed the death penalty for convicted witches.

KENT

TUNBRIDGE WELLS, 1565

A Tunbridge widow, Alice Latter was accused of bewitching to death the daughter of a Tunbridge butcher, and also the son of one William Harris, also bewitched at Tunbridge Wells. She was found not guilty.

MAIDSTONE, 1565

A widow from Maidstone, Joan Byden, was found guilty of using witchcraft to cause the fatal illness of Mary Huett, the daughter of a local pewterer, Robert Huett; of causing the sickness of the son of a merchant named Arthur Startowte; and of destroying by magic thirteen turkeys belonging to Ralph Moore. She was found guilty of all charges but her fate is not recorded.

BOUGHTON MONCHELSEA, 1567

In 1567 Agnes Bennett of Boughton Monchelsea was accused of using 'her enchantment and potion', having been 'incited by the instigation of the Devil', to kill John Lyttelhare, also of Boughton Monchelsea. She was found guilty and punished accordingly, although exactly how is not recorded.

BETHERSDEN, 1567

A woman from Bethersden was found guilty in 1567 of causing by witchcraft the life-threatening illness of Martha Loppam, the daughter of one of her Bethersden neighbours. She was sentenced to a year's imprisonment and quarterly appearances in the pillory.

ALLHALLOWS, 1571

In 1571 a labourer's wife, Ellen Peckham of Allhallows, was found guilty of bewitching to death the infant son of another Allhallows labourer. She was almost certainly hanged.

FOLKESTONE, 1571

In 1571, charged with 'unlawful practices', Margaret Browne was banished from Folkestone for seven years with the threat of a whipping 'at the cart's tail' if she appeared within seven miles of the town.

NORTHFLEET, 1574

Alice Stanton of Northfleet, a yeoman's wife, appears to have come close to receiving a death sentence at the Kent Summer Sessions. She was found guilty of bewitching a heifer and eleven pigs to death, but not guilty of the more serious crime of causing the death by witchcraft of William Allyn. According to the terms of the 1563 Act, assuming this was her first witchcraft offence, she would have been imprisoned for a year and subjected to quarterly six-hour public appearances in the pillory.

WESTWELL, 1574

Reginald Scot recorded the accusation of 'Old Alice' in *The Discoverie of Witchcraft* (1584) as further evidence for exposing some of the more absurd claims of *maleficia*. Her accuser was the seventeen-year-old servant of William Sponer of Westwell, Mildred Norrington, who 'was possessed with Satan night and day'. In this condition she identified another villager, Old Alice, as Satan's former keeper, with whom he had lodged, kept in two bottles, for the last twenty years. Old Alice, allegedly, nicknamed him 'Partener' and he had another demon, by the name of Little Devil, serving him. During this time Old Alice had instructed him to kill three people – Edward, the young son of Richard Ager, an unnamed gentleman from Dig, and a Mrs Wolton, one of her Westwell neighbours. In addition, Satan stole food and drink for the witch from the Petman, Farme, Millen, and Fuller families. After making these confessions, Satan was finally exorcised by the vicars of Westwell and Kennington from the body of Mildred Norrington. However, when these allegations were heard by the authorities they were deemed to be fraudulent and Mildred was punished accordingly.

BOXLEY, 1574

Alice Daye, though found guilty at the Dartford Assizes in March 1574 of murdering three of her Boxley neighbours by witchcraft and sentenced to be hanged, appears to have evaded her punishment on the grounds of pregnancy. Theoretically, the punishment would have been carried out shortly after the birth of the child and yet Alice appears to have lived long enough to cause further acts of *maleficium*. In July 1578 she reappears in the Assize records, this time accused of employing witchcraft to cause the illness of John Collyns and the death of two cows. When Collyns subsequently died she faced a murder charge and was hauled up before the judge again in March 1579. For a second time she was sentenced to hang and, almost certainly, this time she was executed shortly afterwards.

BRENCHLEY, 1581

By no means all of those accused of witchcraft in the late sixteenth century were found guilty. Margaret Simons was acquitted in 1581 of the charges of killing two of her near neighbours: the wife and fourteen-year-old son of James Champe.

FAVERSHAM, 1586, 1645

Joan Cason was the victim of a lenient but ignorant jury. She was charged in 1586 with the murder of three-year-old Jane Cooke. When Jane sickened, her mother, Sarah, was advised by a traveller that she was the victim of witchcraft and of the way in which she could identify the perpetrator. Accordingly Sarah Cooke stole a tile from the roof of Joan Cason's house and, as instructed, laid it in a hot fire. As foretold by the traveller, it sparkled and flew up into the air. Shortly afterwards the witch herself

THE
EXAMINATION,
CONFESSION, TRIALL,
AND EXECUTION,

Of *Joane Williford*, *Joan Cariden*,
and *Jane Hott*:

Who were executed at *Feversham* in *Kent*, for being Witches, on Munday the 29 of *September*, 1645.

Being a true Copy of their evill lives and wicked deeds, taken by the Major of *Feversham* and Jurors for the said Inquest.

With the Examination and Confession of *Elizabeth Harris*, not yet executed.

All attested under the hand of
ROBERT GREENSTREET, *Major of Feversham*.

LONDON,
Printed for *J. G.* October 2. 1645.

The examination, confession, triall, and execution, of Joane Williford, Joan Cariden, and Jane Hott, 1645.

came to visit to enquire after the child; within four hours, having looked the witch in the face, Jane Cooke was dead. Investigations revealed that Joan Cason already had something of a reputation. It was revealed that several years earlier she had had a strange pet, presumably her familiar, that looked like a reddish rat with a broad tail: it was heard to speak and somehow evaded being killed by a neighbour's cat. Joan denied the charges and insisted that she was being victimised by her enemies. The jury decided to acquit her of the charge of murder but to declare her guilty of invocation, presuming this would result in a lesser punishment. Although the overseeing judge, Thomas Barming, mayor of Faversham, presumed the same, a learned lawyer on the bench advised the court that, by the terms of the 1581 Witchcraft Act, invocation should now be considered a felony. Consequently, despite the intention of the jury, Joan was executed after all.

In 1645 Faversham became the scene of a significant outbreak of witch-hunting when several local women were accused of making pacts with the Devil and of using their infernal powers against their neighbours. The case, which was heard at the Michaelmas Sessions in Faversham, was typical of many others of the period, depending largely upon confessions extracted under duress and expanding to take in more suspects before it finally petered out. It was publicised in a short pamphlet entitled *The examination, confession, triall, and execution, of Joane Williford, Joan Cariden, and Jane Hott* (1645).

At the centre of the case was Joan Williford, who confessed to indulging in a wide range of witchcraft practices. She had, it was claimed, become first acquainted with the Devil when he appeared to her in the form of a small dog and invited her to give him her allegiance. She accordingly sold him her soul and signed the pact in her own blood in return for revenge against one Thomas Letherland and his wife Mary Woodruff, and was further rewarded by promises that she should never want for money. She was also granted a familiar spirit called Bunnie, whose services to her over the ensuing twenty years included depositing an enemy, Thomas Gardler, in a cesspool.

Also identified as witches in Williford's confession were Jane Holt, Joan Argoll, and Elisabeth Harris. Jane Holt (or Hott) for twenty years kept a familiar that was described as something like a hedgehog. A specific charge against Harris, whose familiar took the form of a large mouse, was that she had put a curse on a boat belonging to one John Woodcott after her own son had drowned while sailing in it. As a result of the curse, it was alleged, the boat was lost. Argoll, meanwhile, had laid curses on a man called Major and another called John Mannington, both of whom had suffered in consequence.

Williford's confession, which ended with a claim that the Devil had twice visited her in prison in the form of a mouse in order to suck her blood, was more than enough to seal her fate. She and her accomplices were all hanged at Faversham on Monday 29 September 1645. It has been suggested that the Faversham trials were inspired by the contemporaneous witch-hunting activities of Matthew Hopkins and his accomplices – and it remains an unverifiable, if remote, possibility that Faversham was among the towns actually visited by Hopkins and John Stearne.

ASH, SANDWICH, 1631

In 1631 Katherine Younge of 'Ash-juxta-Sandwich', a labourer's wife, was found guilty of bewitching another widow at Ash, Mary Randall, to death. For some reason her sentence was deferred to the next Sessions and the outcome is unknown.

GOUDHURST, 1657

In 1657 a labourer's wife, Mary Allen of Goudhurst, and her daughter, Mary, were both found guilty of practising witchcraft and of having an 'evil spirit' in the form of a black dog, which they kept with the intent of causing harm. Both were sentenced to hang even though no specific act of *maleficium* appears in the surviving records of the case.

CRANBROOK, 1652

A major trial of eighteen suspected witches was held during the Kent Summer Sessions at Maidstone in 1652. Of these eighteen, twelve were women, and six were men. Six, all women, were hanged. A record of their trial survives in a pamphlet produced by 'E. G., Gent', 'a learned person, present at their Conviction and Condemnation'. Entitled *A Prodigious & Tragicall History of the Arraignment, Tryall, Confession, and Condemnation of six Witches at Maidstone, in Kent*, it was printed, in London, in the same year.

The 'chief Actresse' in the story was Anne Ashby (also known as Cobler) of Cranbrook. Both she and her accomplice, Anne Martyn, confessed that 'the Divell had known them carnally, and that they had no hurt by it'. The author of the pamphlet claimed to have witnessed Anne Ashby fall 'into an extasie before the Bench' and that she 'swell'd into a monstrous and vast bigness, screeching and crying out very dolefully'. When questioned she claimed that during this fit a spirit called Rug 'came out of her mouth like a Mouse'. She also revealed that the Devil had given them 'a piece of flesh, which whensoever they should touch, they should thereby affect their desires'. She told the court where she had hidden this diabolical object and it was put on public display 'at the sign of the Swan in Maidstone', and both 'seen and felt' by the writer of the pamphlet.

One act of *maleficium* specifically linked by the author to Anne Ashby was the death of 'a certain Groom' who, after her arrest, made a playful remark about Anne's spirit 'Rug', and 'died within a fortnight after'. Of all the eighteen people arraigned, the author commented, 'It is supposed that nine children, besides a man and a woman, were bewitched; 500 pounds worth of Cattel lost, and much Corn at Sea wrack'd, by Witchcraft.' Furthermore, 'They confessed they had bewitched a child, that had been languishing along time; this child died about the time of their trials, whose pourtraicture in wax was found, where they had laid it, under the Threshold of a doore.'

The suspects were subjected to full body searches and pricking. When a pin was 'thrust to the head into one of their arms', neither Mary Browne, Anne Wilson, nor Mildred Wright, all of Cranbrook, felt it, 'neither did it draw bloud from her'. When searched, 'Mary Read of Lenham had a visible Teat under her tongue, and did shew it to many, and it was likewise seen by this Observator'. All four of these women were condemned to death, along with Anne Ashby and Anne Martyn. The fact that five of the six came from the same small town and were tried and condemned at the same assizes implies the discovery of a suspected coven. Three of the women, including Ashby and Martyn, pleaded for a stay of execution by claiming that they were pregnant. However, their pleas were rejected when they confessed they were carrying the Devil's babies. Mary Browne appears to have been reprieved before the execution was carried out but the other five were hanged, parliamentary reprieve orders for two more, Mildred Wright and Anne Wilson, failing to arrive in time. The Assize records reveal that another woman, Susan Pickering of Halden (presumably High Halden near

Cranbrook), was also condemned and hanged for causing, by witchcraft, the death of a girl.

AYLESFORD, 1657

In 1657 an Aylesford widow, Judith Sawkins, was found guilty of causing the wasting disease of a twelve-year-old neighbour, Mary Meadowes. Although the record does not indicate Mary's death, nevertheless Judith Sawkins was sentenced to hang.

LANCASHIRE

YEALAND, 1546

In a very early English witchcraft case, at the end of the reign of Henry VIII, William Walker of Yealand was accused of raising evil spirits to convey by magic a valuable silver spoon, belonging to James Standisshe, to Wigan! Presumably the accusation, essentially, was to do with the handling of stolen goods.

TYLDESLEY, 1594

Described by contemporaries as an itinerant conjuror, herbalist, and faith healer, Edmund Hartlay became disastrously involved in a notorious case of demoniacal possession that erupted at Cleworth Hall, Tyldesley, near Wigan in Lancashire, in 1594 and led to a sensational trial on charges of witchcraft. The case was recorded in two major publications in 1600: John Darrell's *A True Narrative of the Strange and Grevous Vexation by the Devil of 7 persons in Lancashire*, and George More's *A true discourse concerning the certaine possession and dispossession of 7 persons in one familie in Lancashire*.

The trouble at Cleworth began when the children of one Nicholas Starkie, John (aged ten) and Anne (aged nine), were afflicted with violent fits and bouts of nervous shouting. Hartlay, who happened to be in the neighbourhood at the time, treated the children over a period of eighteen months with herbs and charms and seemed to achieve some improvement in their condition. When Hartlay announced that he was planning to leave the country, the two children (who were evidently very fond of the conjuror) were seized by fits and hysteria once more, and it was consequently arranged for him to remain permanently at the Hall.

When Hartlay was paid less than he asked for, however, he threatened a serious deterioration in the situation. Sure enough, two girls living at Cleworth – Margaret and Elinor Hardman (or Hurdman), aged fourteen and ten respectively – and two adults – Margaret Byrom, a poor relation of Mrs Starkie, and Jane Ashton, a servant-woman – then came down with similar symptoms of demoniacal possession, shrieking and generally sending forth 'such a strange, supernaturall, and fearefull noyse, or loud whapping, as the like was never heard at Cleworth'.

Hartlay, who found himself the target of assault by the evil spirits involved, took the extreme measure of drawing out a magic circle (despite the fact that these were forbidden by law) in order to quell the demons threatening the household. The fits, however, continued unabated and Starkie, in desperation, sought advice from the celebrated Dr John Dee (1527–1608), then Warden of Manchester College, a renowned scholar, magician, and one-time confidant of Elizabeth I herself.

Dee criticised Hartlay and declined to involve himself, even when approached by the children themselves. Hartlay, a hot-tempered man who possibly genuinely thought he could help the children, was by now incensed by Starkie's lack of faith in his abilities and the problems in the house redoubled. John Starkie was particularly badly affected, throwing things around and biting people like a mad dog. Hartlay himself was beset with violent fits and had to be held down by others in the household. Margaret Byrom started to act in an increasingly unruly manner and revealed that the Devil had twice manifested himself in her bedroom in Hartlay's form. Hartlay tried to calm her down and was seen to try to kiss her, giving rise to the suggestion that 'whomsoever he kissed, on them he breathed the divell'. Others recalled how Hartlay was given to kissing the children and that all those currently tormented had been kissed by him at some time or other. Questions began to be asked about Hartlay's integrity, and soon allegations were being made that he was a wizard and himself the source of the trouble.

When examined by Dr Dee's curate, Matthew Palmer, Hartlay proved incapable of reciting the Lord's Prayer without breaking down (thus failing a challenge commonly used to test suspected witches). Margaret Byrom now gave Palmer full details of how she had been troubled by a spectral black dog and other supernatural creatures, all of which she attributed to Hartlay's influence. On Palmer's advice, Hartlay was swiftly

Contemporary image of a learned magician.

arraigned before the local magistrates and sent to the court in Lancaster. Attempts to get evidence from the various witnesses who had been allegedly bewitched by Hartlay proved difficult, as they tended to bark and howl or go into fits when examined. The story of the magic circle Hartlay had drawn up in order to vanquish the demon, however, proved damning evidence of his guilt. He was sentenced to death as a witch at the Lancaster Assizes and went to the gallows in March 1597. The first attempt to hang him failed when the rope broke, but at the second attempt he died.

After Hartlay's death the case was put in the hands of the controversial Puritan exorcist John Darrell, who only the year before had been imbroiled in the case of the so-called 'Burton Boy'. Accompanied by his assistant George More, Darrell spent three days subjecting the seven possessed people in the house to a regime of fasting, prayer, and preaching, and then declared six of them to be free of their tormenting devils. The seventh victim, Jane Ashton, was a Roman Catholic and it took another day's effort before she too was cured.

Both exorcists wrote accounts of the affair, each contending that they individually were due the lion's share of the credit. Not long afterwards, the pair courted renewed controversy through their involvement with another case of demoniacal possession resulting from witchcraft, that of the 'Boy of Nottingham'.

Cleworth Hall, the scene of the hysteria that led ultimately to Hartlay's demise, was demolished in 1805.

CASTLETON, 1597

Alice Brerely of Castleton, near Rochdale, was found guilty of the murder by witchcraft of James Kirshaw and Robert Scolefield and condemned to death. However, on 3 May 1597, for reasons not stated, she received a pardon.

PENDLE, 1612

The mass trial in 1612 of a coven of witches allegedly active in the Pendle Forest in Lancashire remains one of the most notorious episodes in the history of witch-hunting in England.

Post-Reformation Lancashire was a scene of considerable religious conflict in the early seventeenth century, with a largely Roman Catholic population living under Protestant rule, and everywhere there was suspicion and counter-suspicion between neighbours. In this climate of mistrust, accusations of witchcraft inevitably had a deep effect upon local communities, and the nascent hysteria finally erupted on a major scale when two old women long reputed to be witches were publicly accused.

The Pendle Forest, in east Lancashire, was home to two rival peasant families. The Sowtherns were headed by the eighty-year-old blind beggar Elizabeth Sowthern (or Southernes), a woman known as 'Old Demdike' and described as the 'rankest hag that ever troubled daylight'. The Whittles were led by a 'very old, withered, spent, and decrepit creature, her sight almost gone ... her lips ever chattering and walking: but no man knew what' dubbed 'Old Chattox', otherwise called Anne Whittle.

With their wild, unattractive appearance and malevolent natures, both women fitted the popular image of a witch perfectly. Local legend had it that many mysterious deaths in the district could be attributed to the lethal potions that the two women concocted as heads of a coven based in the Forest. Certainly the two women appear to have capitalised on their reputations in order to exert influence over their neighbours and to promote their own trade in simple herbal potions and remedies.

The train of events that led to the eventual trial started around 1601, when the two old women, formerly close friends, fell out. This parting of the ways, which resulted in members of the two families embarking on a lengthy and ultimately bloody feud, resulted from the theft of some linen clothing and some meal from Alison Device, the young granddaughter of Old Demdike. The following Sunday, Alison Device claimed that she saw a missing band and coif being worn by Anne Redfearne, the married daughter of Old Chattox, and soon the two families were trading accusation and counter-accusation. In an attempt to prevent Old Chattox, apparently the more powerful of the two witches, using her supposed supernatural powers against his family, John Device, Alison's father, promised to pay her a yearly tribute of meal. This seems to have brought about a temporary truce that lasted until John Device's death a few years later.

Early in 1612, the revived feud between the two sides led to numerous complaints about both families reaching the ears of Roger Nowell, a local justice of the peace, and he determined to investigate the quarrel. A crucial factor in the downfall of the Sowtherns and the Whittles was the introduction of the third witchcraft law passed in England in 1604, which extended the capacity of the authorities to condemn witches by making intent to cause physical harm or death to a person a capital offence. Starting by interviewing the young Alison Device on 13 March, Nowell had little trouble persuading members of the two families to give evidence against each other, and accusation piled up on accusation until all involved were hopelessly compromised.

It emerged that Elizabeth Sowthern had become a witch many years before after meeting a 'spirit or devil in the shape of a boy' at a stonepit in the forest and agreeing to exchange her soul with him in return for anything she might want. The Devil, who called himself Tibb, reappeared to her from time to time, variously assuming such guises as a brown dog or a black cat, in order to enquire if she had any new tasks she wished him to carry out on her behalf. Subsequently Elizabeth Sowthern had her son Christopher Howgate, her daughter Elizabeth Device, and Elizabeth's children James and Alison also recruited as witches. Other converts included Anne Whittle, who sold her soul to a 'thing like a Christian man', and various neighbours and relatives.

After questioning Old Demdike, Old Chattox, and Anne Redfearne, Roger Nowell decided that there was a case to answer and all three were confined in the damp dungeons of Lancaster Castle to await trial at the next Assizes. There they were joined by the eleven-year-old Alison Device on charges of bewitching an itinerant pedlar called John Law. It appeared that she and Law had had an altercation after he had refused to give her some pins, as related in Law's statement to the court at the subsequent trial:

> He deposeth and saith, that about the eighteenth of March last part, hee being a pedler, went with his packe of wares at his back thorow [through] Colne-field: where unluckily he met with Alizon Device, now prisoner at the barre, who was very earnest for pinnes, but he would give her none; whereupon she seemed to be very angry; and when hee was past her, hee fell downe lame in great extremitie; and afterwards by meanes he got into an ale-house in Colne, neere unto the place where hee was first bewitched.

As detailed by Law, the exchange had culminated in Alison cursing him, upon which he had collapsed, complaining of sharp pains in his side (modern medical opinion suggests that he suffered a stroke). Law's son Abraham took up the story at the trial, explaining how he went out to find the woman his father suspected of afflicting him:

...and having found her, brought her to his said father ... whose said father in the hearing of this examinate and divers others did charge the said Alison to have bewitched him, which the said Alison confessing did ask this examinate's said father forgiveness upon her knees for the same; whereupon this examinate's father accordingly did forgive her.

Alison Device obligingly admitted that she had cursed the pedlar, and further claimed that she believed she was responsible for his illness and for the permanent disabilities he had suffered as a result. Old Demdike, meanwhile, also freely admitted to being a witch.

The trial of no fewer than ten alleged witches, mostly members of the two families, was the largest mass witchcraft trial staged in England to that date and inevitably attracted much attention. (Another accused witch, Jennet Preston, was tried in her home town of York.) Huge crowds arrived at the court in Lancaster to witness the proceedings and to catch a glimpse of the accused, whose very appearance confirmed in many minds their guilt. The younger Elizabeth Device in particular seemed the absolute epitome of a witch, with a deformed face and eyes that looked in different directions at the same time – a sure sign to many that she possessed the power of the evil eye.

The trial itself lived up to expectations, and was in many respects typical of hundreds of other similar proceedings. Several of the charges laid against the accused involved murder by witchcraft. Old Demdike, it was claimed, had enlisted the aid of the Devil in the form of the demonic Tibb to kill the child of one Richard Baldwyn after he had threatened to have her and her granddaughter Alison executed as witches. Old Chattox, allegedly aided and abetted by a familiar in the form of a 'spotted bitch',

Steps leading down to the 'Witches' Well', the dungeon under Lancaster Castle where the Pendle Witches were imprisoned before trial and execution.

was accused of using sorcery to kill a local landowner called Robert Nutter (a charge that was also laid against Anne Redfearne). Perhaps belatedly realising the danger she was in, Old Chattox made some attempt to shift the blame by stressing that it was Old Demdike who had first introduced her to the Devil and that it was she who had arranged Nutter's death. Alison Device, meanwhile, wept bitterly when the pedlar she had accused of maiming was led into court, and begged his forgiveness.

Further charges related to a sensational report that ten days after the original arrests various members of the two families had plotted to blow up Lancaster Castle in order to rescue their imprisoned relatives. According to the court, the two families had temporarily shelved their differences and had met on Good Friday at Malking Tower, the Pendle home of Elizabeth Device, in order to plan a breakout. Over a substantial meal that included mutton stolen by James Device, the assembly hatched a plot to kill the gaoler at the Castle and to use gunpowder to release the prisoners (parallels have been drawn between this and the Guy Fawkes Gunpowder Plot of 1605). Suggestions that the eating of a feast made this one of the very few occasions when English witches celebrated an actual sabbat exaggerate the significance of what was probably an ordinary meal: no Devil was present and there was no performance of occult rites or dancing, sacrifices, orgies, and so forth.

Of the eighteen women and two or three men who attended the meeting, sixteen were readily identified – although only nine were located and brought to trial. Among these was a surprising name, that of the wealthy Alice Nutter of Roughlee, mother of the deceased Robert Nutter, who was further charged with using witchcraft to murder a man named Henry Mitton. Her participation in the event was confirmed by several of the accused, but there was absolutely no concrete evidence against her (rumour had it that the charge was fabricated by those who stood to profit by her execution, and that Roger Nowell himself bore a grudge against her following a dispute over a boundary marker). In any event, to the very end she declined to admit any involvement in the affair.

Besides Jennet Preston (who had already been acquitted of witchcraft once and now stood accused in York of having come over to Pendle from Gisborne-in-Craven

A continental style sabbat.

to ask for aid in killing Thomas Lister of Westby), the others indicted were Anne Whittle, Elizabeth Device, James Device, Anne Redfearne, Alice Nutter, Katherine Hewit (popularly known as Mould-heels), Jane and John Bulcock (a mother and son), Margaret Pearson (of Padiham), and Isabel Robey. Elizabeth Sowthern, 'Old Demdike', was missing, having died in Lancaster Castle prior to the opening of the Assizes.

With a break for the court to deal with the so-called Samlesbury Witches (all of whom were acquitted), each defendant was dealt with in turn on a variety of charges, most of the trials lasting less than a day. Katherine Hewit, for instance, was alleged to have used witchcraft to kill Anne Foulds, identified as 'a child of Colne', while the Bulcocks had through their magic brought about the madness of a woman named Jennet Deane. Isabel Robey had used witchcraft to inflict physical pain upon parties identified as Jane Wilkinson and Peter Chaddock. In all, the accused witches were charged with responsibility for some sixteen deaths in the locality, as well as with causing harm to livestock and property and other lesser offences.

The case for the prosecution rested largely on the testimony of Old Demdike's daughter Elizabeth Device, Elizabeth's son James (a labourer with learning difficulties, then in his twenties) and her nine-year-old daughter Jannet. Jannet's appearance in the witness box was unexpected and also illegal, as the testimony of children under fourteen was not admissible – a ruling that the court, under Sir Edward Bromley and Sir James Altham, set aside for its own convenience. The young girl was placed on a table in the middle of the room and her subsequent confirmation of all that had been alleged prompted her mother to make a full confession (which she later retracted).

According to James and Jannet, their mother was served by a familiar in the form of a brown dog called Ball; she had caused at least three deaths through the use of image magic and by other supernatural means. James informed the court that he had himself encountered 'a thing like a hare', which had begged from him some communion bread that he had been instructed to steal by his grandmother: the creature had disappeared when he made the sign of the cross. For his pains, James too was accused of keeping a familiar, a dog by the name of Dandy, and of recruiting its powers to commit the murder of a Mistress Towneley, of the Carre.

At the close of proceedings the assembled crowd was not best pleased when Anne Redfearne was acquitted of the murder of Robert Nutter, but was somewhat mollified when she was found guilty of killing his father, Christopher Nutter, who on his deathbed had blamed witchcraft for his demise. On the strength of the confessions made by the accused and on the allegations they had traded between themselves, ten of the prisoners were sentenced to be hanged. Alone among those condemned, only Old Chattox made no attempt to deny her culpability, though she begged the court to spare her daughter; the others all protested vehemently that the charges against them were false.

Old Chattox, Anne Redfearne, Elizabeth Device, James Device, Alison Device, Alice Nutter, John and Jane Bulcock, Katherine Hewit, and Isabel Robey died on the gallows at Lancaster on the day following the end of the trial, 20 August 1612, by which date Jennet Preston had already been hanged (on 27 July) in York as the murderer of Thomas Lister. Significantly, the judges at her trial were also Sir Edward Bromley and Sir James Altham. Margaret Pearson, who was found guilty of bewitching a mare to death, was sentenced to a year in gaol and made four appearances in the pillory, at the towns of Clitheroe, Padiham, Whalley, and Lancaster.

The sensational details of the case were published the following year in a chapbook entitled *The Wonderful Discovery of Witches in the County of Lancaster*, written by Thomas Potts, clerk of the court, and approved as accurate by the presiding judge, Sir Edward Bromley. As a result, people became familiar with the episode throughout

A particular Declaration of

the moſt barberous and damnable Practiſes, Murthers, wicked and diueliſh Conſpiracies, practized *and executed by the moſt dangerous and malitious* Witch *Elizabeth Sowthernes* alias *Demdike*, of the Forreſt of *Pendle* in the Countie of *Lancaſter* Widdow, who died in the Caſtle at *Lancaſter* before ſhe came to receiue her tryall.

Hough publique Iuſtice hath paſſed at theſe Aſſiſes vpon the Capitall offendours, and after the Arraignement & tryall of them, Iudgement being giuen, due and timely Execution ſucceeded; which doth import and giue the greateſt ſatisfaction that can be, to all men: yet becauſe vpon the caryage, and euent of this buſineſſe, the Eyes of all the partes of *Lancaſhire*, and other Counties in the North partes thereunto adioyning were bent: And ſo infinite a multitude came to the Arraignement & tryall of theſe Witches at *Lancaſter*, the number of them being knowen to exceed all others at any time heretofore, at one time to be indicted, arraigned, and receiue their tryall, eſpecially for ſo many Murders, Conſpiracies, Charmes, Meetinges, helliſh and damnable practiſes, ſo apparant vpon their owne examinations & confeſsions. Theſe my honourable & worthy Lords, the Iudges of Aſſiſe, vpon

B.   great

The Wonderful Discovery of Witches in the County of Lancaster, 1613.

the whole of northern England, and its influence was fated to be felt in many other trials.

SAMLESBURY, 1612

Following on from the first part of his account of the Pendle witch-hunt, Potts provided details of the trial of four more Lancashire 'witches' from Samlesbury, also in 1612. This trial revolved around fourteen-year-old Grace Sowerbutts, who accused four women, including her grandmother and an aunt, of various acts of witchcraft and *maleficium*. These included turning themselves into black dogs, the murder of a child and associated acts of ritual cannibalism, and of being carried by some form of transvection across the River Ribble to attend a sabbat-like meeting that involved dancing and sexual intercourse with four demons. Tried by Sir Edward Bromley at the same assizes in Lancaster as the Pendle witches, this time the judge found in favour of the accused and the case was thrown out. According to Potts, Grace confessed that she had been persuaded to make these allegations by a Catholic priest named Thompson. This allegedly occurred in the context of a family feud that focused upon the recent conversion to Protestantism of certain family members, including the three accused. While it is less certain in the case of the Pendle witches, religious views certainly seem to have helped provoke and to determine the outcome of the Samlesbury witch trial.

WALTON-LE-DALE, 1614

Cecilia Dawson of Walton-le-Dale was hanged for witchcraft in 1614. She had been found guilty of causing the wasting sicknesses of three people, and the death of at least one.

BUTTERWORTH, 1623

Anne Butterworth, a widow of Butterworth in Rochdale, like Cecilia Dawson of Walton-le-Dale nine years earlier, was charged with causing wasting sickness and the death of two supposed victims. However, unlike Cecilia Dawson, she was found not guilty and released.

MANCHESTER, 1633

An alleged conspiracy of witches based to the north of Manchester, that led to the death after a period of illness of Richard, the son and heir of Ralph Ashton of Middleton, was exposed at the Lancaster Sessions in 1633. Those accused were Robert Smethehurste, a husbandman of Radcliffe, Smethehurste's wife, Elizabeth, Henry Bordman of Bury, and Richard Uttley, a yeoman farmer from Langfield in Yorkshire. They were found guilty of conjuring evil spirits to attack the Ashton family. All four were found guilty and hanged. The case is unusual in its high proportion of male protagonists.

PENDLE, 1634

In 1633, some twenty years after the sensational trial of the original Pendle Witches, the county of Lancashire was again rocked by another alleged outbreak of witchcraft in the Pendle Forest area – an episode that became known as 'The Pendle Swindle'. The first Pendle case had depended upon the evidence of a girl well below fourteen, the age when evidence from a minor might legally be heard; this time, too, the case stemmed from a minor, a ten-year-old boy called Edmund Robinson. On this occasion, however, the judge at the Lancaster Assizes showed himself to be altogether more demanding when it came to accepting the testimony of a mere child.

Edmund Robinson (b.1624) was the son of a mason living and working in the Pendle Forest. As such, he was doubtlessly familiar with the notorious events that had traumatised the whole of Lancashire a few years before his birth. Whatever the inspiration, the boy startled locals when he began to tell odd stories about various neighbours that strongly suggested occult activity. According to the lad, on All Saints' Day 1633, he had encountered two greyhounds and had tried to persuade them to chase a hare. When the dogs had refused to obey him he had beaten them, only for the creatures to be transformed at once into human beings. One of these was a little boy whom he did not know, while the other he identified as a woman called Frances Dicconson. She tried to buy his silence with a shilling, but Edmund declined the money. Dicconson had then transformed the unidentified small boy into a white horse and had made Edmund ride on it to a sabbat in a barn.

With encouragement from two lamentably gullible magistrates, Richard Shuttleworth and John Starkie, before whom Edmund Robinson repeated his story at Padiham on 10 February 1634, the boy gave a full description of the witches' sabbat he had

Eighteenth-century image of Lancashire witches.

witnessed. Some sixty men and women were present at the gathering, of whom he
was able to recognise nineteen. Some of these already had local reputations as witches;
ironically, they included Jannet Device, whose evidence as a child had hanged the
witches in the 1612 case. Robinson related how meat was cooked on the fire and how
he was invited to taste some of the food and drink. After trying a sample, however, he
declined the offer. More food was produced for the company by pulling on six ropes
suspended from the ceiling. By magically 'milking' these ropes hot meat, milk, and
butter fell out of thin air. Three of the women, meanwhile, thrust thorns into three
portraits, clearly intending harm to the person depicted. At this point Edmund had
run home, terrified out of his wits:

> ...he saw six of them kneeling and pulling, all six of them, six several ropes, which
> were fastened or tied to the top of the barn. Presently after which pulling, there came
> into this informer's sight, flesh smoking, butter in lumps, and milk as it were flying
> from the said ropes ... And during all the time of their several pulling they made
> such ugly faces as scared this informer, so that he was glad to run out and steal
> homewards.

With memories of the 1612 episode thoroughly evoked, the magistrates had some
thirty people arrested and committed seventeen of them for trial at the Lenten Assizes
in Lancaster. All the suspects except one resolutely protested their innocence of all
charges. Margaret Johnson, though, broke down and confessed that she was indeed
a witch: 'I will not add sin to sin. I have done enough already, and will not increase

it. I pray God I may repent.' Under pressure from the court, Johnson explained how she had sold her soul to the Devil, who manifested in the form of a black-suited man named Mamilion, in exchange for the fulfilment of all her wishes. She confirmed that a sabbat had been celebrated at Hoarstones on the date in question, although she herself had not attended. Since her exposure as a witch, however, her familiar had deserted her 'and she never saw him since'.

Margaret Johnson's confession, coupled with memories of 1612, had a deep impression upon the jury in the case and the accused were found guilty. The judge, however, was uneasy about the convictions – the sum total of the testimony against one of the accused, twenty-year-old Mary Spencer, for instance, was that she would roll her pail down the hill, running before it and calling to it to follow her. Because of his doubts about Edmund Robinson's story he referred the matter to the Privy Council. John Bridgeman, the Bishop of Chester, was asked to interrogate some of the prisoners, after which he agreed with the judge that the allegations were the product of Robinson's imagination. Four of the accused – Frances Dicconson, Jennet Hargreaves, Margaret Johnson, and Mary Spencer – were despatched to London, where they were questioned further by Dr Harvey, royal physician to Charles I, and others. These eminent authorities discounted the witch's marks that had allegedly been located on their bodies, and they too concluded that fraud was at play. Charles I himself interrogated Robinson and the four suspects and quickly came to the conclusion that the boy's story was a pack of lies.

Robinson himself eventually admitted the deception, confirming that he had made up the allegations on the basis of what he had heard about the 1612 trial. At the time of the alleged sabbat he had been picking plums. His only motive, he claimed, had been a desire to make mischief. Others, however, suspected that he had been put up to it by enemies of those accused, pointing out that Edmund Robinson's father was known to have quarrelled with Frances Dicconson over the sale of a cow.

Like other notable child accusers, the boy might also have been seduced by the opportunity to enjoy some local celebrity: certainly, before his exposure he seemed to derive some satisfaction from being invited to one parish after another to identify witches who had been present at the notorious sabbat (and he received a fee for each suspect identified). Dr John Webster, in his *Displaying of Supposed Witchcraft* (1677), related how he met Edmund Robinson after he was taken to the parish church at Kildwick during this period:

> After prayers, I enquired what the matter was; the people told me it was the boy that discovered witches; upon which I went to the house where he was to stop all night, and here I found him and two very unlikely persons, that did conduct him and manage the business. I desired to have some discourse with the boy in private, but that they utterly refused. Then, in the presence of a great many people, I took the boy near me and said: "Good boy, tell me truly and in earnest, didst thou see and hear such strange things at the meeting of witches as is reported by many thou didst relate?" But the two men, not giving the boy leave to answer, did pluck him from me...

Whatever the reasons behind the Edmund Robinson hoax, the consequences of it were regrettable. Although the accused were released without charge, not all survived the experience. Three of those charged as witches, one man and two women (John Spencer, Alice Higgins, and Jennet Loynd), died in prison before the case was resolved.

Nothing is known of Robinson's life after his exposure.

BURNLEY, 1638

A major trial of witches took place in Lancaster in 1638. At least six women were charged and it is likely there were more; unfortunately the court rolls are incomplete, seemingly having been 'deliberately torn or cut'[68]. At least three, probably more, were found guilty. The charges included the invocation of evil spirits to cause wasting diseases and subsequent deaths, and the bewitching of livestock. Those accused came from places to the east of Burnley, including Colne and Todmorden.

LIVERPOOL, 1664

Margaret Loy of Liverpool was released from Lancaster Castle gaol in 1664 having been found not guilty of the deaths by witchcraft of two people, James Burton and Thomas Radcliffe, both of whom had suffered from a period of sickness before their death.

HINDLEY, 1666

In 1666 Isabella Rigby, the wife of a husbandman of Hindley near Wigan, was hanged as a witch. She was found guilty of causing by witchcraft the wasting sicknesses of three people: Anne Rothwell, Jane Grundy, and Thomas Ashton. Ashton certainly lived in Hindley and it is likely that the others named were also Isabella's near neighbours.

WESTHAUGHTON, 1666

Jane Gregory, the wife of a Westhaughton weaver, testified in 1666 against two neighbours: Agnes Hurst and her daughter, Margaret. She claimed that her husband had witnessed a strange scene in which Agnes Hurst was carried in a chair to the top of a hill, Daisy Hillock, by eight or nine people. He joined in and Hurst took him by the hand before they parted. Shortly afterwards he fell ill with acute pains in his back as if he was being stabbed with an awl. Convinced he had been bewitched by the Hursts, he accused Agnes to her face. Apparently she had been suspected of being a witch for the past twenty years. These claims were corroborated by Thomas Gregory's brother and Mary Gregory, probably Thomas' sister or daughter-in-law. This interesting case of a feud between neighbours hints at the possibility of some kind of supposed sabbat meeting – a most unusual element in the English tradition. The outcome of the case is unknown.

BOLTON, 1667, 1671

Margaret Sharples of Bolton, imprisoned at Lancaster Castle gaol, was charged in 1667 with causing by witchcraft the wasting conditions of Elizabeth Lomax and Elizabeth Hough. She was found not guilty.

Richard Greenhalgh of Edgeworth, Bolton, recorded as a husbandman, was imprisoned in Lancaster Castle gaol on a charge of causing the wasting diseases of John Whitehead. When his case was heard in September 1671 he was found not guilty and acquitted. In December he faced further charges of causing the illnesses of

Roger Brindwood and his son, Abraham; Jennett Entwhistle; and Andrew Entwhistle. At least two of these had died by the time Greenhalgh's case was heard. The *bella vera* statement in the records, identifying a 'true bill', in other words one for which the evidence was strong enough for the case to be heard in the first place, suggests Greenhalgh was in real danger a second time in 1671. The outcome, however, is unknown.

DUXBURY, 1668

Alice Dewhurst of Duxbury was tried in 1668 for causing the death by witchcraft of Elizabeth Hodgson of Chorley. She was found not guilty.

INCE-IN-MAKERFIELD, 1673

Margaret Green a widow of Ince-in-Makerfield, seems to have been a woman of some notoriety and a good example of how witch reputations might be built over several years. She first appears in the records in 1666 on a charge of causing by witchcraft the death of a baby, Henry Blackhurst, and also of one Anne Booth. On these charges she was found not guilty. She reappears (assuming it is the same widow Margaret Green of Ince-in-Makerfield) seven years later, charged with causing by witchcraft the lingering sickness and death of Thomas Hodgkinson, who, because he is described as the son of one W. Hodgkinson, was probably also a child. The outcome of her case is unknown.

BUTTERWORTH, 1680

In 1680 a widow, Mary Turner of Butterworth, was tried for causing by witchcraft the wasting sicknesses of Sarah, Mary, and Abigail Stocke. She was found not guilty.

THE FOREST OF ROSSENDALE, 1681

In 1681 Mary Ashworth, the wife of a husbandman from the Forest of Rossendale, was tried for causing the wasting sicknesses by witchcraft of Mary and Elizabeth Nuttall. She was found not guilty.

LEICESTERSHIRE

LEICESTER, 1597, 1616

A record of the fate of Mary Cooke in 1597 appears in the Leicester Chamberlain's Accounts at the very end of the Tudor period. Reference is made to 'the charges of meate and drincke of oulde Mother Cooke', suspicions regarding her 'witchrye', and her subsequent imprisonment in the county gaol, trial, and execution by hanging.

In 1616, ten accused witches met their deaths directly or indirectly on the strength of accusations made by John Smith, a thirteen-year-old boy from Husbands Bosworth near Leicester. The son of Sir Roger Smith, and an ancestor of the earls of Derby, John Smith had made such accusations before, at the age of four or five, but nothing had come of it. By the time he reached thirteen, however, his fits had grown so convincingly violent that it took several strong men to hold him down. He publicly ascribed his affliction to various women of the town, providing full details of their familiars – as described in a contemporary letter:

> Six of the witches had six several spirits, one in the likeness of a horse, another like a dog, another a cat, another a foulmart, another a fish, another a toad, with whom every one of them tormented him. He would make some sign according to the spirit, as, when the horse tormented him he would whinny; when the cat tormented him, he would cry like a cat...

Nine of the women were in due course tried as witches at the Leicestershire Summer Assizes, found guilty and, on 18 July 1616, hanged. Another six women were thrown into prison to await similar examination.

A few short weeks after the first wave of executions, news of the case reached the ears of James I, who was then passing through Leicester. On the King's orders, Smith was brought into the royal presence and closely questioned. In the face of such stern examination the boy broke down and confessed that he had fabricated his evidence in order to enjoy the celebrity it brought him. The Archbishop of Canterbury, to whom the boy was despatched for further questioning, agreed with the King that there was no reason for suspecting witchcraft and the King turned his wrath on the judges, Sir Humphrey Winch and Sir Randolph Crew, who had presided over the original trials. Five of the six women in prison (the sixth had died) were released and the judges were roundly condemned by James for their gullibility. He also permitted the playwright Ben Jonson to ridicule the judges for their foolishness in his play *The Devil Is an Ass.*

no pest, Whereuppon sodenly in the waie she
hard a greate noise, and presently there appe=
red vnto her a Spirite of a white colour in see=
mynge like to a little rugged Dogge, standyng

Above: A witch's familiar.

Right: Ben Johnson's play
The Devil is an Ass.

THE DIUELL
(2)   IS
AN ASSE:

A COMEDIE
ACTED IN THE
YEARE, 1616.

BY HIS MAIESTIES
SERVANTS.

The Author BEN : IONSON.

HOR. de ART. POET.
Ficta voluptatis Causâ, sint proxima veris.

LONDON,
Printed by *I. B.* for ROBERT ALLOT, and are
to be sold at the signe of the *Beare*, in *Pauls*
Church-yard. 1631.

As a result of this very public rebuke English judges became more circumspect in accepting uncorroborated accusations in witchcraft cases, especially if they came from the mouths of children.

BELVOIR, 1618

The activities and fate of Margaret and 'Phillip' [i.e., Philippa] Flower, the daughters of Joan Flower, is described in a substantial pamphlet, *The Wonderful Discoverie of the Witchcrafts of Margaret and Phillip Flower, daughters of Joan Flower neere Bever Castle ... Together with the severall Examinations and Confessions of Anne Baker, Joan Willimot, and Eilen Greene, Witches in Leicestershire*, dated 1619, the year after their trial in 1618. Old Mother Flower and her daughters were the beneficiaries of the generous Francis Manners, Earl of Rutland who helped his poor neighbours out with alms and employment in his household at 'Bever' [i.e., Belvoir] Castle. The daughters both worked for him as general cleaners and Margaret subsequently lived at the castle, carrying out duties that including looking after the poultry and the wash-house.

All was well until rumours of the bad character of these women, particularly the mother, were heard by the earl's wife, his 'honourable Countesse'. According to local gossip, Joan Flower 'was a monstrous malicious woman, full of oaths, curses, and imprecations irreligious, and ... a plaine Atheist'. Indeed, 'the whole course of her life gave great suspition that she was a notorious Witch' and 'some of her neighbours dared to affirme that shee dealt with familiar spirits, and terrified them all with

The witches of Belvoir, 1618.

curses and threatening of revenge'. Furthermore, it was rumoured that Margaret was stealing provisions from the castle to take home to her mother. As for Philippa, she was accused of using bewitching Thomas Simpson into falling in love with her for her own lewd gratification. Apparently these negative views of the Flowers had been developing in their neighbourhood over many years. When their enemies won support from above by turning first the countess and then the earl against the Flowers the consequences would prove fatal.

Eventually Margaret was discharged from her work at the castle and paid off with forty shillings and gifts of a bolster and a woollen mattress. The writer of the pamphlet assumed that, if they had not already made a diabolical pact with the Devil, now that they were down on their luck and eager for revenge, he would, at this point, have easily made 'instruments' of them 'to enlarge his Kingdome'. Soon the earl and the countess were suffering strange illnesses and 'extraordinary convulsions', surely the work of 'these damnable Women'. They then, allegedly, targeted the earl's three children – all fell seriously ill and his eldest son, Henry, subsequently died.

Shortly before Christmas 1617, the women were arrested and taken to Lincoln Gaol. Old Joan Flower, doubtless in a state of great distress, died before they even got there and was buried at Ancaster, about ten miles north-east of Belvoir Castle. After a lengthy spell in prison, during which time they were interrogated and examined by both the earl and his brother, they were finally tried at the Lincoln Assizes, found guilty of murder and executed in March 1618.

At the same assizes three more 'witches', Anne Baker, Joan Willimot, and Ellen Greene, were examined: all of them contributed evidence in the Flower case. Anne Baker of Bottesford in Leicestershire was charged with the death by witchcraft of Elizabeth Hough, who, when Anne begged for some food, had angered the witch by giving her bread of the poorest quality. She confessed to having a familiar in the form of a white dog. Joan Willimot also confessed to having a familiar she called 'Pretty'.

Statues from the tomb of the Sixth Earl of Rutland in the church of St Mary the Virgin at Bottesford, Leicestershire, depicting the earl's two children allegedly killed by witchcraft.

Pretty, a fairy in the shape of a woman, had been given to her by magical means by William Berry, of Langholme in Rutlandshire, for whom she had worked for three years. She insisted that she had never used her spirit for the purpose of hurting others. She also revealed that a local shepherd, Gamaliel of Waltham, also had a familiar that took the form of a white mouse. In addition, she claimed to have witnessed Joan Flower giving suck, under her right ear as far as she could tell, to two spirits, one in the form of an owl, the other a rat.

However, the third woman, Ellen Greene of nearby Stathern (or Stathorne), declared that she had been persuaded by Willimot to give her soul to the Devil, who then gave her two spirits, one in the form of a 'kitlin' [i.e., kitten], the other of a 'moldiwarp' [i.e., mole]. With these she claimed to have bewitched to death two of her neighbours when she was living in Waltham – someone named Baker, who had called her a witch and struck her, and Anne Dawse, who had called her a 'witch, whore, jade etc.' She then used her familiars to kill a farmer and his son, the Willisons, who lived in Stonesby. Having moved to Stathern, she then assisted Joan Willimot by using her evil spirits to kill the child of a yeoman farmer, John Patchet, whose wife had offended Willimot.

Unfortunately the fate of these further three witches, in this exceptional set of trials, is not recorded in the 1619 pamphlet. As a footnote to the sorry affair, the tomb in Bottesford church of the Sixth Earl of Rutland, who died in 1632, was adorned with carvings representing his children and a note that they 'dyed in their infancy by wicked practice and sorcerye'.

SWITHLAND, 1620

An interesting record of a witchcraft accusation survives in the Records of the Borough of Leicester. It is unusual in that the accused was both male and, being a minister, a member of the local elite. Using sorcery, it was alleged that he had broken the arm of Christopher Monke's wife and caused Monke's son to cut his own throat. The outcome of this dramatic episode is unknown.

GREAT WIGSTON, 1717

The charges brought against Jane Clarke and her daughter and son mark the last serious attempt to bring about a trial for witchcraft under English law. Since the laws that allowed for such a possibility remained on the statute books until 1736, the case demonstrates the fact that the decline of witch-hunting in England was not the direct result of legislation. Details of the case survive in the notes, held by the British Museum, of the foreman of the Grand Jury, Sir G. Beaumont.

No less than twenty-five of the Clarkes' neighbours were prepared to provide testimonies regarding their malefic activities. The accusations included mysterious illnesses, in one case the vomiting up of 'a great quantity of gravell and dirt and thatch of a house and stones which were so big, that it was incredible how they could come out of any [...] mouth'. Others suffered similar symptoms and in some cases they 'had seen and felt great black bees to come out of their own and other peoples [sic] noses and mouths, which bees could not be struck down or taken but would make a terrible humming and then fly up ye chimney'. One 'young maiden' produced with the local midwife's assistance 'and with as much pain as if it had been a child birth a great number of stones of a large size'. The body of a young woman, presumed to have been 'bewitched to death', had 'monstrous wounds ... which appeared to be the bites of some human teeth, and others like the gnawing of dogs'. Although old Jane Clarke had no teeth with which she could have caused such damage, her accusers were quick to point out that 'her son and daughter had'.

As remarkable as the accusations was the thoroughness with which the supposed witches were subjected to the conventional tests by their tormentors before their complaints were presented to the authorities. Jane Clarke was searched 'publickly before a great number of good women in their town [who] found in her secret parts two white pieces of flesh like paps and some swore they were like the teats of an ewe, and some like the paps of a cat'. The swimming test was also applied:

> ...all the supposed witches had severally their thumbs and great toes ty'd together and [...] they were thrown so bound into the water, and [...] they swam like a cork, a piece of paper, or an empty barrel, tho they strove all they could to sinck.

The case also sheds light upon contemporary practices to lift a witch's curse. Since the local priest could not cure their illnesses, the witches' victims and their families resorted 'to a cunning man or white witch' by whom:

> they were directed to put the afflicted party's water into a bottle and set it near the fire which accordingly they frequently did and corked it well and ty'd down the cork with 20 rounds of packthread, notwithstanding which the water would always give a crack like a gun, and the cork fly out leaving the bottle and pack thread as it was, while the water was in the bottle the parties had ease but upon its bursting out their pains and illness returned.

One cunning man's advice to the afflicted was:

> to put rosemary balm and mary gold flowers in a bagg to the patients brest as a charm and to give them inwardly a decoction made of the same in a quart of ale and their own blood [...]

However, 'the most infallible cure' was the scratching, or 'blooding', of the witch who was responsible. It seems that this was done on a number of occasions 'but the witches would be so stubborn that they were often forced to call the constable to bring the assistance of a number of persons to hold them by force to be blooded'. Old Jane Clarke presented a particular problem since 'the old woman's skin was so tough that they could get no blood of her by scratching so they used great pins and such instruments for that purpose'.

The three suspects were committed for trial at the Autumn Assizes held in Leicester in 1717, but in the event the case was thrown out by the jury and no verdict was passed. As much as the evidence presented suggests popular beliefs in witchcraft were as vibrant as ever, the fact that the case never got to court is indicative of the scepticism that, by the early eighteenth century, was the prevailing attitude among those in authority.

MIDDLESEX AND
GREATER LONDON

WIMBLEDON, 1569

At the Surrey Summer Sessions of 1569 Jane Baldwyn, a yeoman's wife from Wimbledon, was found guilty of bewitching to death a woman of Wimbledon named Elena Lingarde and also a baby, Richard Hollingworth. Of two other charges she was found not guilty – the bewitching to death of another Wimbledon neighbour, Elizabeth Bonham, and the bewitching of four pigs. Presumably she was hanged.

CROYDON, 1570

A Croydon labourer, Richard Marshall, and a widow named Clemence Marshall, probably his mother, were accused in 1570 of bewitching to death the livestock of three of their neighbours. They were found to be not guilty.

WESTMINSTER, 1574-91

Joan Ellyse, the widow of a Westminster brewer, was found guilty in 1574 on four counts of witchcraft. These comprised two charges of bewitching to death livestock belonging to one of her Westminster neighbours, Edward Williamson, and two more of causing the sickness of Williamson and that of a labourer, William Crouche of Westminster. The outcome of the case is not known.

A couple of years later, Marion Lytman, also of Westminster, was found guilty of bewitching to death a Westminster clerk named William Hereford. For this she was probably hanged, although it is interesting to note that at her hearing she was found not guilty of two further charges concerning the death by witchcraft of two boys – a four-year-old and a one-year-old.

In 1591, Stephen Trefulak, a gentleman, was found guilty of using love magic to bring together another gentleman, George Southcott, and Eleanor Thursbye. He was given a one-year prison sentence.

The unexplained death of livestock often gave rise to suspicions that witchcraft was the cause.

HARMONDSWORTH, 1575

The wife of a tailor, Elizabeth Ducke of Harmondsworth was found not guilty on a charge of witchcraft in 1575. She had been accused of bewitching to death an ox belonging to a neighbour, Edward Brandon.

LALEHAM, 1577

Helen Beriman of Laleham was found not guilty on a charge of witchcraft in 1577. She had been accused of bewitching to death four calves and an ox belonging to a neighbour, Lionel Dockett.

CLERKENWELL, 1582, 1611

Marjory Androwes, a widow of Clerkenwell, was accused of bewitching to death a child. The outcome of her case is not known. Some years later, Olive Cooper, a labourer's wife from Clerkenwell, was in trouble in 1611 because she had professed 'herselfe a wizard, and goes up and down the country to cozen the king's subjects'.

HARROW WEALD, 1585

A Harrow Weald labourer's wife, Joan Barringer, was accused of bewitching to death Rose, the daughter of Richard Edlyn. She was found not guilty.

WHITECHAPEL, 1591-1656

A married woman from Whitechapel, Alice Cutler, was accused of bewitching to death Sibil, the daughter of William Chappel. She was also accused of causing the sickness, by witchcraft, of the wife of a Whitechapel baker. She was found not guilty on both counts. Many years later, in 1652, Temperance Foster, also of Whitechapel, was facing charges of causing by witchcraft the sickness of a yeoman's wife, Elizabeth Peirson; the outcome of her trial is unknown. In 1653, Elizabeth Newman, a Whitechapel weaver's wife, was accused of using witchcraft to cause the illnesses of a vintner's three children. She was found guilty and hanged. In 1656, Grace Box, a widow, was accused of causing the sicknesses, by witchcraft, of several people, at least two of whom died as a consequence. However, she was found not guilty.

HOLBORN, 1597, 1614

Josia Ryley, a Holborn widow, is recorded as having died in court during her trial, in 1597, for killing by witchcraft Herbert Apshawe, who died after a short illness lasting about thirty hours. Some years later, in 1614, the appositely named Dorothy Magicke, another Holborn woman, was found guilty of bewitching two people and sentenced to the pillory and a year's imprisonment. Her curious surname is likely to have been a nickname, possibly even one she gave herself, indicating a woman with a particular reputation, probably formed over many years.

ST GILES-IN-THE FIELDS, 1597

Helen Spokes of St Giles-in-the-Fields was faced with a charge of witchcraft in 1597. She was accused of bewitching to death a St Giles-in-the-Fields neighbour, Anne Whitworth, but the court found her innocent.

BROKEN WHARF, 1599

Anne Kerke of Castle Alley, near Broken Wharf, fell out with one of her neighbours and warned her she 'would be meet with her or hers'. Sure enough, as soon as the neighbour arrived home she suddenly fell ill and eventually died. When one of her children subsequently met Anne Kerke she suffered some kind of a fit, foaming at the mouth and gnashing her teeth. She recovered as soon as the alleged witch departed, although she did suffer recurrences of the condition. The child of another woman who crossed Anne Kerke was similarly afflicted. A local innkeeper was shown the image of Anne Kerke in a cunning man's glass when he was investigating the reason for the recent illness and death of his child. Shortly after telling a neighbour of his discovery, he too became ill and died. Kerke was also accused of causing the deaths of two more children, George and Anne Taylor of nearby Thames Street, and of causing a fit-inducing evil spirit to enter the body of their sister Joan in revenge for being turned down when she begged for money at Anne's burial. She was interrogated by three justices, one of whom, learning that it was impossible to cut the hair of a true witch, decided to put the tradition to the test by requesting a sample of ten or so hairs from Anne's scalp. Sure enough, a 'serjaunt attempting to cut them with a pair of barber's scissors, they turned round in his hand, and the edges were so battered, turned, and spoiled, that they would not cut anything'.

The original trial records for Anne Kerke's case have not survived. According to the pamphlet in which her story is preserved, *The Triall of Maist. Dorrell, or a Collection of Defences against Allegations* (1599), she was hanged at Tyburn on 4 December 1599.

LONDON, 1600

In 1600, a yeoman of London, Richard Nelson, was facing charges of bewitching to death, at St Katherine's, an infant by the name of Katherine Corwell. The outcome of the case is not known.

WEST DRAYTON, 1601

In 1601, a married woman from West Drayton, Elizabeth Robertes, was accused of causing the deaths, by witchcraft, of four of her neighbours, at least one of whom was an infant. She was found not guilty.

ALLHALLOWS, 1602

Elizabeth Jackson, 'an old charwoman' of Upper Thames Street in the parish of Allhallows the Less, had the misfortune of being tried by Lord Anderson, who warned the jury at her trial that England was awash with witches and that he had already dispatched twenty-six of them by passing hanging sentences at previous hearings. The record of Elizabeth's trial survives in the form of a 1603 pamphlet, *Mary Glovers late woefull case together with her joyfull deliverance*, written by Stephen Bradwell, a member of the College of Physicians. It reveals the discovery of 'divers strange marks' found by the women employed to search for the Devil's mark on her body. Elizabeth was duly found guilty of bewitching a neighbour's daughter, fourteen-year-old Mary Glover, causing her to suffer from fits and trances. She was also accused of cursing a man with the words 'I pray God he may break his neack or leg'; the man then fractured a leg. When the judge required Elizabeth Jackson to repeat The Lord's Prayer she was unable to say the words 'Forgive us our trespasses' and 'Lead us not into temptation'. When searched for the Devil's mark several 'unnatural' marks were found on her body. Although a physician summoned to give evidence, Dr Jordaine, declared he considered the girl's condition a purely natural one, Lord Anderson, the judge, was convinced that it was the consequence of witchcraft. Jackson was extremely fortunate to have been tried before the passing of the 1604 Witchcraft Act and her punishment was a term of one year in prison together with four appearances in the pillory. Had she been tried a year or so later it is likely she would have faced execution.

An alternative account of this case survives in *A True and Briefe Report of Mary Glover's Vexation*, by John Swan, a 'student in divinity', printed in 1603.

WHITECROSS STREET, 1607

Rose Mersam of Whitecross Street, was found not guilty on a charge of witchcraft in 1597. She had been accused of causing the sickness of Margaret James.

HAMPSTEAD, 1607-15

A Hampstead widow, Alice Bradley, was accused of several acts of *maleficium* in 1607. These included bewitching to death pigs and cattle belonging to her Hampstead neighbours, and killing a six-year-old boy. She was found not guilty. Likewise, in 1614, William Hunte and his wife, Joan, also of Hampstead, were acquitted of charges that they had killed a gelding and bewitched a woman to death. A year later, however, in 1615, Joan Hunte was found guilty of killing a three-year-old by witchcraft, and hanged.

ENFIELD, 1610

An Enfield woman, Agnes Godfrey, was charged with bewitching both animals and people. Although she was found not guilty of some charges, guilty verdicts were passed on two counts – that of killing livestock belonging to William Durante, and of causing the fatal sickness of an infant, Thomas Phillippes. No sentence is recorded but execution by hanging seems likely.

FINCHLEY, 1615, 1619

In 1615 a Finchley widow, Elizabeth Rutter, was charged with bewitching four people. Although their ages are not specified, they appear to have been children and to have included the son and two daughters of James Fielde, all of whom died as a consequence of their sicknesses. Elizabeth was found guilty and hanged. A few years later, in 1619, a yeoman's wife, Agnes Miller, was found not guilty of bewitching to death Richard, the son of Salomon Harte.

THE TOWER OF LONDON, 1616

The apparent murder, in the Tower of London, of the renowned English courtier and poet Sir Thomas Overbury (1581–1613) caused a sensation at the time, with the blame for it being attributed by many contemporaries to witchcraft. Overbury had been a prominent member of the court of James I, and his death was an appropriately dramatic last chapter in a life of scandal and intrigue.

The Tower of London, scene of a witchcraft scandal involving members of the aristocracy.

The train of events that led to Overbury's murder had begun when he attempted to prevent the marriage of the King's favourite, Robert Carr (later Earl of Somerset), to Frances Howard, the beautiful and precocious daughter of the Earl of Suffolk. By an arranged marriage in 1606, when she was thirteen, Frances Howard was already the wife of Robert Devereux, Earl of Essex, but it was not until 1609 that the Earl of Essex arrived at court to claim his bride, by which time the young girl had fallen in love with Carr. Faced with the urgent need to get rid of the Earl of Essex and the equally pressing desire to win the love of the King's favourite, Frances Howard turned to her friend Mrs Anne Turner, the court dressmaker, who was known to be a source of magic potions and spells. These she in turn got from a Dr Simon Forman of Lambeth, a renowned magician who had already only narrowly escaped the gallows on charges of necromancy.

From Dr Forman, Frances Howard obtained a love potion to capture the heart of Robert Carr and another philtre to make the Earl of Essex impotent (some accounts suggest that a wax figure was used to this end). Allegedly as a result of this magic, Carr fell passionately in love with Frances Howard and the Earl of Essex failed to consummate his marriage, leaving his wife free to have the union annulled.

Able at last to marry her lover, Frances Howard then experienced a setback in the opposition of Sir Thomas Overbury, who, it is speculated, had a homosexual attachment to Carr and was blackmailing him into refusing her hand. Infuriated by this, Howard used her influence to have Overbury posted overseas, but he declined the position – upon which he was imprisoned in the Tower of London for disobedience to the King. At this point Howard allegedly turned once again to Mrs Turner (Forman having died in 1611) and procured from her poisons (reportedly supplied by a Dr Franklin, another magician, Forman having died in 1611), which were then secretly administered through a servant to Overbury while in the Tower. The poisons made Overbury seriously ill but did not lead to his death, probably because his doctors were giving him regular purges and enemas. To finish him once and for all, Howard persuaded one of the doctors to mix poisonous mercury sublimate into the prisoner's next enema. This ploy successfully brought about his death.

Overbury's agonizing demise in the Tower was unexpected, but murder was not at first suspected. However, when the doctor who had administered the fatal enema fell ill and, believing he was dying, made a full confession, an investigation was started. Letters between Howard and Mrs Turner were found and, as proof of the employment of witchcraft, incriminating wax figures were discovered during searches of Anne Turner's home, along with written spells and a piece of human skin. Anne Turner, Frances Howard, and the Earl of Somerset were arrested and sent to the Tower of London themselves. When Frances Howard discovered she was being kept in the very room in which Sir Thomas Overbury had died she kicked up such a row that it was decided to lodge her in another chamber.

In 1616, Frances Howard and her husband the Earl of Somerset, alongside Mrs Turner and others, were tried for Sir Thomas Overbury's murder. Sir Edmund Coke, Chief Justice of England, presided over the initial stages until James I himself decided to watch over events in person, in company with Sir Francis Bacon. The accused were all found guilty but only Mrs Turner, Sir Thomas Overbury's servant, and the Lieutenant of the Tower (who had taken no steps to prevent the murder) were actually hanged. In 1621, the King pardoned his former favourite and his wife, leaving them to a quiet (and unhappy) married life together in obscurity, obliged never to venture more than three miles from their home in Kent. Frances died ten years later, her mental and physical health wrecked by her experiences. The Earl of Somerset eventually died many years later, in greatly reduced circumstances.

TOTTENHAM, 1617

A married woman of Tottenham, Anne Branche was charged, in 1617, with causing by witchcraft the illnesses of three people, at least one of whom, a three-year-old, died. She was found not guilty.

EDMONTON, 1621

One of the best-known English witchcraft cases concerns Elizabeth Sawyer of Edmonton, who was hanged on 19 April 1621. Her story was familiar to audiences of Jacobean drama after it was turned into a play, *The Witch of Edmonton*, by William Rowley, Thomas Dekker, and John Ford in the same year. The earliest account is Henry Goodcole's *The wonderfull discoverie of Elizabeth Sawyer a Witch* (1621). The Reverend Goodcole was the ordinary and visitor for Newgate gaol and he interviewed Sawyer during her imprisonment.

She was, according to his account, every inch the archetypal witch: 'Her face was most pale and ghost-like without any blood at all, and her countenance was still dejected to the ground'. 'Her body was crooked and deformed', and she was prone to cursing, blaspheming, and swearing.

Sawyer had been suspected of being a witch for many years. Goodcole recorded the 'ridiculous' old tradition that confirmed her status in the eyes of her neighbours – that of stealing a piece of thatch from the suspect's house and burning it in the belief that, if

The witch of Edmonton.

a witch, the suspect would soon visit the house in which the sample had been burned. Suspected of causing the sickness and death of cattle and infants in the neighbourhood, Elizabeth was tested positive with the burning thatch trick. From that point on, with the support of an equally convinced local JP, her neighbours were resolved 'to find out by all means they could endeavour her long and close-carried witchery, to explain it to the world and, being descried, to pay in the end such a worker of iniquity her wages ... namely shame and death...'. Once discovered, Goodcole commented, Sawyer was abandoned by her master the Devil and left to defend herself as best she could.

Sawyer was accused of causing the death by witchcraft of Agnes Ratcleife, a neighbour who had incurred the witch's wrath by striking with her 'washing-beetle' Sawyer's sow after she had placed a piece of soap she had been using on the ground. Agnes fell ill that very evening and died within four days, declaring on her deathbed that she believed Elizabeth Sawyer was the cause of her illness.

Three women searched Elizabeth's body, much to her anger and distress, and 'they all three said that they a little above the fundament of Elizabeth Sawyer ... found a thing like a teat, the bigness of the little finger which was branched at the top like a teat and seemed as though one had sucked it, and that the bottom thereof was blue and the top of it was red'. This was enough to convince the jury and she was found guilty of causing the death, 'by diabolical help', of Agnes Ratcleife, and sentenced to be hanged.

Following her trial, Sawyer made a full confession to Henry Goodcole. She admitted to making a pact with the Devil eight years before and that she had used his power to cause the deaths of cattle and two babies. The Devil, in the form of a black or a white dog, visited her a couple of times each week to suck her blood from the teat discovered

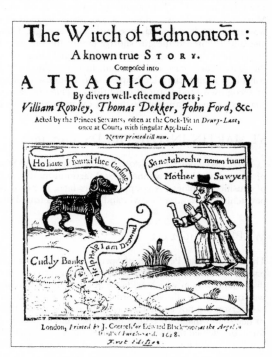

The Witch of Edmonton:
a Tragi-Comedy.

by the searchers. In return, he would do 'the mischief that I did bid him to do for me'. She nicknamed him 'Tom'. However, among other accusations, she categorically denied causing the death of Agnes Ratcleife.

In 1625, another Edmonton woman, Anne Bever, faced an accusation of murder by witchcraft, but she was found not guilty.

The dramatised version of the witch of Edmonton story is a genuine tragi-comedy in its mix of bawdy humour and diabolical deeds. It remains a diverting read and provides fascinating insights into contemporary ideas of how witches were made and the extent and limit of their malefic powers. In the play Elizabeth Sawyer is provoked into calling upon a demon in the form of a black dog to help her take revenge against her tormenter, Old Banks, who has beaten her with a stick. Interestingly, the dog-demon's powers are limited – when she implores him to kill Old Banks, it appears the man has just enough decency in him to limit the demon's powers to the destruction of his corn and livestock. In any case, the demon has one objective in mind and that is the seizing of Sawyer's soul; his acts of *maleficia* are merely his part in their diabolical deal, and, once the deed is done, Elizabeth Sawyer's fate is sealed. She is exposed as a witch when one of her neighbours sets fire to a handful of thatch from her cottage and she comes running home, having been magically alerted to the fire. She is promptly arrested, tried and hanged.

ISLEWORTH, 1622

When the thirteen-year-old daughter of Lady Jennings fell ill with convulsions in 1622 and named, in her ramblings, several women, including an old woman named Margaret Russell, also known as 'Countess', as the cause of her illness, a witch-hunt was more or less bound to ensue. Sure enough, Countess, who, apparently, had met and frightened the girl shortly before the onset of her illness, was arrested and interviewed. Meanwhile, various experts, including a wise woman, were consulted in the search for a cure for the child. In the event, Lady Jennings, able to afford one, consulted a physician, Dr Napier, who diagnosed the girl's illness as a combination of recognised (and natural) conditions – *epileptic matricis* and *morbus matricis*. All charges against Margaret Russell on the grounds of *maleficia* were lifted.

ST MARTIN-IN-THE-FIELDS, 1650, 1652

In 1650, two women – a widow, Elizabeth Smyth, and Dorothy Brumley – were accused of bewitching Jane Gwynne in St Martin-in-the-Fields. They were found not guilty of causing her illness. A couple of years later, in 1652, Margery Scott was accused of bewitching Cassandra Godwin and she too was found not guilty and released.

WAPPING, 1652

The case of Joan Peterson, of Spruce Island, Shadwell, London, recorded in a short pamphlet entitled *The Witch of Wapping* (1652), is remembered chiefly for the disgraceful way in which evidence at her trial for witchcraft at the Old Bailey in 1652 was rigged or disallowed in order to secure a conviction.

Peterson did not contest accusations that she was a 'wise woman' skilled in the use of herbs and magic to relieve headaches, unwitch cows, provide love potions, and so forth, but denied that she ever used her power for evil ends. The prosecution at her trial, however, maintained that Peterson had used magic for much more sinister purposes.

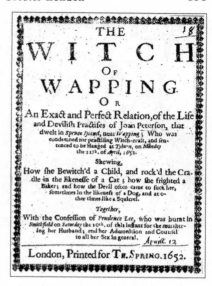

The Witch of Wapping, 1652.

Among other nefarious doings, she kept a familiar in the unusual guise of a squirrel and had allegedly cast a spell over a child, sending a ghostly black cat to rock its cradle:

> ...about midnight, they espied (to their thinking) a great black cat come to the cradle side, and rock the cradle, whereupon one of the women took up the fire-fork to strike at it, and it immediately vanished, about an hour after the cat came again to the cradle side, whereupon the other woman kicked at it, but it presently vanished, and that leg that she kicked with, began to swell and be very sore, whereupon they were both afraid, and calling up the master of the house, took their leave; as they were going to their own homes they met a Baker, who was likewise a neighbour's servant, who told them that he saw a great black cat that had so frighted him, that his hair stood an end...

When the ailing Christopher Wilson came to Joan Peterson seeking a remedy for his sickness, but then failed to pay her after he got better, she apparently threatened him and he began to suffer from 'very strange fits, and for twelve hours together would slabber out his tongue, and walk up and down like a meer changeling'. It was also alleged that Peterson was also the source of the headaches that she later offered to cure.

The magistrates at Peterson's trial included Sir John Danvers, a confidant of Oliver Cromwell, and it was in large part he who ensured – for reasons that remain unclear – that the accused was found guilty of the charges against her. Witnesses wishing to testify on Peterson's behalf were frightened into staying away from the court, while others were bribed not to voice their support for the accused. The court also had no compunction against hearing the evidence of Joan Peterson's own son, who was no more than seven or eight years old, to the effect that the squirrel kept by his mother 'taught her what she should do'.

In the face of such determined opposition, there was little chance for Joan Peterson: she was found guilty as charged and hanged as a witch at Tyburn on 12 April 1652. It

English witches were widely believed to rely on familiars to carry out their acts of *maleficia*.

was subsequently rumoured that Joan Peterson had been silenced by certain favourites of Oliver Cromwell after she had refused to use her magic to get rid of a Mistress Levingstone, the only person who stood between these favourites and a substantial legacy.

STEPNEY, 1653

In 1653, a widow, Barbara Bartle of Stepney, was accused of causing the illness by witchcraft of Elizabeth Gyan, a spinster. She was found not guilty. In 1657, facing similar charges, another Stepney woman, Elizabeth Crowley, was found not guilty, although a record survives of a decision to detain her in the House of Correction. In 1659, Elizabeth Kennit, also of Stepney, was accused of the same and found not guilty.

SPITALFIELDS, 1682

The witchcraft accusation against Jane Kent seems to have evolved from a dispute over the sale of two pigs. A man called Chamblet refused to part with his two pigs until Jane Kent had the money to pay him. He believed that, in revenge, she bewitched his pigs and then caused the illness that brought about the premature death of his five-year-old daughter Elizabeth. He also accused her of bewitching his wife. Chamblet consulted a cunning man in Spitalfields, who advised him to mix a quart of his wife's urine with some of her nail parings and some of her hair, and to boil them in a 'Pipkin'. He claimed that when this was done he heard Jane Kent's voice at his door, screaming in pain, and that when he saw her the next day she seemed more bloated than before. Another witness swore she had searched Jane and found a teat on her back and curious holes behind her ears. A further witness, a coach man, declared that his coach overturned shortly after he had refused to give Kent a ride. However, despite these damning accusations, investigations revealed that Jane Kent was an honest, church-going woman. The Old Bailey jury that heard the evidence found her not guilty.

NORFOLK

GREAT YARMOUTH, 1575-1603

An early witchcraft accusation was levelled against Katherine Smythe in 1575 and recorded in the gaol delivery records. She was accused of using witchcraft to kill Mary Dogeon at Great Yarmouth. In 1583, Elizabeth Butcher and Cecilia Atkins, both of Great Yarmouth, were found guilty of witchcraft. They were to suffer a spell in the pillory, 'in the market, every market-day, till with contrition of heart they confessed'. Elizabeth Butcher is also recorded as being given a term of imprisonment later in the year, to last until she confessed publicly. This appears to have worked since, in 1584, she and another woman, Joan Lingwood, were hanged for witchcraft. In 1587, Helenea Gill of Great Yarmouth was indicted for causing the wasting disease of Catherine Smythe, a widow from the town and conceivably the same Katherine/ Catherine Smythe who had been accused of witchcraft back in 1575. Alice Moore was imprisoned, suspected of dabbling in witchcraft, in 1603.

KING'S LYNN, 1590, 1616

Benjamin Mackerell's *History and Antiquities of King's Lynn* (1738) records the burning of Margaret Read for witchcraft in 1590. Either this story is apocryphal or an extremely rare example of an English witch-burning, an exceptional and horrific sentence that was reserved for the witch who had used her magic to kill her husband, an act that constituted treason. Another *History of King's Lynn*, this one by H. J. Hillen, reported the hanging of Dorothy Floyd (or Lloyd) for witchcraft in 1650.

Mary Smith, the wife of a King's Lynn glover, was hanged as a witch in her home town on 12 January 1616. Her case has been preserved in a contemporary account entitled *A True Narration of some of those Witch-crafts which Marie, wife of Henry Smith, Glover, did practise*, by Alexander Roberts, printed in 1616. According to her own confession, Smith sold her soul to the Devil having formed a dislike of her neighbours because, at a time when brewing and cheese-making were regular domestic activities, they were more successful than her in finding buyers for their cheese. An early victim of her *maleficia* was a sailor who had struck her son; as a consequence he fell seriously ill with something akin to gangrene, which caused the putrefaction of his fingers and toes. When a neighbour, Elizabeth Hancocke, falsely accused Mary Smith of stealing one of her hens, Mary cursed her and Hancocke became very sick, only recovering after her father consulted a local cunning man, who gave advice on how to lift the witch's spell. This included baking a 'witch cake' that among other ingredients included the victim's own urine. This was designed not for eating, but for placing on the patient's chest and back. Elizabeth later married but, unfortunately, the feud revived after her husband caused the death of the witch's cat by running it through, twice, with his sword and striking it on the head with his pikestaff. Amazingly, the cat did not immediately die of what must have been horrendous injuries. Subsequently Elizabeth's malady returned.

Among others, another victim, Edmund Newton, had an argument with Mary Smith over the purchase of some of her cheese. He believed himself bewitched by her when he suffered terrifying dreams and visions, and was further inconvenienced by the invasion of his house by Mary's imps in the form of a toad and crabs. When he attempted to scratch the alleged witch to lift her curse his fingernails were reported to have turned as soft as feathers.

HOCKHAM, 1600

Margaret Francis, who was about eighty years old, was confined in Norwich Gaol on a charge of bewitching a young woman named Joan Harvey. Joan suffered severely from fits, 'she tearing her hair, and beating herself ... sometimes foaming, sometimes dolefully shrieking and blaring like a calf; groaning, howling, and barking like a dog: and biting like a mad dog'. She would sometimes spit in people's faces and would lash out at her parents and others attending her, possessing 'extraordinary strength' when fitting. Furthermore, 'stinking smells and savours came sometimes out of her mouth' and she would make strange speeches, sometimes blasphemous, often in voices other than her own. In some of her ravings she would name Mother Francis as her tormentor, and list the names of the imps with which she did her diabolical deeds, as well as the names of others in the town she had bewitched.

Investigations into Margaret Francis' activities revealed that she had been considered a witch by some of her neighbours for the past thirty years and that she was suspected of bewitching and destroying cattle. She was also alleged to have caused the deaths of at least two of her neighbours, 'Edmund Fall and one Fit's wife'.

Margaret Francis did, however, have her champions. A learned Norwich alderman, Augustine Styward, decided Joan Harvey's illness was a natural medical condition and prevailed upon the authorities to have Francis released. Before she was set free, Joan visited Margaret in gaol and subjected the old woman to a 'scratching', drawing her blood in the belief that this would lift the witch's curse. Margaret died, still in gaol, soon afterwards. Ironically, the record of this case survives not as a compilation of evidence to condemn a witch but as evidence regarding the possibility of foul play in the death of a former suspect.

NORWICH, 1659

Witch-hunting could prove a costly business and the property of the accused was a potential source for recovering the expenses. When Mary Oliver was executed as a witch in 1659 it is recorded that her goods were sold 'for the city's use'.

NORTHAMPTONSHIRE

GUILSBOROUGH, 1612

A twenty-six-page pamphlet entitled *The Witches of Northamptonshire* (1612) provides a fascinating account of the persecution of four women and one man, all of whom were found guilty of witchcraft and executed on 22 July 1612. Agnes Brown of Guilsborough, described in the pamphlet as poor and 'borne to no good', appears to be the archetypal 'witch' who fell foul of her more respectable neighbours and was condemned accordingly. She was, allegedly, 'of an ill nature and wicked disposition, spitefull and malitious'. As was often the case in the records of trials, such as that of the Pendle trials of the same period, her inclination to witchcraft was deemed to be hereditary or, at least, something that was likely to be passed from parent to child. In this instance, her daughter, Joan Vaughan or Varnham, was 'as gratious as the mother, and both of them as farre from grace as heaven from hell'. The mother's reputation appears to have been built up over a period of time and she was 'long suspected'. Joan offended a 'gentlewoman', one Mistress Belcher, with her conversation, which was considered 'unfitting and unseeming the nature of woman-hood'. In disgust, Mistress Belcher rose and slapped Joan, who accordingly declared she would have her revenge. A few days later Mistress Belcher suffered an apparent fit:

> [Mistress Belcher] being alone in her house, was sodainely taken with such a griping and gnawing in her body, that she cried out, and could scarce bee held by such as came unto her. And being carried to her bed, her face was many times as disfigured by beeing drawne awrie that it bred both feare and astonishment to all the beholders, and ever as she had breath, she cried, 'Heere comes Joane Vaughan, away with Joan Vaughan.'

When Mistress Belcher's brother, Mr Avery, attempted to confront the Browns at their home he found the front door, miraculously, would not give way to his attempts to force it open. Believing the women had diabolical aid in resisting him, he returned home. Shortly afterwards he too started suffering from fits. The Browns were promptly arrested and confined in Northampton Gaol.

Popular superstition held that the way to release a victim from a witch's curse was for the victim to draw the witch's blood. This was arranged accordingly and Mistress Belcher and her brother were conveyed to the gaol in order that they may scratch the skin of the witches until they bled. Sure enough, they were 'sodainely delivered of their paine'. As soon as they left the gaol, however, the fits returned and they were 'more violently tormented than before'.

Joan and her mother were found guilty of causing their victims' fits. It transpired that they had also, allegedly, used magic to kill a child. They stoutly denied these charges throughout the trial. Both were hanged.

A curious woodcut appears on the front page of the 1612 pamphlet. It is explained in the closing paragraph:

> It was credibly reported that some fortnight before their apprehension, this Agnes Browne, one Katherine Gardiner, and one Joan Lucas, all birds of a winge, and all abiding in the town of Gilsborough, did ride one night to a place (not above a mile off) called Ravenstrop, all upon a sowes backe, to see one Mother Rhoades, an old witch that dwelt there, but before they came to her house the old witch died, and in her last cast cried out that there were three of her old friends coming to see her, but they came too late, howbeit she would meete with them in another place within a month after.

At the same assizes Arthur Bill of Raunds was accused of causing the death by witchcraft of Martha Aspine (otherwise called Jeames). The pamphlet records the water test to which he, together with his parents, was subjected. In King James' *Demonologie* it had been declared that God's intervention would ensure that a true witch would float when he or she was tested. The floating or 'swimming' of the witch involved binding the accused and securing them by ropes held by men on the banks of the designated pool. This is the earliest surviving record of the practice in England.

The witches of Northamptonshire riding upon a sow's back.

All three floated, but Arthur alone was sent to prison by Gilbert Pickering of Titchmarsh, quite likely the same Gilbert Pickering associated with the witch-hunting at nearby Warboys some twenty years earlier. However, presumably in despair for the fate of her son and terrified that she and her husband might yet be condemned, his mother subsequently cut her own throat and bled to death. Arthur Bill pleaded his innocence as the evidence, including the keeping of three imps named Grissil, Ball, and Jack, stacked up against him. After two months in gaol he was found guilty and executed with the Guilsborough witches, pleading his innocence even as he stood at the gallows.

Helen Jenkinson of Thrapston, also executed at Abingdon near Northampton on 22 July 1612, appears to have shared the same socio-economic circumstances as the other women who died with her. She had 'lived many years poore, wretched, scorned, and forsaken of the world'. Her alleged crimes included the bewitching of cattle and the murder by witchcraft of a child. Prior to her imprisonment she was searched by one Mistress Moulsho and others for the 'Devil's mark' – some blemish or area of skin insensible to pricking that the Devil left with her on sealing their diabolical pact. Shortly afterwards, Moulsho's maid was shocked on hanging out her mistress' washing to discover that a white smock was 'bespotted with the pictures of toades, snakes, and other ougly creatures'. Being a 'gentlewoman of stout courage', Moulsho returned to Helen Jenkinson's house and threatened to scratch out her eyes unless she restored the linen to its former unpatterned white and by the time she got home again the garment was back to normal. Doubtless, though, her accusations helped secure Helen's subsequent arrest, trial, and execution. Mistress Moulsho's enthusiasm for convicting Helen may well have been due to the fact that she had herself been 'strongly suspected' of witchcraft.

The fifth victim of this bout of witch-hunting was Mary Barber of Stanwick:

[She] was one in whom the licentiousnesse of her passions grew to bee the master of her reason, and did so conquer in her strength and power of all virtue, that shee fell to the apostacy of goodnesse, and became diverted, and abused unto most wilde actions, cloathing her desperate soule in the most ugly habiliments that either malice, envy, or cruelty could produce from the blindnesse of her degenerate and devilish desires.

She, too, had bewitched cattle and also, allegedly, brought about a man's death by some act of *maleficium*. Old, impoverished, and despised, she was executed with the others at Abingdon on 22 July 1612.

OUNDLE, 1705

The alleged trial and execution of two witches in Northampton at the relatively late date of 1705 is a source of controversy among historians of the subject.

The story of Mary Phillips, or Philips, and Elinor Shaw is typical of hundreds of other such cases recorded throughout the British Isles. The case against the pair was never more than circumstantial, and it was more by their reputation than by their deeds that they came to be condemned.

Mary Phillips was born into poverty in the town of Oundle, Northamptonshire, and as a young woman eked out a meagre living weaving stockings in the cottage she shared with her only close friend, Elinor Shaw of Cottestock. Both women had a reputation for immoral conduct and when they ventured outside children were said to follow them in the street, calling them whores. They were the outcasts of the local community and many inhabitants of the town, speculating that the couple were really witches, blamed them for the deaths of several people.

In 1705, the gossip crystallised in the form of complaints to the authorities, and the two women were taken to Northampton for trial, on 7 March 1705, at the Assizes. The indictments against them included murder by witchcraft of the wife of Robert Wise of Benefield, of four-year-old Elizabeth Gorham of Glapthorn and of twelve-year-old Charles Ireland of Southwick. Under pressure from two local constables, the pair confessed that they were witches and provided full details of how they had been admitted to a local coven by a tall dark man, who pricked the tip of their third finger as a way of baptising them into the service of the Devil.

Whether or not the women really believed they were witches is unclear, but they certainly made the most of her short-lived notoriety, shocking listeners with their account of their lives as witches and howling with laughter in court. According to Elinor Shaw, over a period of nine months they had been responsible for the deaths of fifteen children, eight men, and six women, as well as accounting for forty hogs, one hundred sheep, eighteen horses, and thirty cows. When, as they were being taken by cart to Northampton gallows, they were asked by the attending priest to repent, they merely laughed and invoked the name of the Devil. Before they could blaspheme any further, both women were hastily hanged until nearly dead and then thrown into a fire and burned to ashes.

The most controversial aspect of the case is the fact that, although it appears in many lists of historical witchcraft trials, it may well be a complete fiction, the sole authority for it being a 1705 pamphlet, *An account of the Tryals, Examination and Condemnation of Elinor Shaw, and Mary Phillips, &c. by Ralph Davis*, a publication

A diabolical baptism.

of highly dubious authenticity. Real or fictitious, the description of the women's execution in the tract is particularly vivid:

> They were hardened in their wickedness that they publicly boasted that their master (meaning the Devil) would not suffer them to be executed, but they found him a liar, for on Saturday morning, being the 17th inst., they were carried to the gallows on the north side of town, whither numerous crowds of people went to see them die, and being come to the place of execution the minister repeated his former pious endeavours, to bring them to sense of their sins, but to as little purpose as before; for instead of calling upon God for mercy, nothing was heard of them but damning and cursing; however, a little before they tied up, at the request of the minister, Elinor Shaw confessed not only the crime for which she dyed but openly declared before them all how she first became a witch, as did also Mary Phillips; and being desired to say their prayers, they both set up a very loud laughter, calling for the Devil to come and help them in such a blasphemous manner as is not fit to mention; so that the sheriff seeing their presumptious impenitence, caused them to be executed with all the expedition possible, even while they were cursing and raving, and as they lived the Devil true factors, so they resolutely dyed in his service to the terror of all the people who were eye witnesses to their dreadful and amazing exits … So that being Hang'd till they were almost Dead, the fire was put to the Straw, Faggots and other Combustable matter, till they were Burnt to Ashes. Thus Liv'd and thus Dyed, two of the most notorious and presumptious Witches, that ever were known in this Age.

NORTHUMBERLAND

CHATTON, 1645-50

In the late 1640s, three Northumberland women – a widow called Dorothy Swinow and two sisters, Margaret and Jane White – were suspected of witchcraft and infanticide. Their tale was told in *Wonderfull News from the North, or, a True Relation of the Sad and Grievous Torments Inflicted upon the Bodies of three Children of Mr George Muschamp, late of the County of Northumberland, by Witchcraft*, a thirty-page pamphlet published in 1650 that is exceptionally unusual among the pamphlets written about English witch-hunts by named authors in that it was written by a woman, Mary Moore.

Where most witch-hunts focused on the lives of people from pretty humble backgrounds, the alleged witches often being impoverished elderly women falling out with their neighbours, this is also an unusual case in that both the chief protagonists seem to have had fairly well-to-do, 'respectable', backgrounds. Dorothy Swinow was the wife and widow of a colonel; the family that accused her appears to have had at least one highly literate member – Mary Moore herself, the author of the 1650 account. As further evidence of her social standing, Mary Moore seems also to have possessed a virginal, since her possessed daughter vomited the wire strings used in such an instrument, and was apparently wealthy enough to consult a range of physicians.

In 1645, Mary Moore's eleven-year-old daughter from her first marriage, Margaret Muschamp, began to suffer from fits and trances in which she saw angels and fought an imaginary foe that took the form of a dragon or other wild creatures. Mary 'sent for physicians, both of soule and body' and was comforted by Lady Selby, Lady Higgarston, Countesse Lendrik, and other friends. Astonishingly, despite eating and drinking scarcely anything for a full sixteen weeks, Margaret did not appear to lose any weight. Her recovery was as sudden as her collapse, although she had frequent relapses, brought on particularly by the sound of muskets being discharged when the family moved for a short time to the nearby garrison town of Berwick.

Meanwhile, Margaret's older brother George fell ill with a consumptive sickness. His mother, to no avail, sent for doctors from Newcastle, Durham, and Edinburgh, but it was all to no avail. All agreed that the boy had less than a month to live 'which was sad newes to his sorrowful Mother, God knowes'.

In one of her trances, Margaret wrote down the abbreviated names of the people who were tormenting her brother: 'Jo. Hu.' and 'Do. Swo.'. Mary's niece suggested the 'Do. Swo.' might stand for Dorothy Swinow who, apparently, had once visited the house to see Margaret when her mother was away and, according to the niece, had said unpleasant things about Mary in her absence. At some point Mary linked

Wonderfull News from the North, 1650.

Wonderfull News from the North.

OR, A TRUE

RELATION

OF THE SAD AND
GRIEVOVS TORMENTS,

Inflicted upon the Bodies of three Children of
Mr. *George Muschamp,* late of the County
of *Northumberland,* by Witch-craft:

AND HOW MIRACULOUSLY IT
pleafed God to ftrengthen them , and to
deliver them :

As alfo the profecution of the fayd Witches, as by
Oaths, and their own Confeffions will appear,
and by the Indictment found by the Jury
againft one of them, at the Seffions of
the Peace held at *Alnwick,* the 24.
day of *April,* 1650.

Novemb. 25. 1650.
Imprimatur, J O H N D O VV N A M E.

L O N D O N,
Printed by *T. H.* and are to be fold by *Richard Harper,* at his fhop in Smithfield, 1650.

Although most witchcraft cases were
concerned with the witch's propensity for
acts of *maleficia,* some revolved around the
Devil's seduction of an elderly woman and
their subsequent diabolical pact.

the 'Jo. Hu.' with John Hutton, a man – possibly a recognised cunning man – of whom 'it was suspected [...] could do more than God allowed of'. Mary confronted Hutton, 'bidding him confesse who had wrong'd her child, or she would apprehend him'. Hutton obliged and named Dorothy Swinow. Furthermore, he declared that she had caused brother George's sickness and also the death of Mary's sister, Lady Margery Hambleton. A complex section in Mary Moore's account suggests that Dorothy Swinow's *maleficia* was to do with the very earthly matter of the inheritance of property:

> Saying her angels bid her now be bold to speake out [...], saying, thy name is John Hutton, and hers is Dorothy Swinow, she hath beene the death of my Aunt Hambleton, the consumer of my brother, and the tormenter of me; the knowing my Aunts estate was but for life, and her onely sonne had marryed Fauset's daughter, who to enjoy the estate, he having but one sonne, was the cause of yong James Fauset's unnaturall fits.

Ironically, John Hutton, who already had a reputation, was arrested and imprisoned at Newcastle, where he subsequently died, but the 'witch' he had helped expose, Dorothy Swinow, was still at liberty when Mary Moore wrote her pamphlet in 1650. No doubt her reason for writing it in the first place was to try to convince her readers that Swinow really was the cause of her family's misfortunes. Fortunately for Dorothy, it seems that the judges were sceptical; at least one who witnessed Margaret's fits thought she was faking. According to her mother's account, when she got home after being accused of feigning, the distraught girl vomited 'stones, coals, brick, lead, straw, quills full of pins' and 'virginal wire'. In her lengthy statement in her mother's account, Margaret gave full details of how Dorothy Swinow had caused another sibling to fall ill with a similar condition, her sister Betty. The pamphlet goes on to include the confession before John Sleigh, JP, of one of Swinow's supposed accomplices, an illiterate woman named Margaret White. White confessed to forming a pact with the Devil and having sex with him, in the form of a man in blue clothes, on several occasions. She also described satanic parties that she attended with the Devil, Dorothy Swinow, and her sister, Jane Martin, at the latter's home. She confirmed that she and the other witches had inflicted sicknesses on several children and caused the death of at least one, Thomas Yong of Chatton. At the time of writing, a warrant for Dorothy Swinow's arrest, a version of which concludes the pamphlet, had apparently been issued but she was 'as yet not taken'. Her fate is unknown. Jane Martin, however, was hanged.

EDLINGHAM, 1653

Several charges against Margaret Stothard were presented before Henry Ogle of Edlingham, JP, in January 1653. Although the outcome of the case is unknown, it is an interesting one in that Margaret's witchcraft, allegedly, was used for both beneficial and malevolent purposes.

According to the testimony of William Collinwood of Edlingham, a local woman, Jane Carr, took her sick child to Margaret for a magical cure, presumably because she was already recognised as one of the cunning folk. Margaret took the child from her mother and 'put her mouth to the child's mouth and made much chirping and sucking', declaring 'she would warrant the child well enough'. As soon as she finished, a calf fell ill with convulsions and had to be killed. It was Jane Carr's belief that Margaret had transferred the child's sickness to the calf. Isabel Main of Shawdon also claimed she approached Margaret for advice on how to improve the quality of the cheese she was employed to make for Jacob Pearson. Margaret gave her a charmed piece of rowantree wood to carry with her when milking and, sure enough, the quality of the milk, and thus the cheese, was much improved. Margaret would not take any money for her good deed but she did accept the gift of a fleece.

Jacob Mills of Edlingham Castle provided a classic 'charity-refused' model for a witchcraft accusation. He explained how Margaret begged for alms from Alexander Nickle and his wife, and was refused. As she departed she waved, ominously, something white three times. The next morning a child, presumably the daughter of the Nickles, fell very ill, crying out that a woman was pressing her with such force that she thought her back and heart would be broken. She died shortly afterwards.

TYNEMOUTH, 1660

Another case that conforms to the 'charity-refused' model for explaining witch-hunting is that of Elizabeth Simpson of Tynemouth whose case was heard by Luke Killingworth, JP, in 1660. Elizabeth Simpson, the wife of a fisherman, was refused a pot of beer by the daughter of Michael Mason, a soldier. Elizabeth assured her she would repent of her meanness and, sure enough, Frances lost the use of her legs and became bedridden. Her pain subsided a little when she scratched and bled Elizabeth, but she remained sick and unable to walk at the time of the hearing. The outcome of the case is unknown.

NEWCASTLE-UPON-TYNE, 1650, 1660-85

According to nineteenth-century historians, the parish records of St Andrew's, Newcastle, recorded a significant episode of witch-hunting that culminated in a mass execution on 21 August 1650:

> The 21 day of August (1650) these parties here under named were executed on the Town moor for Witches, - Isab' Brown, Margrit Maddeson, Ann Watson, Ellenor Henderson, Ellenor Rogers, Elsabeth Dobson, Mathew Bonner, Mrs Ellsabeth Anderson, Jane Huntor, Jane Koupling, Margrit Brown, Margrit Moffet, Ellenor Robson, for stealing of silver spoons, Kattren Wellsh for a Witch, Aylles Hume, Marie Postes.[69]

Tradition has it that these witches were buried in St Andrews' churchyard with nails driven through their legs to prevent them from escaping from their graves.

Charges of witchcraft, typically, were made in the small, close-knit rural localities in which most people lived. However, assize records survive for a string of cases concerning the inhabitants of this busy port in the first half of the reign of Charles II, king from 1660 to 1685. In most instances these were charges brought against women for causing serious wasting diseases; interestingly, in most of these cases, the victim was still alive at the time of the indictment. Unfortunately, the records do not comment on the outcome of any of these cases.

Although anything resembling sabbat meetings is almost unheard of in English witchcraft trials, it was not unusual for small groups of witches, operating together, to be identified. A good example of this is the indictment in 1661 of three Newcastle women – Anne Mennam, a labourer's wife, and two widows, Margaret Cawtserwood and Jane Bamborow – who were accused of bewitching a one-year-old boy, Daniel Philip. Another three women were accused of causing the illness of a Newcastle labourer, Robert Philip, who testified that one night when he was in his sickbed with the doors shut they had manifested before him, had a short conversation, and vanished.

Four more cases from 1661 concern the bewitching of John Jackson by Margaret Shevell; of Robert Johnson by Isabella Story; of Katherine Cudworth by Jane Watson; and of Elizabeth Gibson by Emma Haskin. All of those charged were Newcastle women apart from Story, who was from nearby Seaton Delavel. Conforming to the witch stereotype, three of the four were widows; Haskin is described as being the wife of a skipper. Some dramatic details of the Jane Watson case have survived: according to the testimonies of three witnesses, all women, she had bewitched the children of Jonas Cudworth, one of whom was presented with an apple by the witch, shortly before cries of 'Fire! Fire!' were heard from people in the house. The witness, Winifred Ogle, claimed to have seen 'a flash of fire, and a round thing like fire go up the chimney'. Jane Patterson claimed to have seen the witch when she went to visit the Cudworth children; immediately the witch hid under the children's bed and when a Mr John Ogle thrust his rapier under the bed a sound like the cry of a pig was heard. The witness provided a rare detail – the witch was dressed in a red waistcoat and a green petticoat. A third testimony, that of Elizabeth Richardson, commented on how she had called upon the services of Jane Watson, clearly a known 'wise woman', when she fell sick. The witch took her by the hand and Elizabeth's pain immediately dissipated but her pet dog promptly died.

Further cases in the district were recorded for 1663, including the bewitching to death of Anne Charleton by Christian Hearon, a labourer's wife from Acomb, and of two further deaths in Great Whittington, for which Mary Gibson, also of Great Whittington, was indicted.

A group of witches.

An interesting record from 1664 tells of the suffering of Jane Milburne of Newcastle, who was tormented by Dorothy Stranger after Jane refused to invite her to her wedding feast. Sometimes transforming herself into a grey talking cat, Dorothy allegedly made death threats towards Jane, bit her arm, pushed her to the ground, and even, on one occasion, tried to strangle her with a rope. Jane fell ill, getting just a brief respite after scratching the witch and drawing her blood. Dorothy Stranger was also implicated in bewitching to death her own niece, according to the testimony of the deceased's mother, Elizabeth Stranger. Nevertheless, a non-guilty verdict was recorded.

In the same year another two Newcastle women, Jane Simpson and Isabella Atkinson, were accused of causing the sickness of Dorothy Heron, a baker's wife, who had fallen out with Atkinson, the wife of a labourer. Both Dorothy and her husband saw Isabella standing by Dorothy's bedside 'clothed with a green waistcoat' before she vanished as mysteriously as she arrived. Both women were found not guilty and released. Yet another case in the same year records the testimony of William Thompson of Newcastle, whose 17-year-old daughter, Alice, reportedly became perilously ill through the bewitchment of a local widow, Katherine Curry. These little-known cases endorse the argument of many historians that witchcraft accusations emanated 'from below' in the day-to-day squabbles of neighbours and relations, heightened by anxiety and sorrow.

In 1665, one 'Mistress Pepper' of Newcastle was accused of dabbling in witchcraft. Described as a midwife, hers appears to be a certain example of the targeting of the local 'wise woman'. She may have fallen foul of her neighbours when her cures did not work. When she gave Robert Pyle, a sick miner, some water to drink, he immediately had a fit. Mrs Pepper responded by grabbing his small children and 'laid them to his

Many witchcraft trials began in a refused act of charity to a supposed witch, who was then suspected of using her craft to exact revenge.

mouth', claiming the 'breath of the children would suck the evil spirit out of him'. When Richard Rutherford, a tailor, fell ill she treated him with holy water, which she sprinkled over his inflamed hand, and a silver crucifix, which she placed in his mouth. Interestingly, the testimonies were made by the two men's husbands, presumably, being too sick or, perhaps, disinterested to make formal allegations themselves. As was often the case, the accusers as well as the accused in this witchcraft trial were women.

A classic 'charity-refused' witchcraft episode occurred in Newcastle in 1667. When Emma Gaskin, a beggar, was turned away empty-handed from the house of Thomas Sherburne, a watchmaker, Gaskin cursed his maid, who fell ill with fits thereafter. Conceivably, a combination of fear and guilt had provoked in the maid a form of psychosomatic illness.

A 'cunning man' appears in the Newcastle Assize records for 1674. Peter Banks, a Newcastle labourer, is revealed as being well known for practising charms producing spells to give ships safe passage. Since he charged twenty shillings for one of these spells, it is not surprising that, sooner or later, he would fall foul of his customers. The precise nature of their complaints, however, is not recorded.

BEDLINGTON, 1673

Two women of Morpeth, Dorothy Himers and Isabel Fletcher, testified against a third, Margaret Milburne of Bedlington. Each of her accusers had quarrelled with Margaret Milburne and then fallen ill. Also, they each had had encounters with Margaret, or perhaps a vision of Margaret, at night, manifesting out of a bright white light.

STOCKSFIELD-ON-TYNE, 1673

The trial of Anne Forster and others on charges of witchcraft in 1673 is interesting for the wealth of detail surrounding the allegations, and also because it implied, for some observers, the existence of a loosely organised system of covens throughout Northumberland during the seventeenth century.

At the heart of the case against Anne Forster was the evidence of Anne Armstrong, a maidservant at Burtree House near Stocksfield-on-Tyne, who claimed that she had been bewitched by Forster into carrying her to a sabbat one night just before Christmas. According to Armstrong, she had first met Forster when sent to buy some eggs from her on behalf of her mistress, Mrs Mabel Fouler. The pair could not agree on a price for the eggs and, after checking each other for lice, they parted. Soon afterwards, however, Armstrong was much troubled by fainting fits. A beggar she met warned her that Anne Forster was a witch and that she would try to ride her spirit like a horse.

With Christmas approaching, Armstrong met Forster once more and this time the alleged witch forced a bridle over Armstrong's head, upon which the maid lost all power to resist the other's will. Armstrong was subsequently obliged to carry Forster cross-legged to join her companions at Riding Mill Bridge, where the witches held their sabbats. In so doing she got a good look at Forster's confederates, who included several people she knew (and named in court). Most striking of these was a 'long black man riding on a bay galloway, as she thought, which they called their protector'. The members of the coven ordered Armstrong to sing for them while they danced and amused themselves changing from one shape to another. Anne Baites, a witch from Morpeth, in quick succession changed into a cat, a hare, a greyhound, and a bee in an effort to please the Devil, described here as 'a little black man in black clothes'. At the end of the proceedings the luckless Armstrong was obliged to carry Forster back home again.

According to Armstrong's testimony before the justices at Morpeth, Anne Forster met her friends on numerous occasions; sometimes it was Forster who used Armstrong as her mount, although other witches demanded similar service of her too. Armstrong was garrulous in describing the details of the ceremonies that she witnessed, recalling in particular a lavish banquet at which no fewer than five covens of thirteen witches each were present. A rope hung down over the gathering from the ceiling, and the witches pulled on it to obtain any food they desired, which was magically produced. The maidservant also described how she had seen the witches bow down in obeisance before a certain large stone, reciting the Lord's Prayer backwards in the course of their veneration.

Armstrong went on to make further serious allegations that Forster and the other witches had used their magic to harm enemies and their livestock, saying that she had learned of their misdeeds when they boasted of them to the Devil. Mary Hunter and Dorothy Green had cast a spell over John March's mare, resulting in the animal's death – an accusation that tallied with the story of John March himself, who described how his horse had been pestered by a swallow one evening and had then become ill and died four days later. Another of the witches, Elizabeth Pickering of Wittingstall, was said to have boasted of procuring the death of a neighbour's child through magic.

Anne Forster and the other accused witches all denied Armstrong's extraordinary accusations and it seems from the inconclusive trial records that they were all acquitted (although two of the group were briefly imprisoned).

LONGWITTON, 1680

Nicholas Raynes, on behalf of his wife, Anne, made some extraordinary allegations against Elizabeth Fenwick of Longwitton in 1680. He claimed that Elizabeth, a reputed witch, would ride on his wife and force her to the floor, and that his wife had seen her dancing with a black man (probably indicating an individual in black clothing with dark hair and complexion). Sir Thomas Loraine, JP, was unimpressed and the case was dropped.

NOTTINGHAMSHIRE

NOTTINGHAM, 1597

In November 1597, William Somers, the teenaged apprentice of a Nottingham musician, attracted attention when he began to show symptoms of demoniacal possession, which locals were quick to attribute to witchcraft. Among other things, he appeared to swallow his tongue, to be seized by weeping fits, and to lie on the ground as if dead. Word of the alarming behaviour of the so-called 'Boy of Nottingham' spread quickly and the assistance was sought of John Darrell (c. 1562–1602), a preacher who already had a widespread, if dubious, reputation as an exorcist.

Exorcists were much employed to counter possession resulting from witchcraft on the Continent, but Darrell remains virtually unique in the role in the annals of English witchcraft. He had already, over the course of more than ten years, attempted to establish a reputation as a self-styled exorcist in witchcraft cases but, after initial success, had succeeded only in coming into conflict with the Church authorities.

A graduate of Cambridge University, Darrell began his career as a preacher in his home town of Mansfield, Nottinghamshire, and was subsequently ordained. The opportunity to involve himself in witchcraft cases came in 1586, when seventeen-year-old Catherine Wright was persuaded by Darrell to make accusations of witchcraft against a woman named Margaret Roper, on the grounds that Roper had ordered a demon called Middlecub to torment her. Unfortunately for Darrell, under examination Wright admitted to the authorities that she had made up the whole affair and the aspiring exorcist was lucky to escape gaol.

Darrell does not appear to have learned his lesson, for ten years later, in 1596, he was at it again, conducting services of exorcism in the widely reported case of Thomas Darling, the 'Burton Boy' (which was later revealed to be a hoax). His next case was that of Nicholas Starkie and his family at Cleworth Hall, Leigh, Lancashire, during the course of which Darrell successfully exorcised no fewer than seven people allegedly possessed by demons.

A year after the case of the 'Burton Boy', Darrell arrived in Nottingham with another priest called George More, his confederate in such matters, to see William Somers. The case was to prove the climax of Darrell's controversial career.

Darrell confirmed the diagnosis of demoniacal possession and performed a successful service of exorcism over the boy. When Somers was then repossessed by his demons, Darrell laid the blame for the lad's suffering upon the sins being committed by the people of Nottingham. Darrell accordingly requested married couples in the city to refrain from physical intimacy and gave a sermon in which he described the boy's symptoms in graphic detail, with Somers himself obligingly demonstrating

A late sixteenth-century exorcism.

these to anyone who cared to see. When encouraged to name those responsible for his condition, Somers produced the names of thirteen local witches. Whenever these women came near him he had a fit (though critics noted that this 'test' was not always infallible).

By now the city was at fever pitch, with arguments raging between those who questioned Darrell's methods and those who feared their very lives were under threat from the covens he appeared to be revealing in their midst. According to Samuel Harsnett, the hysteria affected everyone:

> The pulpits rang of nothing but devils and witches; wherewith men, women, and children were so affrighted as many of them durst not stir in the night, nor so much as a servant almost go into his master's cellar about his business without company.

Next, Mary Cowper, who happened to be Darrell's sister-in-law, identified one Alice Freeman as a witch. When Freeman attempted to evade questioning by claiming that she was pregnant, Darrell was quick to allege that, if she was, the child was almost certainly that of the Devil. Freeman's brother, however, managed to get Somers brought before the town council, where the boy confessed that he had faked the possession. Darrell refused to accept this confession and claimed that this was simply a trick by the Devil to forestall further investigation. A public inquiry followed in 1598. Somers, realising that if he was exposed as a fraud he risked the death penalty, now retracted his confession about his possession, opening the way for Alice Freeman and another of the accused women to be brought to trial.

Once in court, the whole case disintegrated. Somers changed tack again and admitted that he had deceived his interrogators by a variety of simple tricks. It transpired that

Somers had dreamed up the whole business in order to get himself released from his apprenticeship to the musician, which he found irksome. He had discovered how to stage demoniacal possession by reading widely available pamphlets about other recent witchcraft cases, such as that of the Warboys Witches, and had gleaned further tips from Darrell himself, who had described the symptoms of the Burton Boy so that he might imitate them.

The collapse of the trial of the Nottingham witches was a major embarrassment to Darrell and caused the exorcist to be sent to Lambeth Palace for questioning by the Archbishop of Canterbury and other high-ranking Church officials. Although some prominent Church dignitaries sympathised with Darrell's mission against demons, he and More were censured for their conduct, defrocked, and thrown into prison for a year. In 1599, one of Darrell's examiners, Samuel Harsnett, wrote a book about the affair under the title A Discovery of the Fraudulent Practises of John Darrel, Bachelor of Arts.

Although Darrell himself wrote extensively in defence of his conduct, there is no record that he resumed his former activities as an exorcist. The notoriety attached to his name meant that in 1603 exorcism by clergymen was forbidden altogether in England 'under pain of the imputation of imposture or cozenage, and deposition from the ministry' unless the person in question had a licence and the sanction of his Bishop to do so.

WITCHCRAFT ACCUSATIONS IN EARLY SEVENTEENTH-CENTURY NOTTINGHAMSHIRE

Although the details of their cases are not known, a number of people were indicted for witchcraft in Nottinghamshire during early Stuart times. These included widow Margaret Frore of Harby, indicted in 1606; Isabella Cotton of Hayton, 1608; Joan Clark, the wife of a labourer of Sutton in the Clay, 1609; widow Barbara Daste of Broughton Sulney, 1609; Helen Beckett of West Drayton, 1621; Alice Busse of Bagthorpe and an unnamed woman of Boughton, 1623; and another widow, Katherine Brown of Cromwell, indicted in 1629. In 1616, three women from North Muskham – a widow called Christian Clark and two women by the name of Hudson – were accused of 'using incantations against Anna Strey'.

OXFORDSHIRE

NORTH MORETON, 1605

The daughter of a prosperous gentleman of North Moreton, Oxfordshire (though then in Berkshire), Anne Gunter was at the centre of a sensational witchcraft trial held at Abingdon in 1605.

Anne Gunter began to fall victim to fits and hysteria in 1604, when she was around twenty years old. Her symptoms included foaming at the mouth and temporary blindness and deafness, along with a tendency to produce pins from various parts of her body. According to Benedict Allen, a gentleman of Calne, Wiltshire, these were 'wrung out of her breast, some with the head and some with the points forward'. The young woman was also said by witnesses to become unnaturally heavy when in her fits, and her clothes were frequently unlaced by unseen hands. These ailments Anne Gunter herself blamed upon the sorcery of three local women – Elizabeth Gregory, one of the most unpopular individuals in the parish; Agnes Pepwell, who was already thought of as a witch; and Agnes' illegitimate daughter Mary Pepwell.

The allegations caused a considerable stir and in March 1605 Elizabeth Gregory and Mary Pepwell were sent for trial at Abingdon (Agnes having run away before she could be detained). The case was, however, thrown out and Anne Gunter herself came under suspicion of fraud. Her father, Brian Gunter, would not let the case rest, however, and through his contacts at Oxford arranged to have Anne brought before James I himself. The King examined the young woman on three occasions, at Oxford, Windsor, and Whitehall, but doubted the veracity of her story and had her committed to the care of the chaplain to the Archbishop of Canterbury, Samuel Harsnett, and Doctor Edward Jorden, an expert in hysterical conditions. Jorden soon confirmed the King's doubts about Anne Gunter's honesty. The King assured the young woman that she would not be punished if she told the truth; she subsequently admitted that the entire story had been a fabrication and that she had exaggerated her symptoms at the order of her father. He, she explained, wished to have revenge upon the Gregory family in the course of a feud that had arisen after he had fatally injured two Gregorys during a brawl at a village football match in 1598.

Both Anne Gunter and her father were charged with conspiracy and brought before the Star Chamber early in 1606. The verdict is unknown. Local tradition says that Brian Gunter, by all accounts a difficult man who had a tempestuous relationship with his neighbours, died at an advanced age in Oxford in 1628. It is also claimed that Anne Gunter fell in love with a man she met while she was being kept in custody and eventually married him, James I provided the dowry.

The case of Anne Gunter was significant in that it was the first important trial investigated by James I in which fraud was seen to be manifestly at work, and the outcome doubtless had a considerable impact upon the King's subsequent attitude to the assessment of evidence in witchcraft trials (and consequently that of his judges). Historians have noted similarities between the Gunter case and that of the widely reported Warboys witches and it seems probable that the girl got her inspiration largely from pamphlets about the earlier trial.

SOMERSET

DITCHEAT, 1584

The Devil was abroad in Ditcheat in 1584. The tale told in a pamphlet, *A true and most Dreadfull discourse of a woman possessed with the Devill*, published in London that year, reveals something of the mentality of the age which, in part, explains the witch-hunts of the seventeenth century. It concerns the manifestation of a hideous creature that appeared in the bedroom of Stephen Cooper's sick wife, Margaret. Hearing his wife making a terrible commotion, Stephen, and six others, all named as witnesses in the document, entered the room and witnessed the following extraordinary and terrifying events:

> Then her husband looking up in his bed espied a thing come to the bed much like unto a bear, but it had no head nor no tail, half a yard in length and half a yard in height: her husband seeing it come to the bed, rose up and took a joined stool and struck at the said thing, the stroke sounded as though he had struck upon a feather bed: then it came to the woman and stroke her three times upon the feet, and took her out of bed and rolled her to and fro in the chamber, and under the bed. The people there present to the number of seven persons were so greatly amazed with this horrible sight, that they knew not what to do ... At the last this monster which we suppose to be the Devil, did thrust the woman's head betwixt her legs, and so rolled her in a round compass like a hoop through three chambers down a high pair of stairs in the hall where he kept her the space of a quarter of an hour. Her husband and they in the chamber above durst not come down to her, but remained in prayer weeping at the stair's head, grievously lamenting to see her so carried away. There was such a horrible stink in the hall, and such fiery flames, that they were glad to stop their nostrils with clothes and napkins.

HINTON, 1612

The record of a petition from Hinton in 1612 details the demands of the locals that a woman in the neighbourhood, Elizabeth Hinton, be 'apprehended and punished' for her acts of witchcraft including 'the untimely Death of men, woeman, and children which she hath hated'.

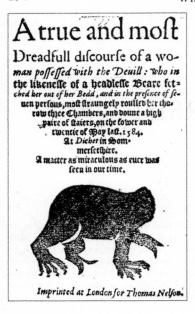

Frontispiece of a pamphlet telling the tale of possession by the Devil in Ditcheat, 1584.

TAUNTON, 1626

Edward Bull and Joan Greedie were accused at Taunton Assizes in 1626 of reducing, by witchcraft, Edward Dynham to bouts of catatonic collapse. In his 'trances' he would seem dead for hours at a time and that when those attending him 'thrust pins and needles through his hands and nostrils [...] he is insensible, neither does any blood appear'. Furthermore, during these fits two voices, presumably emanating from him, could be heard conversing but neither voice was his own. The outcome of the case is unknown.

GLASTONBURY, 1653

It was reported by many witnesses that 'after Elizabeth, wife of Thomas Castle of Glastonbury, had visited their houses to borrow or buy, their stock fell ill and their beer did not work'. In this classic 'charity-refused' example of witchcraft accusation, it was also claimed that Elizabeth Castle would threaten those who refused to help her. One witness saw Castle's cat play with a very large toad. The outcome of the case is not known.

WELLS, 1655-1707

Jane Ridwood of Wells seems to have run into trouble in 1655 since 'The opinion of several women taken on oath [...] was that Jane, wife of John Ridwood of East Wells, was an unlucky [...] witch, that is one who brought ill luck or misfortune.'

The outcome of her case is unknown. In 1670 Anne Blake was found not guilty of bewitching an infant to death or of laming Elizabeth Pinney by witchcraft. Likewise, in 1679, Ann Rawlins evaded prosecution for supposedly causing Grace Atkins' wasting sickness by witchcraft. Brief records of several more witchcraft accusations heard at Wells survive, the last in 1707. They all follow the typical pattern of a single woman accused of causing harm to another, usually female, person. There is no evidence of a guilty verdict being found in any of these cases.

SHEPTON MALLET, 1658

The activities of Jane Brooks of Shepton Mallet were recorded by Joseph Glanvill of Frome, a member of the Royal Society, in his important treatise *Saducismus Triumphatus*, first published in 1681. He received his information from Robert Hunt, one of the two JPs who heard the case at the Somerset Lent Sessions held in the town of Chard in 1658.

One Sunday afternoon in November 1657 Jane Brooks arrived at the house of Henry Jones, where she met his son, Rich, 'a sprightly youth, about twelve years old'. She begged of him 'a piece of close bread', in return for which she presented him with an apple, 'After which she also stroked him down on the right side, shook him by the hand, and so bid him goodnight.' Shortly afterwards he fell ill with a pain in his right side. His illness became a good deal more severe when, having roasted it, he ate half of the apple Jane Brooks had given to him, causing him to suffer from fits and the loss of speech. When Jane Brooks was brought into his view, as one of a number of women, in a bid to discover who had cursed the boy, he lost his sight for a time before being able to identify her as his persecutor. His father, Henry Jones, 'immediately scratcheth her Face, and drew blood from her' – the recognised method of undoing a witch's spell. Rich, accordingly, recovered but about a week later he encountered Jane Brooks' sister, Alice Coward, and again fell ill. In his distress he had visions of both sisters and, on many occasions, having described the clothing in which they were dressed, 'the Constable, and others' would visit Brooks' house which 'was at a good distance from Jones's [...] and always found the Boy right in his Descriptions'.

On one occasion he pointed out to his father and a man named Gibson the place on the wall where he could see the figure of Jane Brooks. Immediately Gibson struck it with a knife 'upon which the Boy cryed out, "O Father, Coz. Gibson hath cut Jane Brooks's hand and 'tis Bloody."' Taking the Constable with them, the two men repaired to Brooks' home where, sure enough, they found her tending a wounded hand that she claimed had been 'scratched with a great pin'.

Jane Brooks and Alice Coward were hauled up before the justices at Castle Cary in December 1657. Having given his initial testimony, Rich Jones temporarily lost the power of speech on catching sight of the two women. At a subsequent hearing in Shepton Mallet the appearance of Jane Brooks precipitated another of the boy's fits. Meanwhile, the women, he claimed, appeared miraculously before him in his room, trying to bribe him on one occasion with the gift of twopence to keep him quiet. His torments also included remarkable feats of levitation:

On the 25th of February between two and three in the afternoon, the Boy being at the House of Richard Isles in Shepton Mallet, went out of the Room into the Garden; Isles' wife followed him, and was within two yards when she saw him rise up from the ground before her, and so mounted higher and higher, till he passed in the Air over the Garden Wall, and was carried so above ground more than 300 yards, falling at last at one Jordan's door at Shepton, where he was found as dead for a time. But

The
transvection
of Rich Jones.

The levitation
of Rich Jones.

coming to himself, told Jordan that Jane Brooks had taken him up by the Arme [...] and carried him in the Air [...]

On another occasion the boy could not be found where he had been left but was discovered in a state of collapse in another room. More extraordinarily still, he was once found 'strangely hanging above ground, his hands being flat against a great Beam in the top of the room, and all his body two or three foot from ground. There he hath hung a quarter of an hour; and afterwards come to himself, he told those that found him, that Jane Brooks had carried him to that place, and held him there.' According to Glanvill, this phenomenon was witnessed by nine people.

When the two women were sent to gaol, Rich Jones ceased having fits. Jane Brooks was found guilty at Chard Assizes on 26 March 1658 and executed.

TAUNTON, 1663

Mrs Julian Cox (c. 1593-1663) was a beggarwoman tried for witchcraft at Taunton in 1663. Her case is interesting in that it sheds light on such alleged phenomena as flying on broomsticks and shape-shifting. It was recorded by Joseph Glanvill of Frome, a member of the Royal Society, in his important treatise *Saducismus Triumphatus*, published in 1681.

The trial had its roots in a confrontation between Mrs Cox and a servant maid, who had declined to give the old woman money when she demanded it. The girl was subsequently much tormented by visions of the vengeful beggarwoman, who supposedly appeared to her in spectral form and forced her to swallow large pins. It transpired from other evidence that the old woman kept a familiar in the shape of a toad and was skilled at transforming herself into a hare. According to one witness, when his hounds cornered a hare in a large bush and he tried to seize it, to save it from his dogs, the creature changed into a woman, whom he identified confidently as Mrs Julian Cox. The transformation had a profound effect on the witness, as later reported: 'He knowing her was so affrighted that his hair stood on end; and yet spake to her asked her what brought her there; but she was so far out of breath that she could not make him any answer.'

Cox was also alleged to have used magic to make a neighbouring farmer's cows go mad and to have flown on a broomstick (she was spotted flying through her own window). The prisoner herself described how she had seen two witches and an unidentified 'black man' approaching her on broomsticks 'about a yard and a half from the ground'. When the court tried to test her guilt by ordering her to recite the Lord's Prayer she made the fatal mistake of leaving out the 'not' in 'And lead us not into temptation'. The accused was found guilty and executed as a proven witch.

BREWHAM AND WINCANTON, 1664

Evidence for the existence of witch covens was rarely presented in English courts. In 1664, however, two such covens were exposed in the course of official investigations in the vicinity of Brewham and Wincanton. The resulting trial is particularly significant in the annals of English witchcraft as the accused persons actually admitted to membership of organised covens. The case was recorded by Joseph Glanvill, a former vicar of nearby Frome, and a member of the Royal Society, in his important treatise *Saducismus Triumphatus*, published in 1681.

According to the prosecutors, the covens active at Brewham and Wincanton were presided over in person by the Devil, answering to the name Robin, who was described by his minions as a deep-voiced and handsome, though little, man in black.

Witches were commonly supposed to be capable of shape-shifting. They were often suspected of changing into hares or other animals.

The commonly encountered notion of witches flying on broomsticks at night. This was a contemporary belief although witches were as likely to confess to flying mounted on horses or other animals, or even people.

Somerset witches and Robin, the man in black.

The Brewham coven comprised ten women and a single man and included Henry Walter, Margaret Agar, four women called Green, and three named Warberton. The investigations into the Wincanton coven culminated in accusations of witchcraft against a total of six women and eight men, at whose head stood Ann Bishop. Other members of the coven included Elizabeth Style and Alice Duke. The man in black, possibly a member of the local gentry, was never identified.

The covens were accused of feasting after dark at open-air sabbats, the food being provided by the mysterious man in black. The accused witches – who variously claimed to be present 'in the flesh' or only in spirit – danced to his music and plotted harm against their enemies by sticking pins or thorns into wax images. These poppets were formally baptised by the Devil, with himself and two of the witches standing as the godparents, and named after the intended victim. A man called Dick Green was said to have died as the result of such a spell cast by the Brewham group.

Alice Duke provided interesting details about how she was initiated into the coven by Ann Bishop. She and Bishop had walked backwards three times around the local church. On the first circuit the man in black appeared; on the second a large black toad leapt up at them; on the third a rat-like creature ran past them. The man in black then spoke to Ann Bishop and shortly afterwards Alice Duke was accepted into the coven, the Devil pricking the fourth finger of her right hand to make his Devil's mark on her. Elizabeth Style, recalling her own initiation, said that she had traded her soul for money and for twelve years of pleasure on Earth, signing a pact to this effect in her own blood. The Devil had then given her sixpence and disappeared.

The accused also described how they had soared through the air to meetings of their covens, first smearing themselves with flying ointment that allowed them the power of flight. According to Elizabeth Style, she and the other witches smeared their foreheads and wrists with a raw-smelling grease that was given to them by their spirit contacts. After reciting the words 'Thout, tout, a tout, tout, throughout and about' they were then able to fly wherever they chose. When the time came to fly to a sabbat, they observed the same procedure but recited the words 'Rentum tormentum'. Anne Bishop, meanwhile, described how she was carried off to the sabbat after similarly anointing her forehead with a feather dipped in oil. When the time came to go home from the sabbat they shouted, 'A boy! Merry meet, merry part' and repeated the 'Rentum tormentum' charm, after which they were quickly returned whence they came.

Most of the witches were accused of keeping familiars. Alice Duke, for instance, had a cat, which sucked at her right breast, while Christian Green suckled her imp in the

The Devil presiding over a sabbat in Somerset.

form of a hedgehog. Elizabeth Style claimed that the Devil manifested himself to her in the form of a black dog and would personally grant her wishes, which she expressed with the words 'O Sathan, give me thy purpose.'

The trial of the witches of Brewham and Wincanton was pursued with considerable zeal by a local justice, Robert Hunt, until his superiors – responding to changing views of the whole issue of witchcraft – obliged him to desist from further enquiry. Joseph Glanvill, in his *Saducismus Triumphatus*, complained bitterly at this interference, claiming that there were many more covens to be uncovered in the county.

BECKINGTON, 1689

A two-page pamphlet, *Great News from the West of England,* published in London in 1689, tells the remarkable story of supposed bewitchment in the village of Beckington, a couple of miles from the town of Frome in Somerset. It was attested by the Rector of Beckington (who probably wrote it), the village's two churchwardens, two overseers of the poor, and two constables. It concerns an unnamed 'old woman', aged 'about fourscore' (i.e., about eighty), who lived in the village alms-house. Here she was the target of verbal abuse from William Spicer, an eighteen-year-old who 'would call her Witch'. She was so upset by this that she reported him to the local Justice of the Peace, who issued a warrant compelling William to apologise and to promise to leave her alone. However, despite his apology, a few days later 'this young man fell into the strangest fits that ever mortal beheld with eyes', which continued for a fortnight. He claimed that when he had a fit 'he did see this old woman against the wall in the same room of the house where he was, and that sometimes she did knock her fist at him; sometimes grin her teeth, and sometimes laugh at him in his fits.' Furthermore, he sometimes threw up great quantities of 'crooked pins', 'to the number of thirty, and upwards'.

Another neighbour of the supposed witch was Mary Hill, also aged around eighteen. Like William, Mary earned the wrath of the old woman first by using threats to try to get her to hand over a ring, secondly by refusing to accompany the old woman to Frome to help her look for spinning work (Frome was a major woollen

(1)

Great News from the
West of England.

Being a True Account of Two Young Persons lately Bewitch'd in the Town of *Beckenton* in *Somerset-shire* : Shewing the sad Condition they are in, by Vomiting, or Throwing out of their Bodies, the Abundance of *Pins, Nails, Pewter, Brass, Lead, Iron,* and *Tin,* to the Admiration of all Beholders.

And of the old Witch being carryed several Times to a great River ; into which, her Legs being tied, she was Thrice thrown in ; but each Time, she Swam like a *Cork.*

Great News from the West of England, 1689.

cloth manufacturing town in this period), and thirdly, having bought some apples, by refusing to give one to the old beggar. Subsequently, like William, she suffered from fits and visions of the old woman. She also began to throw up crooked pins. However, according to the pamphlet, she was afflicted even more severely than William:

>...she began to throw up nails and pins ... and handles of spoons, both of pewter and brass; several pieces of iron, lead, and tin, with several clusters of crooked pins, sixteen or seventeen in a cluster, seven pieces of pewter, four pieces of brass, being handles of spoons, six pieces of lead; some whereof were handles of spoons, and some, the lead of a window, besides one solid piece of lead, which weighed full two ounces; six long pieces of latten, with wire belonging to them; five pieces of iron, one whereof was round, but hollow, and very big; and two and twenty nails, some whereof were board-nails, above three inches and a quarter long.

Consequently, the villagers rounded on the old woman and the JP ordered a search for the Devil's mark to be carried out. The women who searched her found several purple marks on her skin and when these were pricked with a needle 'she felt no pain'. Next she was given a swimming test in the river near to the village and more than 200 people witnessed her floating 'like a piece of cork'. This, seemingly, was an incredible feat since when a 'lusty young woman' was thrown into the river as a test she sank immediately and would have drowned but for assistance from those on the bank. With this evidence stacked up against her, the old woman was sent to the County Gaol at Ilchester to await trial at the next Assizes. When the pamphlet was published the old woman was still awaiting trial and Mary Hill, allegedly, was still throwing up nails and spoon-handles.

The case later appeared in *The Certainty of the Worlds of Spirits* in 1691, a book written by the prolific polemicist Richard Baxter.

STAFFORDSHIRE

BURTON-ON-TRENT, 1596

Sixty-year-old Alice Gooderidge of Stapenhill near Burton-on-Trent was sentenced for witchcraft at the Derby Assizes in 1596. A record of the proceedings, *The most wonderfull and true storie, of a certain Witch named Alse Geederige of Stapenhill,* was published in London in the same year. Alice's mother, Elizabeth, was the well-known 'Witch of Stapleton' and so it would have come as no surprise to locals to learn that Alice was accused of bewitching a fourteen-year-old boy, Thomas Darling, when she met him while he was hunting hares in Winsell Wood on 26 February 1596. When he returned home he was very sick, suffering from fits, hallucinations, and vomiting. On being questioned he declared he had met 'a little old woman, who had a gray gown with a black fringe about the cape, a broad thrumd hat, and three warts on her face'. This woman, the archetypal witch, cursed him when, 'as he passed her by in the coppice, he chanced (against his will) to let a scrape' (i.e., he farted). She retorted with the exclamation 'Gyp with a mischief, and fart with a bell: I will goe to heaven, and thou shalt go to hell.'

Once she had been identified as the woman in the wood, Alice Gooderidge was subjected to certain tests. When instructed to repeat the Lord's Prayer she failed to say the words 'And lead us not into temptation'. When she was searched for signs of the Devil's mark or teats for suckling imps, her searchers found 'upon her belly, a hole the bigness of two pence, fresh and bloody, as though some great wart had been cut off the place'. Her explanation that she had injured herself when she slipped off a ladder failed to convince her interrogators since her clothes were not torn. Her mother, husband, and daughter were also questioned but Alice alone was sent to Derby Gaol to await sentencing. In desperation she confessed to cursing the boy and promised to cure him in return for forgiveness. Instead she was subjected to a subtle form of torture. This involved putting a pair of new shoes on her feet and then placing her 'close to the fire till the shoes became extreme hot'. The following day she confessed 'I met the boy in the wood, the first Saturday in Lent and passing by me, he called me witch of Stapenhill, unto whom I said, Every boy doth call me witch, but did I ever make thy arse itch?' The next day she added more to her confession, declaring 'forthwith I stooped to the ground, and the Devil appeared to me in likeness of a little partie coloured dog, red and white, and I called him Minny, seeing that every boy calleth me witch, therefore go thy ways and torment this boy in every part of his body at thine own pleasure, forthwith I strained every part of my body, enforcing myself to vomit, saying, after this sort, vex him.' Meanwhile, the boy continued to suffer from fits and it was concluded that he was possessed by some kind of satanic spirit.

The moſt wonderfull

and true ſtorie, of a certaine Witch named *Alſe Gooderige of Stapen hill*, who was arraigned and conuicted at Darbie at the *Aßiſes there*.

As alſo a true report of the ſtrange torments of Thomas Darling, *a boy of thirteene yeres of age, that was poſ-ſeſſed by the Deuill, with his horrible fittes and terri-ble Apparitions by him vttered at* Burton vpon Trent *in the Countie of* Stafford, *and of his maruel-lous deliuerance.*

Printed at ~~London for I. O.~~ 1597.

The most wonderfull and true storie, of a certain Witch named Alse Geederige of Stapenhill, 1596.

Alice Gooderidge was sent to trial before Sir Edward Anderson at Derby, where she was found guilty of witchcraft and condemned to death. Shortly afterwards, presumably sentenced to a year in prison, she died in Derby Gaol. The fate of her mother is not recorded.

On 27 May 1596, the infamous exorcist and preacher John Darrell of Ashby-de-la-Zouch, who ten years earlier had only narrowly escaped prison for his involvement in another witchcraft investigation, was sent for to treat the ailing 'Burton Boy', Thomas Darling. He went on to perform a bizarre service of exorcism, which seemed to bring about a marked improvement in the boy's condition.

Three years later, in 1599, Thomas Darling finally admitted that he had invented the affair 'to get myself a glory thereby'. Under pressure from the Archbishop of Canterbury, Darrell admitted that he had faked much of the exorcism ritual he had performed (although he did try subsequently to retract this admission). Darrell continued to entangle himself with cases of alleged witchcraft and possession and a year after the 'Burton Boy' trial he resurfaced at Cleworth Hall in Leigh, Lancashire, where he exorcised seven members of the household of Nicholas Starkie, and again at Nottingham, where he performed a pubic exorcism over William Somers (the 'Boy of Nottingham'). In 1603, as a student of Merton College, Oxford, his tongue was to get him into further trouble when he fell foul of the authorities at Oxford University, being sentenced to be whipped and have his ears cropped after he libelled the Vice-Chancellor.

STAFFORD, 1621

Thirteen-year-old William Perry, of Bilson near Stafford, became known as 'The Bilson Boy' after he levelled accusations of witchcraft against an elderly woman called Jane Clark in 1620. The resulting trial at the Staffordshire Assizes acquired notoriety as one of most widely reported hoaxes of the early seventeenth century.

According to Perry, Jane Clark had bewitched him and caused him to suffer fits. The court, however, was inclined to scepticism, especially in the light of the fraudulent Leicester Boy case four years earlier. In the end, the trial was abandoned and Perry admitted that he had faked the fits because he enjoyed the attention they brought him.

Remarkably, not long after the trial, Perry tried the same ruse again. This time the affair came to the attention of Thomas Morton, Bishop of Lichfield and Coventry. Morton examined the boy and reluctantly conceded (for he realised that his reputation was at stake) that the symptoms, which included the throwing up of various odd objects, must be genuine when Perry passed black urine. As a test, a spy was set to watch Perry secretly in his chamber. This proved the boy's undoing: thinking he was unobserved, Perry revealed the means by which he had made his urine black – an inkpot under the bed. When the boy further claimed that demons sent him into fits whenever the first words of St John's Gospel were read, Thomas Morton seized his chance to test the truth of this:

> Boy, it is either thou or the devil that abhorrest these words of the Gospel; and if it be the devil, he (being so ancient a scholar, as of almost six thousand years' standing) knows and understands all languages, so that he cannot but know when I resite the same sentence out of the Greek text. But if it be thyself, then thou art an execrable wretch, who plays the devil's part.

THE BOY
OF BILSON:

OR,

A TRVE DISCOVERY OF
THE LATE NOTORIOVS IM-
POSTVRES OF CERTAINE ROMISH

Priests in their pretended *Exorcisme,* or expulsion of
the Diuell out of a young Boy, named WILLIAM
PERRY, *sonne of* THOMAS PERRY *of*
Bilson, *in the County of* Stafford, *Yeoman.*

Vpon which occasion, hereunto
is premitted

A briefe Theologicall Discourse, by way of
Caution, for the more easie discerning of such
Romish spirits; and iudging of their false
pretences, both in this and the
like Practices.

2. Thef. 2. 10, 11.
Because they receiued not the loue of the truth, that they might be saued.
For this cause God shall send them strong delusion, that they should be-
leeue a lye.

AT LONDON,
Imprinted by *F. K.* for *William Barret.* 1622,

A 1622 account of the notorious 'Bilson Boy'.

The offending verse was then read in Greek (a language Perry did not understand). The boy entirely failed to respond in the expected way and his imposture was confirmed. It eventually transpired that Perry had been taught to feign possession by a Roman Catholic priest, who had shown him how to perform such tricks as vomiting pins, rags, and straw. The priest had hoped to fake a successful exorcism in collaboration with the boy, and thus to win favour with his superiors. On the order of Thomas Morton, Perry was obliged to admit his fraud in public and to beg forgiveness from Jane Clark at the Summer Assizes held in Stafford in 1621.

The fact that the court refused to be taken in by Perry's evidence tends to mask the telling fact that it agreed to listen to him in the first place, as he was still below the statutory age (fourteen years old) that he needed to be in order to give evidence against anyone.

SUFFOLK

HAWSTEAD, 1576

In 1576, Margery Spencer of Hawstead was found guilty of using witchcraft to cause the fatal sicknesses of another spinster, Mary Foxe, also of Hawstead, and of the one-year-old daughter of another Hawstead neighbour. It can be assumed she was hanged.

IPSWICH, 1580

An Ipswich yeoman, William Randall, was charged with conjuring evil spirits to help discover the whereabouts of treasure and stolen goods. In his activities it was alleged that he had been helped by four other men, all described as yeomen. In a contemporary manuscript they were described as 'a company together in a nest of as arrant knaves as were found in England to this day'. These four, after a lengthy period of imprisonment were eventually released. The fate of Randall is less certain but his 'guilty' verdict and, in his case alone, the absence of reference to a reprieve, implies he was executed.

FRAMLINGHAM, 1591

Alice Stamperde, a Framlington widow, was found guilty, in 1591, of bewitching to death two married women in her neighbourhood – Margaret Cock and Margaret Irelond. Her initial sentence of death was changed to one of imprisonment.

STRADBROKE, 1599

According to a tract published in 1599, *The Triall of Maist. Dorrell, or a Collection of Defences against Allegations,* Olive 'Doll' Barthram fell out with Joan Jorden when the latter refused to give her some of her master's belongings. In retaliation, Olive, a witch, sent three toads to disturb Joan's rest each night by croaking at her bedside until, with some difficulty, Joan was able to get rid of them, throwing the first out of her bedroom window and incinerating the others. Next, Olive sent an imp in the form of a talking cat that called itself Gyles. Gyles visited Joan:

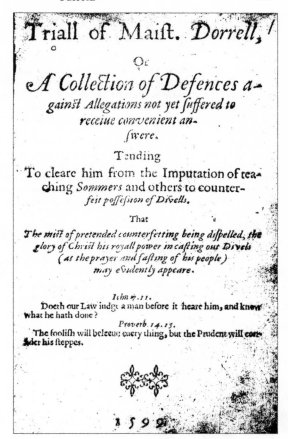

Triall of Maist. Dorrell,

Or

*A Collection of Defences a-
gainst Allegations not yet suffered to
receiue convenient an-
swere.*

Tending

To cleare him from the Imputation of tea-
ching *Sommers* and others to counter-
feit possession of Divells.

That

*The mist of pretended counterfetting being dispelled, the
glory of Christ his royall power in casting out Divels
(at the prayer and fasting of his people)
may evidently appeare.*

Iohn vij.11.
Doeth our Law iudge a man before it heare him, and know
what he hath done?

Proverb. 14.15.
The foolish will beleeue: euery thing, but the Prudent will consider his steppes.

1599

*The Triall of Maist. Dorrell,
or a Collection of Defences
against Allegations,* 1599.

at 11 o'clock at night, first scraping on the walls, then knocking, after that shuffling in the rushes: and then ... he clapped the maid on the cheeks about a half score times as to awake her ... kissed her three or four times, and slavered on her, and (lying on her breast) he pressed her so sore that she could not speak, at other times he held her hands that she could not stir, and restrained her voice that she could not answer.

Once he had woken her, Gyles, now taking the form of something resembling a dark 'sugar loaf, white on the top' and about a foot high, proceeded to tell her he was Doll Barthram's servant (and had been for twenty years) and that his task was to kill Joan. On a subsequent visit he possessed Joan's body and witnesses observed a lump moving around her body. It took six strong men to restrain her and on another occasion, possessed again, she was hurled violently out of her bed in a dramatic fit. As a consequence of these remarkable occurrences Olive Barthram was tried by the Lord Chief Justice at the Suffolk summer sessions and executed at Bury St Edmunds on 12 July 1599.

THE WITCH-HUNTS OF MATTHEW HOPKINS, WITCHFINDER GENERAL, 1645-47

The name of Matthew Hopkins is notorious as that of England's most famous witchfinder, the instigator of the biggest witch-hunt in English history. Estimates of the number of accused witches who met their deaths as a result of the Hopkins witch-hunt in the eastern counties have varied over the years, but it is now generally agreed that probably around 100 people went to the gallows after being implicated by his investigations.

The younger son of James Hopkins, the vicar of Great Wenham in Suffolk, Matthew Hopkins was born around 1620 and lived through a period of considerable social unrest. In 1645, when he embarked on his fourteen-month campaign against suspected witches, the country was experiencing further trauma in the shape of civil war between the forces of Parliament and the Royalist armies of Charles I. East Anglia, where Hopkins grew up, was a heartland of puritanism, and it was puritanical fervour combined with anxiety arising from social turmoil that created the ideal conditions for a witchcraft panic in the area.

Little is known for certain about the early life of Matthew Hopkins, which seems to have been spent largely at Great Wenham and, from the early 1640s, in the environs of Mistley and Manningtree, on the Stour estuary in Essex. Doubtlessly, as a child he absorbed his father's impassioned religious views about witchcraft, papism, and idolatry and was influenced by the growing hysteria in the locality about the satanic forces that were supposed to be at work. In his early twenties he used part of the

Matthew Hopkins, the Witchfinder General.

respectable inheritance passed on by his father to buy the Thorn Inn in Mistley and to set himself up as a member of the minor gentry. He is often said to have received some training in the law, perhaps working as a lawyer's clerk in Ipswich, but there is no firm evidence for this.

The first case with which the name Matthew Hopkins became associated was that of an elderly one-legged widow of Manningtree called Elizabeth Clarke. Suspected of causing the death by witchcraft of the wife of John Rivet, a tailor of Manningtree, the old woman had been identified as a witch before the local magistrates on 21 March 1645 by another Manningtree Puritan called John Stearne. Stearne, who was a little older than Hopkins and in his thirties, evidently shared the concerns that Hopkins had about the threat apparently posed by a network of witches in eastern England. The local magistrates, Sir Harbottle Grimston and Sir Thomas Bowes, gave their permission for Stearne to question Elizabeth Clarke further and for the old woman to be searched by Mary Phillips and other local women for the teats with which she was thought to feed her familiar spirits. Matthew Hopkins promptly volunteered to assist Stearne in his interrogation, possibly claiming a right to involve himself in the case after having been, allegedly, the intended victim back in 1644 of a bear-like demon sent against him by a coven of local witches, of whom Elizabeth Clarke was one, after he had overheard them plotting in fields near his house.

Hopkins and Stearne caused a sensation when they reported back to the magistrates, claiming that during their lengthy interrogation the old woman had admitted her guilt and that several nightmarish familiar spirits belonging to their suspect had, according to the accusers themselves, manifested during her interrogation. Clarke's confession during her interrogation enabled the pair to make accusations of witchcraft against five other local women – Anne and Rebecca West, Anne Leech, Elizabeth Gooding, and Helen Clarke. The accused women were duly confined in the miserable cells of Colchester Castle, where Hopkins continued his interrogation. The witch-hunting fever spread through April and May, with the two magistrates hearing similar evidence against further suspects from neighbouring towns and villages, among them Margaret Moone of Thorpe-le-Soken, Mary Greenliefe of Alresford, Mary Johnson of Wivenhoe, and Joan Cooper and several other women of Great Clacton. As a result of all these investigations, a mass trial of no less than twenty-nine suspected witches – there would have been more but four of the prisoners died while in prison – eventually took place in Chelmsford on 17 July 1645. Elizabeth Clarke was among the nineteen suspects who were condemned to death. On 18 July, fifteen of the condemned prisoners were hanged in Chelmsford, while the remaining four, including Elizabeth Clarke, were taken back to Manningtree to be hanged there on 1 August.

In collaboration with Stearne, Hopkins set out on a systematic campaign to expose those guilty of forging alliances with the Devil against their fellow-men throughout the eastern counties, the pair moving initially north into Suffolk and then splitting up to cover more ground. Locations visited by the pair ranged from villages like Shelley, Polstead, Long Melford, Waldringfield, Bramford, Creeting St Mary, Rattlesden, Wetherden, Bacton, Copdock, Chattisham, and Hintlesham to larger towns like Sudbury and Ispwich, where at least seven suspected witches were questioned. From there they continued north and east, adding the villages of Framlingham, Swefling, Great Glemham, Rushmere, Halesworth, Linstead, Mendham, Fressingfield, Wickham, Horham, Hoxne, and others to the places where they identified further suspects. Often they stayed only long enough to set legal proceedings in motion, leaving others to pursue the cases to trial. This strategy proved highly effective: in the space of little more than a year the two witchfinders caused scores of suspects, typically impoverished and physically unattractive old women who were loathed in the communities in which they lived, to be brought before the authorities in Essex, Suffolk, and beyond.

It is thought that Matthew Hopkins' investigations were the direct cause of the execution of around 100 people, the vast majority of whom were women.

Although the law forbade the use of torture, Hopkins and Stearne, assisted by various women who conducted physical examinations of suspects, extracted confessions by such relatively subtle means as pricking the flesh of suspects with sharp bodkins (to see if they felt anything), swimming them (in the belief that a witch would float while an innocent person would sink) and depriving them of sleep for long periods. The fact that the women whom they charged with witchcraft fitted so closely the conventional idea of a witch probably did much to advance their chances of getting a conviction (although it should be noted that they took little direct part in the trials themselves).

Particularly notorious was the pair's investigation into nearly 200 suspected witches in Bury St Edmunds in August 1645, which culminated in the trial and execution of many of the accused. Victims included an eighty-year-old Royalist clergyman, John Lowes, who had made the mistake of antagonising his parishioners at Brandeston in Suffolk. He had given his enemies ample scope to attack him when he had spoken up in defence of a woman called Ann Annson, who had been accused of witchcraft, publicly stating that she was no more a witch than he was – a statement that was interpreted as a virtual admission of guilt. Encouraged by local sentiment against the clergyman, Hopkins subjected Lowes to swimming in the moat of Framlingham Castle (he floated) and then to the 'unofficial' torture of being forced to walk backwards and forwards with barely a pause for several days and nights (an ordeal known as 'walking a witch') until the accused was in such a state of delirium that he was ready to confess to all manner of forbidden practices. The old man's trials were recorded in the Brandeston parish register:

> ...Hopkins his chief Accusor ... kept ye poor Old Man waking several Nights till he was delirious & then confest such Familiarity with ye Devil as had such Weight with the Jury & his Judges.

It emerged from these confessions that Lowes had made a pact with the Devil, had kept several familiars (the largest of which he knew as 'Thomas') and had sunk a ship off Harwich (with the loss of fourteen lives) by the use of magic, as well as committing other misdeeds such as destroying cattle. Proof that a ship had been lost at the time in question was not considered necessary and although Lowes quickly withdrew the confession when he recovered from his ill-treatment the clergyman was one of eighteen persons condemned to death on evidence provided by Hopkins and Stearne. Refused a clergyman to read the burial service over him, Lowes was obliged to speak the words himself as he stood before the gallows. It is not known whether Hopkins himself was present at the execution, or at any other execution for that matter, but it seems that Stearne at least was there to witness the outcome of their efforts.

Other victims in Bury St Edmunds included Mary Lakeland, a pious woman thought to have been in her fifties, who was burned for the murder of her husband, a barber, by witchcraft. Because she was technically guilty of 'petty treason' against her husband she became one of the relatively few English witches to be burned to death instead of being hanged and, incidentally, the only victim of the East Anglian witch-hunt to die in such a fashion. Her accomplice in various other crimes, Alice Denham, was paraded through Ispwich and hanged.

Reports of the trials at Bury St Edmunds emphasized the commonly-held notion that the witches of East Anglia were working in collaboration with the Royalist armies, as testified by an extract from *The Scotish Dove*:

> It is certified, that at Bury in Suffolke, there were last weeke (besides those formerly) Executed more then 20 Witches, and above 100 more discovered in those parts. Some of them confessed they had beene in the Kings Armie, and have sent out their Hags to serve them ... His Majesties Armie it seemes is beholding to the Devill; you may be sure it is a just cause where the Devill takes part...

As the campaign progressed through eastern England, other unfortunates were hanged at the instigation of Hopkins and Stearne in the adjacent counties of Norfolk, Cambridgeshire, Northamptonshire, Huntingdonshire, and Bedfordshire. It is thought that in all they interrogated around 300 suspected witches, of whom around 100 were put to death. Details of many of the cases are now lost: little is known, for instance, of the twenty witches reportedly put to death, probably based on evidence supplied by Hopkins, in Norwich in July 1645.

The career of the Witchfinder General – a title that Hopkins is thought to have devised for himself but may not have used until around the end of his campaign – was mercifully brief. Doubts about his methods led to the setting up of a parliamentary commission to watch over each trial and to restrict the use of coercive measures by the investigators. Hopkins was forced to give up the swimming test after the Bury St Edmunds trials in August 1645 but he continued to torment victims with sleep deprivation, starvation, and other abuses.

After the trials at Bury St Edmunds were concluded, Hopkins was invited to Yarmouth, on the Norfolk coast, where he oversaw the questioning of several suspected witches recently arrested in the area. After charges against them were successfully laid, he moved on to Aldeburgh, then, via the villages of Yoxford and Westleton, to Dunwich, at each place uncovering more suspected witches. He continued his work through the winter months, visiting, among other places, Stowmarket, to which he probably returned in the early spring of 1646.

By April 1646, the campaign had moved from Thrapston in Northamptonshire into Cambridgeshire, where witches from the villages of Over and Fen Drayton and towns like Kimbolton and St Neots were identified and sent for examination by the magistrates. The witchfinders suffered a serious setback, however, when the Reverend John Gaule of Great Staughton, who had visited an accused witch in Huntingdon Gaol, objected to the presence of Hopkins and his minions in his county and delivered a series of powerful tirades against their investigations and the practice of witchfinding in general. Gaule condemned the duress applied by Hopkins and pointed out that 'every old woman with a wrinkled face, a furrowed brow, a hairy lip, a gobber tooth, a squint eye, a squeaking voice or a scolding tongue' was likely to be pronounced a witch under such circumstances. Magistrates began to resist pressure from the witchfinders and convictions fell off.

Hopkins retreated from Huntingdon and accepted an invitation to help identify witches in the Norfolk port of King's Lynn. A wet summer had spoiled the harvest, and the return of large numbers of soldiers from the civil war had spread plague and other infections: the local population were more than ready to blame their woes upon any witches Hopkins could uncover.

After King's Lynn, Hopkins gave his attention to the witches of Upwell, where he interrogated an accused witch called Ellen Garrison, and to those of Littleport, where one Anne Green was searched for the teats with which she was alleged to feed her imps. When the latest batch of nine accused witches were brought before the judges in King's Lynn, however, only two were condemned to death, with six of the others being acquitted and another being found unfit to be tried. Other unexpected acquittals followed at Ely, where Ellen Garrison was set free, and elsewhere. In the spring of 1647, after another exacting winter, Hopkins attended the Norfolk assizes, only to be subjected to hostile questioning from critics who argued that because of their superstitious methods witchfinders were no better than the witches they sought to expose.

After these public humiliations, stunned by the mounting opposition to his campaign, Hopkins suspended his witchfinding activities. Another factor may have been the fact that it was becoming impossible to persuade towns and villages to stump up the fees for employing a witchfinder. It is also likely that Hopkins was experiencing a decline in his health, his constitution having been worn down by long months on the road.

Confined to Manningtree by his consumption, Hopkins sought to defend himself against his critics by giving an account of his methods in a ten-page pamphlet entitled *The Discovery of Witches*, which was published in London and Norwich in May 1647. He insisted that watching suspected witches for long periods was essential to uncover their guilt, and that swimming a witch was sanctioned by no less an authority than James I. To those who accused the witchfinder of operating solely for financial gain, and of concocting allegations against the innocent regardless of the evidence, he answered thus:

You do him a great deal of wrong in every of these particulars. For, first,

1. He never went to any town or place, but they rode, writ or sent often for him, and were (for ought he knew) glad of him.

2. He is a man that doth disclaime that ever he detected a witch, or said, Thou art a witch; only after her tryall by search, and their owne confessions, he as others may judge.

3. Lastly, judge how he fleeceth the Country, and inriches himself, by considering the vast sum he takes of every town, he demands but 20 shillings a town, and doth sometimes ride 20 miles for that, and hath no more for all his charges thither and back again (and it may be stays a week there) and find there three or four witches, or if it be but one, cheap enough, and this is the great sum he takes to maintain his company with three horses.

2

THE
Diſcovery of VVitches:

IN

Anſwer to ſeverall QUERIES,

LATELY

Delivered to the Judges of Aſſize for the County of NORFOLK.

And now publiſhed

By MATTHEVV HOPKINS, Witch-finder.

FOR

The Benefit of the whole KINGDOME.

EXOD. 22. 18.

Thou ſhalt not ſuffer a witch to live.

---

may . 14

LONDON,
Printed for *R. Royſton*, at the Angell in Ivie Lane.
M. DC. XLVII.

Matthew Hopkins' *The Discovery of Witches*, 1647.

Hopkins' motivation remains a subject of discussion: he was not an official government or church agent but, conversely, may not have acted out of religious zeal alone. He was probably much attracted by the substantial amounts of money to be made through the exposure of witches, and it seems certain from surviving accounts that he was paid much more generously than he pretended in his *Discovery*. More important, possibly, was the prospect witchfinding offered of making him, while still in his mid-twenties, one of the most feared and respected men in the country – hence his readiness to employ tactics that effectively, if not legally, amounted to torture and, in the first case in which he was involved at least, the use of false testimony.

Whatever his motives, Hopkins frequently declared himself to be convinced of the existence of witches and of the reality of the threat they posed to Christian society. Much of his activity was directed towards identifying the guilty parties on what he claimed was the 'Devil's List', a document that was reputed to name every witch in Britain.

According to legend, Hopkins became the victim of the hysteria he had helped to whip up. Local tradition claims that he was himself accused of being a witch and taken by a mob to a pond between Mistley and Manningtree, where he was bound thumbs to toes and subjected to the ordeal of swimming, after which he died – or was hanged. In reality, his demise was almost certainly much less spectacular. Exhausted by the rigours of travel around eastern England in the depths of winter, his health steadily worsened. John Steame reported him dying 'of a consumption' at his home in Manningtree, an event that is thought to have taken place on 12 August 1647.

The exact location of the grave in which Hopkins lies is unknown, though it is probable he was laid to rest in the graveyard of St Mary's Church at Mistley Heath. His burial is recorded in the Manningtree parish register, but there has been diverting speculation over the years that his death was faked and that he actually went into hiding with the support of well-placed sympathisers. One far-fetched theory has it that he emigrated to New England, where as an old man he had a hand in the notorious trial of the Salem witches.

John Stearne conducted the final stage of the campaign, travelling steadily southwards from Ely and visiting the villages of Haddenham, Stretham, and Sutton, where he unearthed further suspects to be despatched for trial in Ely. Other places visited by Stearne into the autumn of 1647 included Chatteris, March, and Wisbech. Among the last victims of the campaign was Margaret Moore of Stretham, who appeared to believe in the fantasy that she was a witch and effectively talked her way to the gallows. By the time Goodwife Moore was turned off the ladder by the Ely hangman, Stearne was already on his way home to Lawshall in Suffolk. There he devoted his attention to completing the literary legacy left by Hopkins by writing *A Confirmation and Discovery of Witch Craft*, published in 1648, in which he similarly defended the methods they had used and the godly service they had performed. He never resumed his calling as a witchfinder, however, and died early in 1670, a quarrelsome man resented by his neighbours and detested by society at large.

IPSWICH, 1645

The case of Mary ('Mother') Lakeland, recorded in *The Lawes against Witches, and Conjuration* (1645), is exceptional in the history of English witch-hunting in that she was executed by being burned at the stake. Although this was the norm for many parts of Europe in which the victim was likely to be burned alive or shortly after being strangled, it was most unusual in English witchcraft cases. In England in the mid-seventeenth century this punishment was reserved for those found guilty of an

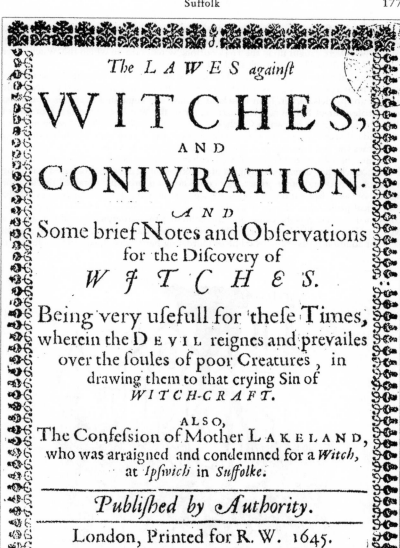

The *L A W E S against*

WITCHES,

AND

CONIVRATION.

AND

Some brief Notes and Obſervations
for the Diſcovery of

W *I* T C H *E* S.

Being very uſefull for theſe Times,
wherein the D E V I L reignes and prevailes
over the ſoules of poor Creatures, in
drawing them to that crying Sin of
WITCH-CRAFT.

ALSO,

The Confeſſion of Mother L A K E L A N D,
who was arraigned and condemned for a *Witch,*
at *Ipſwich* in *Suffolke.*

Publiſhed by Authority.

London, Printed for R. W. 1645.

Pamphlet containing the confession of Mother Lakeland, 1645.

act of treason. Since one of her victims, allegedly, was her husband she was guilty in law of killing her 'lord and master' – an act of petty treason. She was one of the many people who were caught up in the 1645 Suffolk 'witchcraze' in which the 'Witchfinder General' Matthew Hopkins took the lead role.

Mother Lakeland was probably in her fifties when she was condemned. She appears to have been a deeply religious woman of the parish of St Stephen's, and the respectable wife of an Ipswich barber, John Lakeland. It has been suggested from her reputation as 'a professour of Religion, a constant hearer of the Word', and the fact that one of the witnesses against her was a Colchester minister, that she may have been a member of a radical sect.[70] If so, this case might support the theory that witch-hunting was sometimes the consequence of sectarian conflict within the Church.

Accused initially, together with Alice Denham, of using witchcraft to harm William Lawrence, who had demanded payment of a twelve-shilling debt, she confessed to making a diabolical pact and other crimes. Her confession was probably obtained through the agency of sleep deprivation and other strategies that enabled witchfinders to evade the theoretical prohibition of torture in such cases. When Lawrence and his son died, she confirmed that she was the cause. She also confessed to murdering the maidservant of a Mrs Jennings who, like Lawrence, had raised with her, via the maid, the issue of a small debt. In addition to the heinous crime of murdering her husband, she also confessed to

Witches condemned to death in English courts were usually hanged, but they could be burned if guilty of treason, which could include the murder of their husbands, or if they were tried for witchcraft in the Channel Islands.

causing the horrible illness of her granddaughter's former suitor, Henry Reade. Having broken off the engagement, Mother Lakeland punished him first by ruining his business, sending a demon to burn the ship he owned. She then caused the crippling illness that was slowly destroying him – 'halfe of his body is rotten upon him as he is living'.

While Alice Denham was hanged for her part in the murder of William Lawrence, Mother Lakeland was placed in a barrel of pitch and chained to a stake around which a bonfire of faggots and other combustible materials was built. If she was lucky she would have been strangled by the executioner before being burned. Miraculously, following her execution, Henry Reade began to recover from his terrible illness. This, together with the unusual mode of her execution, made the whole tale eminently print-worthy and within a month the story, possibly written by Matthew Hopkins himself, was published in pamphlet form by a London printer.

The burning of a witch was a costly business for the taxpayers of Ipswich, and, at £3 3s. 6d., three times as expensive as a hanging. This, together with the additional costs of such things as terms of imprisonment and the hiring of witchfinders, could, in part, explain why 'panic' proportion witch-hunts in early modern England were extremely unusual and of short duration.

BURY ST EDMUNDS, 1645, 1664

Bury St Edmunds in Suffolk witnessed two of the most notorious witchcraft trials to be held in England during the seventeenth century. The first trial, which took place in August 1645, resulted from the witch-hunting activities of the self-styled Witchfinder General, Matthew Hopkins, and involved the arrest of nearly 200 suspects, of whom the most notable was an elderly clergyman named John Lowes from the village of Brandeston. A 1645 pamphlet records the execution of eighteen people in total, sixteen of whom were women.

The second trial, which was well documented, followed in 1664 and was presided over by a future Lord Chief Justice, Sir Matthew Hale. This latter case was destined to have considerable influence upon the decisions of the judges in the infamous trial of the Salem Witches in America. It is recorded in a later tract entitled *A Tryal of Witches ... at Bury St. Edmunds* (1682).

The 1664 case concerned two widows, Rose Cullender and Amy Duny of Lowestoft, who were charged with numerous acts of witchcraft, including the bewitching of seven children, one of whom died. The two women had allegedly caused infestations of lice, children to fall ill or to suffer fits, farm carts to overturn, and chimneys to fall, as detailed in a contemporary pamphlet:

> The said Amy became tenant to this deponent's husband for a house, who told [the deponent] that if she looked not well to such a chimnay in her house that the same would fall. Whereupon this deponent replied that it was a new one; but not minding much [Amy's] words, at that time they parted. But in a short time the chimney fell down, according as the said Amy had said.

Further damning evidence concerned a toad that had been found in a baby's bedding: on the advice of a Dr Jacob of Yarmouth the toad had been thrown into the fire and shortly afterwards, it was alleged, Amy Duny had been seen to have scorched arms, legs, and face.

The evidence of the children, who complained that the women had caused them to experience paralysis and to vomit pins and nails, was particularly damaging. The pamphlet of the trial detailed their sufferings:

A True
RELATION
Of the
ARAIGNMENT
Of eighteene
VVITCHES.

That were tried, convicted, and condemned, at a Seffions holden at St. *Edmunds-bury* in *Suffolke*, and there by the Iudge and Iustices of the said Seffions condemned to die, and so were executed the 27. day of *August* 1 6 4 5.

As also a Lift of the names of those
that were executed, and their severall Confessions before their executions.

VVith a true relation of the manner
how they find them out.

The names of those that were executed.

Mr. *Lowes* parfon of *Branfon*.	*Rebecca Morris.*	*Anne Wright.*
Thomas Evered a Cooper with *Mary* his wife.	*Mary Fuller.*	*Mary Smith.*
	Mary Clowes.	*Iane Rivert.*
	Margery Sparham	*Sufan Manners.*
Mary Bacon.	*Katherine Tooey.*	*Mary Skipper.*
Anne Alderman.	*Sarah Spinlow.*	*Anne Leech.*
	Iane Limftead.	

Printed at *London* by *I. H.* 1 6 4 5.

A True Relation of the Arraignment of Eighteen Witches, 1645.

A
TRYAL
OF
WITCHES,
AT THE
ASSIZES
HELD AT

Bury St. Edmonds for the County
of *SUFFOLK*; on the
Tenth day of *March*, 1664.

BEFORE

Sir MATTHEW HALE Kt.
THEN

*Lord Chief Baron of His Majesties
Court of EXCHEQUER.*

Taken by a Person then Attending the Court

LONDON,
Printed for *William Shrewsbery* at the
Bible in *Duck-Lane*. 1682.

A Tryal of Witches.

Their fits were various. Sometimes they would be lame on one side of their bodies, sometimes on the other. Sometimes a soreness over their whole bodies, so as they could endure none to touch them. At other times they would be restored to the perfect use of their limbs and deprived of their hearing. At other times of their sight; at other times of their speech, sometimes by the space of one day, sometimes for two, and once they were wholly deprived of their speech for eight days together and then restored to their speech again. At other times they would fall into swoonings, and upon the recovery to their speech they would cough extremely and bring up much phlegm, and with the same crooked pins, and one time a two-penny nail with a very broad head. Which pins, amounting to forty or more, together with the two-penny nail, were produced in court, with the affirmation of the said deponent that he was present when the said nail was vomited up, and also most of the pins.

Consternation greeted the children's claims that the two witches continued to afflict them by appearing to them as ghosts even while the proceedings against them were under way. As additional proof of the presence of witchcraft the court noted that, under the baleful influence of Duny and Cullender, the children stumbled over the name of Christ when asked to read from the Bible and screamed when touched by one of the two women. It was also claimed that examination of Amy Duny – remarkably, by the mother of one of the children involved – had revealed teats for the feeding of her familiars.

In the face of such a wealth of 'evidence', supported by Hale's remarks at the end of the trial to the effect that if so many countries had laws against witchcraft then it must exist, the jurors had no hesitation in finding the two women guilty. They were

A witch's imp.

hanged, though protesting their innocence, four days later. In reality, probably the only crime of the two unfortunate women – who were known to have hot tempers – was to have uttered vague threats against their neighbours after, for instance, being refused the opportunity to buy a few herrings.

Hale, who readily accepted witchcraft as a proven reality, professed himself satisfied with the outcome. Later legal authorities lamented the credence that had been given to unsupported accusations and the manner in which the clearly fraudulent evidence of some witnesses was none the less allowed. Even during the trial, some of those present suggested imposture when one of the girls failed a test designed to prove how the touch of Amy Duny caused her to scream: blindfolded, she screamed just as loudly and fell into a fit when touched by someone else. The conclusion of the trial remains an indelible stain on the reputation of Sir Matthew Hale, one of England's most celebrated legal figures.

Bury St Edmunds became the scene of a further landmark case in the history of English witchcraft in 1694, when Chief Justice Sir John Holt determinedly acquitted another accused witch, Mother Munnings, of causing death by witchcraft. Holt refused to accept charges that dated back to events some seventeen years before and similarly declined to take seriously suggestions that the accused kept an imp in the form of a polecat (as witnessed in court by a man who had been returning home from an alehouse).

SOUTHWOLD, 1646

Ann Camell, the wife of Thomas Camell, a Southwold yeoman, was accused of using witchcraft to injure William Whitten of Southwold. The outcome of the case is not known.

DUNWICH, 1665

The terrible tale of the consequences of Abre (i.e., Aubrey) Grinset's diabolical pact were recorded in a tract by Samuel Petto, a minister at Sudbury, in *A Faithful Narrative of the Wonderful and Extraordinary Fits which Mr Thos. Spatchet ... was under by witchcraft*, printed in 1693. In his preface he claimed to have 'an Eye-witness of a great part' of the events he described.

The treatise is largely concerned with the severe fits suffered by a local middle-aged man, a former Dunwich-based bailiff and official watcher for witches for Matthew Hopkins in Dunwich in 1645, Thomas Spatchet. His fits began in 1661 and continued for several years, during which time he saw visions of a local beggarwoman, Abre Grinset. On one occasion he was observed to be reaching out as if to catch an invisible hand and then biting it. Shortly afterwards Abre Grinset was seen hobbling around with an injured toe.

When apprehended and questioned, Grinset made a remarkable confession. She confessed to being instrumental in causing Thomas Spatchet's affliction and, although she subsequently denied it, of causing harm to others, including the deaths of John Collet of Cookley and Henry Winson of Walpole. She had acquired her powers twenty years earlier as a result of meeting a witch at a wedding and being persuaded by her to enter into a diabolical pact. The Devil took the impish form of 'a blackish Gray Cat or Kitling'. This imp, seemingly, carried out her acts of *maleficium*. When she was searched, a special teat was found on her body from which the Devil would draw her blood.

A Faithful Narrative

OF THE

𝖂onderful and 𝖊xtraordinary FITS

WHICH

Mr Tho. Spatchet

(Late of *Dunwich* and *Cookly*) was under by

WITCHCRAFT:

OR,

A Mysterious Providence in his even Unparallel'd Fits.

With an Account of his first Falling into, Behaviour under, and (in part) deliverance out of them.

Wherein are several Remarkable Instances of the Gracious Effects of Fervent Prayer.

The whole drawn up and written by *SAMUEL PETTO*, Minister of the Gospel at *Sudbury* in *Suffolk*, who was an Eye-witness of a great part. With a Necessary Preface.

Job 2. 6. *And the Lord said unto Satan, Behold he is in thy hand; but save his Life.*

LONDON,

Printed for 𝕵ohn 𝕳arris at the *Harrow* in the *Poultry*. 1693.
Price 6 d.

A Faithful Narrative of the Wonderful and Extraordinary Fits which Mr Thos. Spatchet ... was under by witchcraft, 1693.

3   Item, that one Mother Deuell, dwellyng nigh the Ponde in Windesore aforesaied, beeyng a verie poore woman, hath a Spirite in the shape of a Blacke Catte, and calleth it Gille, whereby she is aided in her Witchcrafte, and she daiely feedeth it with Milke, mingled with her owne bloud.

A witch's familiar.

When she was searched a second time, she was found to be covered 'well nigh over as if scratched with briers and thorns'. Petto concluded: 'It is probable the Devil did much torment her after her Confession'. Suspected but not yet condemned, Abre Grinset died in the spring of 1667, a couple of months after Spatchet's fits, after much prayer, ceased.

The circumstances of Grinset's death were particularly dramatic. About a week before she died, Thomas Spatchet was persuaded to visit her in her final illness. He came close to her but then 'he could not get one step further forward; he ideavoured very earnestly to go on but could not', nor could he depart without difficulty, which included being forced to make many involuntary 'Courtesies (like Women) all the way back again, with many other like actions which were unavoidable.' When a 'Mr. R.' visited Grinset shortly afterwards he found an astonishing sight: 'he never saw such a Spectacle: for all the Skin of her Hands and Arms was scratched or torn off, hardly one place appeared whole as big as his Finger.' This awful condition Grinset declared was the Devil's work, though she had eventually been able to beat him off with the two cudgels that she taken with her to bed. She died soon afterwards.

WITCHCRAFT AT SEA, 1667

For an island nation, surprisingly few examples of witchcraft accusation concerning witchcraft-related storms at sea can be found in the available records for England. However, a contemporary letter written by a Captain Silas Taylor tells of the loss of Captain Jonathan Banticke's ship in 1667. The letter recalls how in a storm at sea two witches sitting on the ship's 'maintop' prevented the sailors from working their sails, with the result that the ship was sunk. The two witches, however, were identified and incarcerated in Ipswich Gaol, presumably awaiting trial. Nothing more is known of the case.

HARTEST, 1694

Philippa Munnings, a destitute widow, was accused of a range of crimes extending over a period of ten years. It was alleged that back in 1684 she had cursed her former landlord, Thomas Pannel, who, in a bid to evict her from his property, had removed the door from her lodgings. Within three weeks Pannell was dead. One witness claimed that, on his way back from the alehouse, he looked through Munnings' window and saw her lift two imps, a black one and a white one, from a basket; one resembled a 'lock of wool, and the black one a shadow'. Nine witnesses swore before the court at Bury St Edmunds that she kept a familiar in the form of a polecat. Other accusations included her causing injury to livestock and people, including one Sarah Wagers, who became lame and lost the power of speech after she had quarrelled with Philippa Munnings. She was also accused of killing by witchcraft two more people – Francis Moulton and James Parkin. However, the willingness of juries in England to convict in witchcraft trials seems to have diminished by the later part of the seventeenth century, and Philippa Munnings was found not guilty.

SURREY

EWELL, 1564, 1682

In 1564, a woman named Eden Worsley was found guilty of bewitching to death the daughter of Elizabeth Dybye. A 'rep' in the margin of the gaol record indicates that she was probably either reprieved or reimprisoned.

Two tracts, *An Account of the Trial and Examination of Joan Buts* and *Strange and Wonderful News from Yowell in Surrey*, published at the time provide information regarding the trial at Southwark in the early spring of 1682 of Joan Buts, a widow and a beggar from Ewell. She was accused of bewitching two people, Mary Farborough ('Farmer' in one of the tracts) and Elizabeth Burridge (or 'Burgiss' depending upon which tract is used). The story provides an interesting account of the use of a form of 'witch bottle', various examples of which have been discovered in recent times.

When Mary Farborough fell ill, her parents consulted a cunning man, Dr Bourne, who, perceiving an act of *maleficium*, 'advised them to save the Child's water, and put it into a Bottle, stopping it close, and bury it in the Earth, and to burn the Child's Clothes'. While the clothes were still burning Joan Buts entered their home and sat down on a stool. Clearly she was very ill herself, having the 'most frightful and ghastly Countenace'. When questioned about her illness and why she had made this appearance, she declared she had been sick for seven weeks and that 'I could not forbear coming to see you'; she then 'threw down her Hat and tumbled down, wallowing on the ground, making a fearful and dismal noise; and being got up, she fell a cursing in a most horrid manner.' Several people, presumably Joan's unfriendly neighbours, swore that they had witnessed this curious episode and some also declared that on many occasions they had taken pins out of the arms and other parts of the sick child. Joan admitted that she was 'a passionate woman', probably one prone to offensive outbursts, but she insisted that 'those things that were sworn against her, were not true'.

Elizabeth Burridge was a maidservant who also lived in Ewell. One day, when her employers were absent from the house, Joan Buts turned up and, after a short chat with the maid, asked her for 'a pair of old Gloves'. The girl, 'knowing her to be a person of ill repute', promptly refused, and Joan Buts went away. However, she soon returned, asking for a pin for her 'Neckcloth' and, this time, the maid obliged. A couple of weeks later the most strange and alarming phenomena developed around the maid and the house in which she served:

> stones flew about the Yard at such a rate, as if it had rained down showers of them, and many of them were as big as a man's fist, and afterwards flew about the house

A witch bottle.

as before they did about the Yard, notwithstanding the doors were close shut, yet for all they flew so thick about, they hit nobody but the Maid, to the great astonishment of her Master, Mistress, and others.

The following day she was suddenly tormented with excruciating pains in her back like the 'unsufferable pricking of Pins'. When her master, Mr Tuers, investigated what was causing her such agony he 'put his hand down her back [...] and to the amazement of all persons present, pulled out a great piece of Clay as full of Pins as it could well be'. He threw the lump of clay into the fire and Elizabeth's pain subsided. However, more unaccountable things happened to her in the days that followed. She became the target of missiles, such as candlesticks, bellows, and stones, hurled by invisible hands. Other curious poltergeist-like activity included great quantities of nuts and acorns flying about, the removal of household objects, such as a fiddle, from one place to another, and the amazing discovery of her grandfather's breeches on the top of the house directly above the bed in which he slept!

Although the sick child, Mary Farborough, died and around twenty witnesses attributed the supernatural activity to Joan Buts, she was found not guilty at the end of a three-hour trial.

COBHAM, 1565

In 1565, a Cobham woman, Joan Gowse, was found guilty of bewitching to death a valuable bull belonging to a Cobham neighbour. At the same Surrey Summer Sessions, Rose Borow of Banstead, a spinster, was found guilty of bewitching to death Alice, the wife of Geoffrey Lambert. A 'rep' in the margin of the gaol record for both of these cases indicates that the accused was probably either reprieved or reimprisoned.

CHERTSEY, 1575

A Chertsey woman, Agnes Crockford, was found guilty of using witchcraft to kill the infant son of a husbandman, the six-year-old son of another, and of bewitching a miiler's wife. Presumably she was sentenced to death, although she may have received a stay of execution having pleaded she was pregnant.

DORKING, 1655

In 1655, a widow of Dorking, Elizabeth Hatton, was found guilty of bewitching to death at Dorking a woman named Elizabeth Stone. For this she was sentenced to be hanged.

GUILDFORD, 1657

In 1657, a husbandman's wife, Mary Wallis of Guildford, was found guilty of bewitching to death, at Guildford, a seven-year-old boy. However, she was not hanged outright: her name appears as a prisoner in the gaol records dated 22 March 1658.

SOUTHWARK, 1701

This fascinating case reveals a good deal regarding popular and elite attitudes towards the whole subject of witchcraft in England at the very start of the eighteenth century. It also exposes the ease with which the credulous could be beguiled by frauds. It is recorded in a pamphlet printed in 1702 entitled *A Full and True Account of the Apprehending and Taking of Mrs. Sarah Moordike, Who is accused for a Witch.*

When Richard Hathaway, a young Southwark labourer, fell sick with a variety of conditions, including being bent double, losing his sight, and barking like a dog, he and his acquaintances came to the conclusion that he was bewitched. Soon suspicion fell on Sarah Mordike, the wife of another Southwark labourer. She had clashed with Hathaway on some previous occasion and doubtless bitter words and curses had been exchanged. But for the intervention of a local minister it is likely she would have been the victim of a lynch mob. The minister devised a plan to expose the absurdity of Hathaway's claims. Knowing that the young man was bedridden and, apparently, unable to talk or see, he arranged for one Mistress Johnson to visit Hathaway, pretending to be Sarah Mordike. When blind Hathaway scratched Mistress Johnson – drawing a witch's blood being the recognised way of undoing a witch's spell – he immediately recovered his sight. However, on discovering the 'witch' was not Sarah Mordike, he promptly lost it again! Only when his friends seized the real Sarah Mordike and dragged her into his room to be scratched did he recover.

Sarah, sensibly, moved from the neighbourhood to Paul's Wharf, London, but Hathaway pursued her and assaulted her. The squabble came to the attention of a local JP, Sir Thomas Lane, who had Sarah Mordike arrested. Despite the failure of a strip search to reveal any obviously diabolical skin embellishments, Sarah was charged with the bewitching of Hathaway. Fortunately for Sarah, the judge and jury were less credulous than Sir Thomas and she was acquitted. Hathaway, however, was not so lucky – he was arrested, gaoled in the Marshalsea prison, and subsequently found guilty of assault. He was also found guilty of using fraudulent means to convince people he was bewitched. These included the pretended vomiting of nails, large quantities of which he kept in his pockets – always conveniently at hand to impress his more gullible friends and neighbours.

SUSSEX

HAILSHAM, 1572

At the Sussex Lent Sessions of 1572, Joan Usbarne, the wife of a Hailsham husbandman, was found guilty of bewitching to death a neighbour's valuable bull, and also a cow belonging to another. According to the terms of the 1563 statute, she is likely to have been imprisoned for a year and placed in a pillory in a local market place for six hours on four occasions during that year.

KIRDFORD, 1575

Margaret Cooper, a surgeon's wife, was found guilty in 1575 of using witchcraft to cause the sicknesses that killed three of her Kirdford neighbours: Henry Stoner, Thomas Fowler's wife, Elizabeth, and William Fowler (possibly their son). It can be presumed she was hanged for murder by witchcraft.

WARWICKSHIRE

A CASE OF CUNNING MEN, 1590

In 1590, three men were suspected of practising 'divers invocations and conjugations of evil spirits' to find treasure. They were named as Anthony Straine, a yeoman from Wolvey; Thomas Rylie, a yeoman from Brailes; Aves Smart, a Leicestershire spinner; and Richard Fysher, a scrivener from Worcester.

COVENTRY, 1617-88

In his book *The Mystery of Witchcraft* (1617), Thomas Cooper declared that Coventry was a veritable hotbed of witchcraft, there being no less than 'three score of that confederacy'. This concept of a full scale 'underground' witch conspiracy, seeking to undermine Christian civilisation, is one that is largely confined to the imaginations of the writers of demonological texts; there is little evidence for widespread belief in such a possibility in the surviving assize records and gaol calendars of the period. However, a letter from Sir Ralph Hope at Coventry to Joseph Williamson, dated 19 October 1668 reported: 'There is much discourse of a strange discovery of witches at Coventry, many of whom are said to be in hold.'

WARWICK, 1652

A 1652 pamphlet by one 'E. G., Gent.' that covered the trial of the Cranbrook witches of Kent also included the curious tale of the bewitchment of Mrs Katherine Atkins, a mercer's wife, of Warwick. It is one of many accounts that reveals the link between witchcraft accusations and charity refused.

On Saturday night, 24 July 1652, Katherine Atkins was standing at her door when she was approached by 'a certain unknown woman' who begged two-pence of her, to which she answered 'two-pences are not so plentifull, and that she would give her no Mony'. The old woman then asked her for the pin in her sleeve, which Katherine agreed to part with. However, the gift would not prove sufficient to spare her the witch's curse:

> Mistris Atkins seeing her so thankfull for a pin, called her again, and told her if she would stay, she would fetch some victuals for her, or give her some thread, or something out of the shop. She answered, she would have nothing else, and bid a

THE
MYSTERY
OF
WITCH-CRAFT.
Difcouering,
The Truth, Nature, Occafions,
Growth and Power therof.

TOGETHER
With the Detection and Punifh-
ment of the fame:

AS ALSO,
The feuerall Stratagems of Sathan,
enfnaring the poore Soule by this de-
fperate practize of annoying the bodie:
with the feuerall Vfes thereof to the
Church of Chrift.

Very neceffary for the redeeming of thefe
Atheifticall and fecure times.

By THOMAS COOPER.

LONDON,
Printed by *Nicholas Okes.* 1617.

Thomas Cooper's *The
Mystery of Witchcraft*
(1617).

pox of her victuals, and swore (by God) saying, You shall be an hundred miles off
within this week, when you shall want two-pence as much as I, and so she went
grumbling away.

Katherine fretted over the curse for some days and, sure enough, at some point
between the hours of eight and nine o'clock on the following Thursday evening she
disappeared, last seen on her way out of the shop, presumably at the very entrance
where she had met the unknown woman less than a week before.

WILTSHIRE

WARMINSTER, 1613

Avis Glasier brought charges against Margaret Pilton of Warminster in 1613. She claimed that, when she was ill, she had been promised by Pilton twenty years of additional life if she gave her her soul. Interestingly, it was suggested in the proceedings that Pilton had been inspired in her wicked behaviour by papists. The outcome of the case is not known.

CLEEVE PEPPER, 1651, 1654

Christiana Weekes of Cleeve Pepper appears twice in the court records on charges of using or claiming to be able to use magical powers to assist in the finding of lost goods. It seems Weekes cultivated her own reputation for being a wise woman; in 1651 she had received a substantial sum of money to use a charm to cure a man of his poorly leg; furthermore, she named the 'witch' who had caused his condition in the first place – one Dorothy Rushton of Clatford.

FISHERTON ANGER, 1653

Mrs Anne Bodenham acquired the nickname 'Dr Lamb's Darling' through her association with the physician and reputed wizard Dr John Lamb, whose notorious career ended when he was stoned to death by a London mob in 1640. The nickname reflected the fact that Mrs Bodenham had lived in Lamb's house, in which she was employed as a servant, rather than with her own husband, a cause of considerable scandal. Though largely uneducated, Anne Bodenham had learned some of the rudiments of Lamb's magic and, after his death, sought to capitalise on this by publishing a small book of charms.

Anne Bodenham's connection with the late doctor bestowed upon her the reputation of a 'Wise Woman' and she made the most of this, settling in the village of Fisherton Anger, Wiltshire, and there selling her services as a fortune-teller and herbalist. If someone sought knowledge of the future from her, for the price of three shillings, she would toss various herbs into a fire set in the middle of a magic circle, causing spirits to appear to answer questions put to them.

According to Nathaniel Crouch's *Kingdom of Darkness* (1688), a man named Mason testified to Mrs Bodenham's abilities, describing how she had raised spirits in order to answer his queries about a lawsuit he planned against his father-in-law. First she drew a magic circle with a staff and then laid a certain book within the circle:

> After that, she laid a green glass on the book, and placed within the circle an earthen pot of coals wherein she threw something which caused a very noisome smell ... and so calling Beelzebub, Tormentor, Satan and Lucifer appear, there suddenly arose a very high wind which made the house shake. And presently, the back door flying open, there came five spirits ... in the likeness of ragged boys, some bigger than others, and ran about the house where she had drawn the staff; and the witch threw upon the ground crumbs of bread which the spirits picked up, and leaped often over the pan of coals in the midst of the circle, and a dog and a cat of the witch's danced with them.

Anne Bodenham's undoing came through her association with the Goddard family. The deranged wife of Richard Goddard, fearing that her own daughters were trying to poison her, sent her young maid Ann Styles to Bodenham to obtain some arsenic to use against her offspring. When news of the plot leaked out, Styles helped herself to some of the Goddard family silver and fled; when apprehended, she attempted to save herself by attributing all blame for the affair to Bodenham. According to Styles, she had been seduced into the Devil's service after Bodenham turned herself into a black cat and then persuaded her to sign a pact with the Devil in her own blood, pricking the maid's finger to wet her pen. As a reward for selling her soul to the Devil, Ann had been given a silver coin by an imp.

The trial of Anne Bodenham depended largely upon the evidence of Ann Styles. Particularly damning was the discovery of a mark on the maid's finger, said to correspond with the wound that Bodenham had inflicted in signing the pact, and the dramatic seizures that Styles suffered when describing the 'black man without a head' who threatened to take her soul. Whenever Anne Bodenham herself was brought into the courtroom Styles appeared to go into a deep trance, from which she only emerged after the defendant had gone. As confirmation of guilt, examination of Bodenham's body revealed two witch's marks, one on her shoulder and another in her genitals.

The trial caused a sensation and, as the antiquary John Aubrey reported, 'the crowd of spectators made such a noise that the judge could not hear the prisoner, nor the prisoner the judge; but the words were handed from one to another by Mr R. Chandler, and sometimes not truly recorded'.

Protesting her innocence to the last and refusing to forgive either her accusers or her gaolers, Anne Bodenham was hanged at Salisbury in 1653. Her plea that she be given some beer so that she would be drunk when the time for execution came was denied.

MALMESBURY, c. 1658, 1672

The deeds of Widow 'Goody' Orchard of Malmesbury and other cases were recounted by an unnamed Justice of the Peace in a series of letters written in 1686. This case appears to have been heard around 1658. It is a classic example of a 'charity-refused' witchcraft episode. The troubles began when Mary, the daughter of a Malmesbury brewer, Hugh Bartholemew, refused to give the beggar, Goody Orchard, some barm (the froth that forms on the top of the liquor in the brewing process) or yeast. The old woman responded by warning her 'Twere better for you you had'. As soon as she had departed, people in Bartholomew's house were amazed to hear a crash in a room above, where Bartholomew kept his money in a great locked wooden chest. It was claimed that Widow Orchard had levitated the chest and smashed it to the floor, causing nails holding it together to be drawn and money getting jammed in the lock mechanism, obliging Bartholomew to call out a local locksmith to repair it.

When, a few months later, the daughter of a gardener from Burbage refused to give her any scraps of food, Goody Orchard once more used her magic in revenge. This involved a piece of ritual spell-making that included the muttering of incantations and pacing out a circle in the girl's garden, in the middle of which she then squatted. She carried out the ritual three times before leaving. Shortly afterwards, when she came to wash her hands, the girl's fingers were crippled. As a consequence, Widow Orchard was hauled before the JP for questioning. She immediately blamed the girl's condition on bad water and performed another spell involving the further immersion of the girl's hands in water, and, miraculously, she got back most of the use of her fingers. However, despite healing the girl, Goody Orchard was convicted of witchcraft and hanged at Salisbury.

The cases against another four women – Elizabeth Peacock, Judith Witchell, Anne Tilling, and Elizabeth Mills (or Williams) – were heard by Sir Richard Rainsford at the Wiltshire Lent sessions held at Salisbury in 1672. The details of the proceedings were recorded some years later by an unnamed Justice of the Peace in a series of letters written in 1686 (see above). The women were accused of causing, by witchcraft, the illness of Thomas Webb, son of respectable Malmesbury parents, Robert and Mary Webb. Mary, it seems, already had experience of witchcraft, for she was formerly Mary Bartholomew, the daughter of a Malmesbury brewer who had offended Widow Orchard some years before (see above). Thomas suffered fits interspersed with bouts of swearing and cursing in which he would name his persecutors. Mary accused Anne Tilling, Elizabeth Peacock, and Judith Witchell of causing her son's condition. Tilling allegedly admitted to Mary that they had indeed caused him harm, Anne having been invited to join their coven when Goody Clark became bedridden. According to Anne Tilling, it took three witches acting together to make their magic work. Elizabeth Peacock was acquitted of all charges, including four of murder by bewitchment, but both Tilling and Witchell were found guilty and executed. Elizabeth Mills also faced trial on a charge of incapacitating a couple of people, but she was also acquitted. The JP, who appears to have been involved in these proceedings, also mentions a further eleven individuals who were arrested at the same time but released without charge. Very likely he was the same sceptical JP who, in the subsequent letters, is reported to have advised his fellow justices, to no avail, that there was little evidence on which to convict Tilling and Witchell, that they might have been targeted by their more respectable neighbours simply because of their bad *reputations* as opposed to bad *deeds*, and that the boy might have been feigning his illness, having been put up to it by his parents.

BISHOPS CANNINGS, 1665

In 1665 Joan Mereweather of Weeke in Bishops Cannings, near Devizes, was indicted for bewitching to death a six-month-old child, Robert Fowler. The child had fallen sick shortly after receiving the supposed witch's kiss. The outcome of the case is not known.

DEVIZES, 1667

In 1689, Joseph Blagrave in his *Astrological Practice of Physick* recorded the witchcraft of a woman from Devizes twenty-two years earlier. According to Blagrave, the woman was gaoled for practising image magic – specifically, for making a model of a man (a 'poppet'), piercing it, and burying it. Consequently, the Devizes man in whose image the poppet was made suffered agonies in one of his limbs. When the poppet was discovered and the thorn was removed he recovered, and when it was replaced his pain returned.

LATTON, 1670

Jane Townsend of Latton flatly denied charges of communing with spirits and other witchcraft activity when she was accused in 1670. All the marks found on her body, she insisted, she was born with. Presumably these included the half-inch long extra nipple that was discovered when she was examined. Allegedly she had tried to teach the daughters of two of her neighbours the dark arts and magic that involved the making of clay figurines that could then be pierced with a hot iron. The outcome of the case is not known.

WORCESTERSHIRE

WORCESTER, 1647

A detailed but erroneous account of the trials of Rebecca West, Margaret Landis, Susan Cock, and Rose Hallybread – 'four notorious witches' – in 1647 survives in an eight-page pamphlet published in London in 1690. While it is most unreliable as a source for the trial and fate of the accused, it provides fascinating evidence for late-seventeenth-century beliefs and assumptions regarding the essence of witchcraft and the forming of the enduring myths surrounding its prosecution.

According to this version of events, some weeks before her trial in Worcester, Rebecca West confessed her crimes to John Edes and also to the notorious 'Witchfinder General' Matthew Hopkins. Having been seduced by the Devil in the form of a young man who, 'cold as Clay', had kissed her and promised to be her loving husband when he appeared in her room one night as she was going to bed, she used his power to kill two men she had a grudge against – John Start, who lived in the same house as her, and one John Hart. As Hart sickened, he declared Rebecca was the cause of his illness and both his son, Thomas Hart, and his doctor became convinced that he was the victim of witchcraft.

Margaret Landish was accused of killing a young girl who had pointed at her and called out 'There goes Pegg the witch'. In return, she cursed the child and that night the girl 'fell sick in raving manner, and dyed within three weeks after'. During her fatal illness the girl often complained 'that *Peg* the witch was by her bed side, making strange mouths at her'. One her accusers claimed that Margaret had tried to entice her into becoming a witch. This woman thus learned of Margaret's need to feed two imps that 'did usually suck two Teats near the privy parts', in order to keep her health. Furthermore, Margaret took this witness to a sabbat meeting 'where she saw the Devil in the likeness of a tall black Man, at which she was so much afrighted that she never went with her any more'. Another woman made similar accusations and blamed Margaret for the death of another young child in the neighbourhood. Quite reasonably, 'the prisoner in her own defence said that they were all malicious people ... insinuating as if they had formerly an old grudge against her, and thereupon made a strange howling in the court, to the great disturbance of the whole bench.' Nevertheless, reminded by the judge that the Bible declares 'that we must not suffer a witch to live', after an hour's consultation, the jury found her guilty.

Susan Cock and Rose Hallybread were tried together for the murder of Mary Peak, John Peak, and the children of Obadiah Peak of Preston. The method of their *maleficia*, observed by Abraham Chad, was as follows:

The Full

TRYALS,

Examination, and Condemnation

Of Four

Notorious 𝔚𝔦𝔱𝔠𝔥𝔢𝔰,

At the

Aſſizes held at *Worceſter*, on *Tuſeday* the 4th of *March*.

With the manner, how they were found guilty of Bewitching ſeveral Children to Death.

As alſo,

Their Confeſſions, and laſt Dying Speeches at the Place of Execution; with other Amazing Particulars concerning the ſaid Witchcraft.

Printed according to Order.

London, Printed by *J. W.* near *Fleet-ſtreet.*

Pamphlet describing the supposed trial of four witches at Worcester in 1647.

...in the house of Susan Cock, the two prisoners having made a great fire, they made the shape of the deceased children in wax, and putting them both on a spit, one of [the] prisoners turn'd it, while the other stuck pins and needles in their bellies, heads, and eyes ... and as the spit wene round, they both muttered to themselves strange kind of words...

The consequence of this was that the children were tormented 'with strange prickings in their eyes, belly and head, and so continued worss, and worss till they dyed, which was about a week after'. As before, the children named the women as the persecutors. When they were examined by a local midwife and other women several large teats for suckling imps were found in 'the secret parts of their bodies'.

According to the pamphlet, very unusually in English witchcraft cases, all four were burned at the stake. However, this particular account is considered unreliable and seems to be based in part upon a 1645 pamphlet concerning the trial of these four 'witches' in Essex, not Worcester. In fact, Rebecca West of the village of Lawford in Essex, according to this more reliable source, was reprieved and Rose Hallybread of St Osyth, Essex, died in prison in 1645. Susan Cock, also of St Osyth, was reprieved but died of plague shortly afterwards.

DROITWICH, 1649

A report by a 'Person of Quality' of trial proceedings at Worcester in 1649 records in *A Collection of Modern Relations of matter of Fact concerning Witches and Witchcraft upon the Persons of People* the maleficent activities of an unnamed elderly woman, who was accused of bewitching a boy. The boy, also not named, apparently met the old woman while he was searching for a lost cow. Suddenly encountering her, she startled him by saying 'Boo!' and he promptly lost the use of speech. When he next encountered her eating a meal in the company of others, he 'ran furiously upon her and threw her pottage in her face and offered some other violence to her'. Suspicions aroused, the old woman was imprisoned and examined. The gaoler withheld food and water from her until she recited the Lord's Prayer and asked God to bless the boy. Upon her doing so, the boy regained his speech. He promptly declared how he had had a vision of the old woman sitting in the window of his room, grinning at him. In retaliation, he claimed 'he took up a form leg and therewith gave her two good bangs upon the arse'. When the old woman was inspected, the marks of these 'two good bangs' were, allegedly, found on her skin.

No comment upon the outcome of the trial appears in the pamphlet.

EVESHAM, 1652

According to Richard Baxter in *The Certainty of the Worlds of the Spirits* (1691), Catherine Huxley was executed after causing the sickness, by witchcraft, of Mary Ellins, who was aged about nine, and of the daughter of an Evesham gardener. Mary had provoked Catherine Huxley by throwing stones at her and calling her a witch. In retaliation, Huxley had warned her she should soon have 'stones enough' and the child immediately fell ill. Within a month the girl was passing stones and her wretched condition continued until the witch was hanged.

KIDDERMINSTER, 1660

A manuscript mentioned in an article in the 'Gentleman's Magazine', 1856, mentions the swimming of four witches from Kidderminster in the River Severn at Worcester in 1660.

YORKSHIRE

KNARESBOROUGH, c. 1500, 1621

Mother Shipton of Knaresborough was, allegedly, a fortune-teller, who was widely renowned for her prophetic skills and remains today perhaps the most famous name in the annals of English witchcraft.

Facts about the life of Mother Shipton are shrouded in obscurity, as no biography about her was published until 100 years after her death. Moreover, Richard Head's *Life and Death of Mother Shipton*, which appeared in 1677, cannot be considered a particularly trustworthy source of information about her, as Head himself had a reputation for being a less than reliable authority. Many of the prophecies attributed to Mother Shipton only emerged after the events she had supposedly envisaged had actually taken place.

Mother Shipton was born Ursula Southeil (or Sontheil) in 1488, the daughter of Agatha Southeil, a sixteen-year-old orphan pauper of Knaresborough. Legend has it that Agatha had been seduced by the Devil in the disguise of a handsome young man, and that during a terrible storm she had given birth to his baby in a cave beside the River Nidd, which runs through Knaresborough. The Devil reputedly bestowed upon Agatha various magical powers, which she used in order to attack livestock and to have revenge upon her enemies in the town, but she did not survive childbirth and her daughter had to be brought up on the parish.

Ursula Southeil suffered from various deformities (it is thought she may have been a hunchback) and as a child she was much feared for the powers she was thought to possess. Many stories were told of strange happenings that occurred in her vicinity, with houses being ransacked by invisible hands and a mysterious black dog manifesting near her at regular intervals as if to confirm that all was well with her. Anyone who taunted Ursula for her deformities was punished by some misfortune or humiliation, all allegedly at Ursula's command.

When she was still a young woman, Ursula Southeil established a reputation as a soothsayer, delivering numerous prophecies in the form of riddles and rhymes. As her fame grew, the curious flocked to Knaresborough from far afield in order to hear her words and to enquire about their own prospects. This was not without its risks, for many people believed that Ursula would punish those who approached her with wicked motives. When one young man asked her to tell him when his father would die, as he was impatient to inherit, she would not reply – the young man himself died shortly afterwards and was buried in the grave intended for his father.

In 1512, in spite of her physical deformities, Ursula married a carpenter, Toby Shipton. Citizens of Knaresborough speculated that she had used a love potion to

Mother Shipton as depicted in Head's *The Life and Death of Mother Shipton* (1677).

The Fire of London, 1666, as depicted in Head's *The Life and Death of Mother Shipton* (1677).

win her husband. The name of Mother Shipton now became a household word, but she remained safe from persecution as a witch – if only because she lived before the witchcraft hysteria had really taken hold in England. She died (as she had foretold) at the age of seventy and was buried in unconsecrated ground outside York, but her fame lived on and was much enhanced by the publication of her prophecies in 1641. One tradition has it that a stone (now gone) was erected at her grave with the following inscription:

> Here lies she who never lied,
> Whose skill so often has been tried.
> Her prophecies shall still survive,
> And ever keep her name alive.

Among other things, Mother Shipton is supposed to have foretold the death of Cardinal Wolsey, to have given details of the deaths and accessions of future kings and queens of England, to have warned of the Great Plague and the Great Fire of London and to have foreseen various wars and other events of national importance, such as the invention of the motor car and the building of the Crystal Palace.

Another rhyme seemed to prophesy the development of modern communications:

> Around the world thoughts shall fly in the twinkling of an eye.

Mother Shipton's cave at Knaresborough.

Other prophecies, fortunately, failed to come to pass:

> This world to an end shall come
> In eighteen hundred and eighty-one.

The cave where Mother Shipton was born in Knaresborough has long since been developed as a tourist attraction, and, though she was principally a fortune-teller rather than a witch, she is commonly depicted as the archetypal witch. There is even a small British moth named the Mother Shipton; it is distinguished by wing markings that suggest the shape of the stereotypical witch's face.

In 1621, charges of witchcraft were made against a number of women who allegedly belonged to a coven operating in the Forest of Knaresborough. The evidence against them was furnished by Edward Fairfax (c. 1580-1635), a scholar and gentleman of Fewston, near Otley in Yorkshire, who in 1621 instigated legal proceedings against six local women.

The affair began when the distinguished scholar's two young daughters started to suffer fits and to complain of visions. The symptoms went on for months and doctors were unable to suggest any medical cause. The two girls laid the blame for their afflictions at the feet of Elizabeth Fletcher, who was the daughter of another renowned witch called Mother Foster, and five other women from the Forest of Knaresborough. These women, it was claimed, ordered their familiars to torment anyone they took against and met at Timble Gill to share midnight feasts with the Devil, who sat at the head of the table. When one of the Fairfax girls, Helen, was found wandering the moors on her own, she alleged that she had been carried there by one of the witches and had got a glimpse of the coven gathered around a blazing fire.

Edward Fairfax, who evidently believed in the reality of witchcraft, found no reason to doubt the testimony of his daughters and consequently took his suspicions to the justices in York. His allegations gained credence when a neighbour, John Jeffray, claimed that his daughter Maud had also been bewitched by the women. The six accused women were ordered to appear before a hearing in York. As soon as proceedings commenced, the Fairfax girls and Maud Jeffray fell into a trance-like state and had to be carried out of the room to recover. Sir George Ellis and the other justices, however, perhaps remembering warnings from James I against accepting unsupported accusations, were not easily impressed by such sensational behaviour and questioned the three girls closely outside the court. It was not long before Maud Jeffray retracted her allegations and confessed that her father, who harboured a grudge against the accused women, had put her up to it. Maud's subsequent attempts to deny this confession were to no avail and her father was thrown into prison.

The young Fairfax girls refused to make similar confessions so the proceedings in court continued, but it was not long before the judges concluded there was no case for the accused women to answer and the charges against them were dropped. It was presumed that the Fairfax girls had been influenced by the Jeffrays and no blame was attached to the name of Edward Fairfax.

Edward Fairfax's transcript of the trial, *Daemonologia* (1622), illustrated by the Reverend Miles Gale of Keighley, provides a fascinating record of the affair.

HULL, 1583

Three elderly impoverished women were tried for witchcraft in Kingston-on-Hull in 1583. Of these one appears to have been found guilty and she was sentenced to a one-year prison sentence and four appearances in the pillory. This was a typical punishment for acts of 'mild' *maleficium* in this period. The witchcraft Act of 1563, at the start of Elizabeth I's reign, reserved the death penalty for witches guilty of murder and second-time offenders of lesser witchcraft crimes.

LEDSTON HALL, 1603

Ten years after the death of William Ledston, Mary Pannel was found guilty of killing him by witchcraft. She was executed near to Ledston Hall on a hill thereafter known as 'Mary Pannel Hill'.

ROSSINGTON, 1605

Joan Jurdie of Rossington, West Riding, was fifty-two years old when she was brought before the court of Hugh Childers, mayor of Doncaster, in 1605. From the surviving evidence of her trial, it seems that her neighbours turned to her for help when, for example, their animals fell sick. However, having acquired a reputation for having special powers such as the ability to predict the outcome of an animal's sickness, when she fell out with her neighbours she was accused of acts of *maleficia*. One of her accusers, Katherine Dolfin, was convinced Joan was a witch because others sought her advice when their animals fell ill. When, having offended the wise woman, her own livestock became sick and an ox died, she concluded she was the victim of Joan's witchcraft. Another woman, Jane Spight, also of Rossington, claimed to have had exactly the same experience. A third woman, Anne Judd of Rossington, accused Joan of causing her child's sickness following a falling out between Joan Jurdie and Anne's brother-in-law, Peter Murfin. As for Joan herself, she denied all charges that she had any powers whatsoever to help people, and, presumably, animals, when they fell sick.

This interesting case, the outcome of which is not known, provides evidence for the link between so-called 'cunning folk' and 'witches'. It is also noteworthy that the charges against Joan Jurdie were made by three women, even though the men they were associated with were equal partners in the quarrel with the 'witch'. As was often the case, women, not men, seem to have initiated the hunt for the witch in their neighbourhood.

RICHMOND, 1606

Ralph Milner, a yeoman, appeared before the court at Richmond on charges of witchcraft and fortune-telling. His punishment appears to have been a mild one – he was instructed to make a full confession before the priest at Muker Church and, presumably, pray for forgiveness.

THIRSK, 1611

By 1611, a woman could find herself in court for merely cursing her neighbours. This is the charge Elizabeth Cooke faced at Thirsk's Quarter Sessions in 1611. Her accusers believed that her curse was sufficiently potent to kill those against whom it was directed. The outcome of her trial is not known.

Probably the most common accusation leading to an execution for witchcraft was that of causing a fatal wasting illness that could last months or even years.

DONCASTER, 1623

A court at Doncaster in 1623 heard how a widow, Jane Blomley, had bewitched Frances, the wife of a yeoman farmer, Marmaduke Craven. Five days after her bewitchment Frances was dead. The fate of Jane Blomley is not known.

NORTHALLERTON, 1623

Elizabeth Crearey was found guilty of bewitching a valuable black cow belonging to one of her neighbours, Edward Bell. She was sentenced to a year's imprisonment and four appearances in the pillory.

POCKLINGTON, 1631, 1649

An intriguing entry in the Pocklington Parish Register, reported in the Yorkshire Archaeological Journal, reads 'Old wife Green burnt in Market for a witch'. The burning of witches in England was exceptionally rare, though not unknown. The Parish Register also commented on the execution in the market place at Pocklington of Petronel Haxby, the wife of the local smith, for being a witch. This, however, did not put a stop to Pocklington's troubles for, a year later, the death by witchcraft and subsequent burial of Thomas Dobson is also recorded in the register.

A shocking account, not verifiable, in the *Records of York Castle* (A. W. Twyford, 1880, p. 177) tells of the hanging and burning of Isabella Billington of Pocklington for crucifying her own mother and also for making a burnt sacrifice of a cock and a calf in 1649. Her husband was also hanged.

WEST AYTON, 1634

Jane Kitchin, Mary White, Barbara Dighton, and Anne Maddison were presented before a court at Thirsk in 1634, charged with using witchcraft to provide information on the location of stolen goods.

HEPTENSTALL, 1646

At much the same time that Matthew Hopkins was finding scores of witches in the south-east, a group of supposed witches was identified in the West Riding. They were Mary Midgley, Mary Kitchinge, Elizabeth Crosley, and Sarah Crosley, Elizabeth's daughter. All four came from Heptenstall. Theirs is a classic tale that conforms to the 'charity-refused' model for witchcraft accusations. Both Elizabeth Crosley and Mary Midgley fell foul of their neighbours over disputes concerning the giving of alms. Henry Cockcroft, who had clashed with Elizabeth Crosley, was convinced by Mary Midgley, who informed him, after she had been beaten about the head by Cockcroft and his acquaintances, she herself 'could witch a little' and that his infant son's illness and subsequent death was

Black dogs frequently appear in witchcraft and witch-hunting traditions, sometimes as familiars, sometimes as the entity into which the witch herself has transformed.

the work of the other three women. Elizabeth was also accused of the lingering illness and death of another infant in the neighbourhood, John Shackleton. Mary Midgley, meanwhile, was accused of causing the sickness of six of Richard Wood's cattle because of a dispute with his wife over alms. All four women denied the charges levelled against them, Mary insisting that her confessions to Cockcroft were made 'in hopes to be freed from further blows'. The outcome of their trial is unknown.

BOWLING, 1650

Henry Tempest, JP, heard the case brought against Mary Sykes of Bowling in 1650. She was accused by two of her Bowling (Bradford) neighbours, and Henry Cordingley from nearby Tonge, of levitating Cordingley's daughter, riding on the back of one of his cows and making his horses sick, one of which died, and of manifesting in the presence of a sick child. She was acquitted of all charges.

SKIPSEA IN HOLDERNESS, 1650

Anne Hudson was charged with being a witch after a sick man recovered when he scratched and drew her blood. According to popular belief, this was the surest way to undo a witch's spell. The outcome of the case is unknown.

KIRKTHORPE, 1651

It is likely that most of those accused in witchcraft cases had a reputation that had been built up over many years. In the case of Margaret Morton this was certainly the case, and it was believed that her mother and sister, both now dead, had also been witches. When the son of Joan Booth of Warmfield fell sick after eating a piece of bread Margaret had offered him, the boy's mother immediately concluded he was bewitched. Sure enough, when Margaret was brought before the lad, very likely by force, she begged his forgiveness three times and, after Joan had scratched her with a pin and drawn blood, the child recovered. Furthermore, Joan Booth suspected Margaret of having something to do with the failure of her butter to churn or her cheese to curdle. Margaret was also implicated in the death of another of Joan's children. Frances Ward, one of Margaret's Kirkthorpe neighbours, was one of four women who searched the supposed witch and declared they had found two curious embellishments at the top of her inner thigh, one of which 'were like a wart, but it was none. And the other was black on both sides, an inch broad, and blue in the midst'.

As usual in English witchcraft trials, the accused and their accusers in this case were all women, the 'witch' probably being a vulnerable, destitute, and despised old woman and her victim a younger woman of modest means with small children.

Margaret was found not guilty and released.

HUDDERSFIELD, 1652

Hester France was accused of bewitching two people – a Huddersfield servant called Elizabeth Johnson, who fell sick after Hester had cursed her, and Robert Cliff, also of Huddersfield. In both cases, Hester was scratched and bloodied by her supposed victims. Hester denied the charges; the outcome of the case is unknown.

SCARBOROUGH, 1652

Anne Hunnam of Scarborough was accused in 1652 of using witchcraft to make children sick with fits. When searched by three women 'a little blue spot upon her left side [...] which grows out of her flesh or skin at her waist of a great bigness' was found. When pierced with a pin, the suspect did not seem to feel it. Anne Hunnam denied the charges; the outcome of the case is not known.

REEDNESS, 1653

Elizabeth Lambe appears to have been the scapegoat of her Reedness neighbours for their various domestic disasters. She was accused of causing the sickness and death of both animals and people. She was treated violently, being routinely beaten, scratched, and bled. Her case was brought to court (outcome unknown) but it is likely that many, many more instances of this kind of cruelty in out-of-the-way English neighbourhoods have left no trace of a record.

FENWICK, 1653

Isabel Emott, a labourer's wife, was charged with bewitching ten cows and a calf belonging to Richard Longbotham. Her case was presented to the sessions at Leeds in July 1653; the outcome is unknown.

GARGRAVE, 1654

Anne Greene, the wife of Thomas Greene of Gargrave, was accused of bewitching three people: Elizabeth Coggill, John Tatterson, and Thomas Shutt, all of whom were 'impaired and wasted'. Facing the possibility of a death sentence, she was found not guilty. Anne's case is an interesting illustration of the dangers facing the practising wise woman or cunning man in early modern England.

Anne fell foul of Tatterson when, having sought it, he rejected her advice that 'black wool' would provide a cure for the pain in his ear. In response she 'got some hair out of his neck without consent' and passed her garter three times across the affected ear. The man's pain increased and, only after threatening her that if she did not 'look to it' he would 'look to her', and thus persuading her to repeat, and thus, presumably, reverse her spell, did his pain subside.

BEVERLEY, 1654

John Greencliffe of Beverley blamed his illness on Elizabeth Roberts, also of Beverley. He had seen her turn 'into the similitude of a cat, which fixed close about his leg, and after much struggling, vanished; whereupon he was much pained at his heart'. The witch-cat also once hit him on the head, causing him to enter a trance. Elizabeth also supposedly transformed herself into a bee, which somehow caused John Greencliffe to fit with such violence that the five or six people with him at the time could not restrain him. The outcome of this case is unknown.

ROTHWELL, 1655

In 1655, Henry Hatfield of Rhodes in Rothwell testified against his neighbour Katherine Earle, the wife of a labourer. He accused her of killing his horse, which fell sick and died shortly after Katherine struck it about the neck with a 'docken stalk'. He also fell ill with a pain in the neck that troubled him for the best part of six months. Katherine, suspected of casting a spell over him, was searched and a curious mark, 'in the likeness of a pap', was found on her body. Katherine pleaded not guilty; the outcome of the hearing is not known.

WAKEFIELD, 1656

Some impressive charges were levelled against Jennet Benton and her son, George Benton of Wakefield, in 1656. Their troubles began when Richard Jackson secured compensation from George Benton following a dispute between George and Jackson's servant, Daniel Craven. The Bentons allegedly threatened Jackson with some kind of reprisal and, sure enough, Jackson's wife became deaf and he started suffering fits in which he heard the sound of dancing and music. He and his wife then witnessed poltergeist-like activity in their home, with doors opening and closing, and heavy objects, including trunks, moving of their own accord. Their pigs broke out of the barn in which they were kept and spectral cats and black dogs manifested about the house. Worse still, the Jacksons lost eighteen of their horses.

The Bentons denied bewitching their well-off neighbours. The outcome of the case is unknown.

STUDLEY, 1656

This is an unusual case in that it directly involved the local elite. The story revolves around a fourteen-year-old girl, Elizabeth Mallory, daughter of Lady Mallory of Studley Hall, Sir John Mallory's widow. For a year, Elizabeth suffered from fits during which she had visions of her tormentor, sometimes in the pose of a cat – Mary Wade, the wife of William Wade. As in the case of several other English witchcraft cases in this period, it was claimed that Elizabeth had been induced by the witch to vomit pins and feathers. When Mary Wade was forced to confess (out of court), the child recovered but when Mary reneged on her confession she fell ill again. Both Mary and her husband, William, were arrested and imprisoned and Elizabeth recovered. William agreed that the girl had been possessed by an evil spirit but denied being involved. The outcome of the examination of the Wades is unknown.

GISBOROUGH, 1658

Another unusual case (outcome unknown), presented before the Quarter Sessions at Helmsley, is that of Robert Conyers, a gentleman and a sorcerer. The vast majority of people accused of witchcraft in England appear to have been members of the labouring classes, and most were women.

WOODHOUSE, 1658

A major witchcraft trial heard in 1568 concerned four people charged with communing with evil spirits and the ghosts of dead men, women, and children, and with using their powers to cause the sickness of their Woodhouse neighbours. The case provides some interesting evidence regarding the gender profile of the accused and their supposed victims: each of the four 'witches' was accused of bewitching a single person, each of which was female; three of the four 'witches' were female; the three women were all found guilty and sentenced to hang but the one man charged, Thomas Jefferson, a labourer, was found not guilty and released. At least two of the women subsequently had their sentences reprieved, but it seems likely that one unfortunate, Margaret Butler, was hanged.

THORNE, 1661

A labourer's wife, Ellen Gray, was accused in 1661 of communing with evil spirits and bewitching James Johnson and Jane Skirlew, both of whom had fallen sick with some kind of 'wasting' condition. The court found her not guilty.

BURTON AGNES AND THORNEHOLME, 1664

At the Yorkshire Summer Sessions held at York Castle in 1664, a widow, Alice Huson of Burton Agnes, confessed to a diabolical pact in which she was promised that her persecution of the family of Henry Corbet, also of Burton Agnes, would be richly rewarded by the Devil. Although the Devil desired the killing of Henry Corbet's wife, Alice, it was her ten-year-old daughter, Faith, who bore the brunt of Alice Huson's *malificia*. Back in 1660, Huson had been employed by the Corbets and had requested the gift of some old linen, previously worn next to the skin of Alice Corbet's children, in lieu of cash. The children, wary of Alice Huson's evil reputation, persuaded their mother to refuse this very particular request. However, it seems that Huson secured an item of clothing nevertheless for, as soon as she had left the Corbets' home, Faith discovered one of her gloves was missing. Shortly afterwards Faith fell ill with a condition that lasted for several years. Frequently she named Alice Huson and another woman, Olive Bilby from nearby Thorneholme, as the cause of her condition. Faith did not recover until Alice Huson was brought before her in her sickbed. However, her recovery was short-lived, for just two days later, she fell sick again when Olive Bilby passed by the house and looked up at the child's bedroom window. Consequently, both women were arrested and examined. Alice confessed to her diabolical pact and the possession of a teat by which she gave her demon suck. She also admitted to using her magical power to will the death of one Dick Warren. Although she was convicted of witchcraft, Alice received a reprieve before the judgement, presumably execution, was enforced. Olive Bilby was found innocent of all charges.

The account is interesting as one that highlights the curious impotence of the Devil who, according to the witchcraft tradition, had to rely upon human agents to complete his demonic work, in this case, unsuccessfully. Furthermore, the outcome coincides with a general shift in English witch trials as scepticism and leniency produced more 'not guilty' verdicts and reprieves.

YORK, 1664, 1680

An unusual accusation of witchcraft appears in the Assize and Gaol Book records for York for 1663 and 1664. It concerns a supposed thief, Richard Readshaw, who was arrested on a charge of stealing £140 from Lord Thomas Fairfax. Readshaw protested his innocence and named a cunning man, Nicholas Battersby, who would be able to say where the money was hidden. Battersby was duly brought to the gaol, presumably to discuss the matter with Readshaw, and the following day Battersby announced that the money had been stolen by Fairfax's servants and hidden in a sack – but also that it would not turn up for another five months. For this fairly hopeless information, Readshaw gave the cunning man five shillings. Battersby, however, was then charged with dabbling in witchcraft. Ironically, when the five months were up and, presumably, the money had not been found, Nicholas Battersby appeared in the 1664 Gaol Book records facing an accusation of obtaining by fraudulent means five shillings from Richard Readshaw!

A York labourer, Kitchell Harrison, found himself in trouble in 1680 when he faced charges of communing with evil spirits and using charms in order to entice Joyce Massey. Unfortunately the rest of this, no doubt, convoluted tale of seduction and betrayal is unknown.

WAKEFIELD, 1665

In his *Life of Oliver Heywood* (1842), the Rev. J. Hunter related how the subject of his book, Oliver Heywood, a non-conformist pastor of Wakefield, had fasted for the benefit of Nathan Dodgson, who was thought to have been bewitched. In his fits Dodgson would sing, become violent, and claim to see the manifestation of the local woman who had cursed him. Unfortunately for her, several witnesses decided to take matters into their own hands and she was killed. They, in turn, were arrested, condemned, and hanged for her murder.

ALNE, 1670

The case of Anne Wilkinson, a widow from Alne, like so many, suggests that witchcraft accusation was especially prevalent within the 'female sphere'. Those testifying were both women, and the supposed witch's magic targeted women. When Mary Earnley fell ill, she declared that Anne Wilkinson had 'prickt her with pins' and cried out 'Burn her! Burn her! She tormented two of my sisters!' when Wilkinson was brought before her. Both of her sisters had died and, allegedly, a black ribbon tied to a crooked pin had been drawn from the mouth of one of the deceased. Margaret Wilson explained how, having been cursed by Anne Wilkinson, her butter would not churn, her husband died, and she herself fell sick for two years. Anne Wilkinson was found to be innocent of the charges.

DENBIGH, 1674

Two married women, Susan Hinchcliffe and Anne Shillitoe, and the husband of one, Joseph Hinchcliffe, a labourer, were accused of various acts of witchcraft, including the bewitching to death of one of their Denbigh neighbours, Anne Haigh. The case was thrown out but one obscure source, *The Life of Oliver Heywood*, by Rev. J. Hunter, declares that Joseph Hinchcliffe hanged himself and his wife went to her grave praying for the souls of her accusers.

Endnotes

1) Levack, B. (2006) estimates 40,000 executions; Anne Llewellyn Barstow (1994), estimates 100,000
2) Cohn, N. (1974), p. 253
3) Dalton, M. *Country Justice*, 1618 p. 261 in A. Macfarlane (1970), p. 16
4) Macfarlane, A. (1970), p. 18
5) Macfarlane, A. (1970), p. 18
6) Macfarlane, A. (1970), p. 18
7) In Sharpe, J. (2001), p. 121
8) Levack, B. (2006), p. 218
9) Levack, B. (2006), p. 23
10) Behringer, W. (1995) in D. Oldridge (2002), pp. 69-86
11) Thomas, K. (1971), p. 15
12) Thomas, K. (1971), p. 16
13) Thomas, K. (1971), p. 17
14) Gibson, M. (2003), p. 91
15) Macfarlane, A. (1970), p. 120
16) Thomas, K. (1971), p. 654
17) Thomas, K. (1971), p. 654
18) Briggs, R. (2002), p. 146
19) Briggs, R. (2002), p. 159
20) Briggs, R. (2002), p. 85
21) Thomas, K. (1971), p. 559
22) Larner, C., in Oldridge, D. (2002) p. 34
23) Thomas, K. (1971), p. 652
24) Macfarlane, A. (1970), p. 161
25) Thomas, K. (1971), p. 674
26) Stephens, J. (1615), *Essays and Characters*, p. 376, in K. Thomas (1971), p. 674
27) Thomas, K. (1971), p. 675
28) Thomas, K. (1971), p. 677
29) Roberts, A. (1616), *A Treatise of Witchcraft*, pp. 42-3
30) *A Tryal of Witches, at the Assizes held at Bury St. Edmunds for the County of Suffolk; on the Tenth day of March, 1664. Before Sir Matthew Hale, Kt., then Lord Chief Baron of His Majesties Court of Exchequer* (1682), pp. 2-5
31) Perkins, W. (1608), *A Discourse of the Damned Art of Witchcraft*, Cambridge, pp. 255-7
32) Sharpe, J. (2001), p. 70

33) Gaskill, M. (2005), p. xv
34) Gaskill, M. (2005), pp. 283-5
35) Gaskill, M. (2005), p. 285
36) Briggs, R. (2002), p. 165
37) Briggs, R. (2002), p. 165
38) Macfarlane, A. (1970), p. 140
39) Gaskill, M. (2005), p. 273
40) Hopkins, M. (1647), *The Discovery of Witches,* p. 51
41) Levack, B. (2006), p. 274-5
42) Macfarlane, A. (1970), p. 202
43) Thomas, K. (1971), pp. 777-8
44) Stone, L. 'Literacy and Education in England, 1640-1900', Past and Present, xlii, 1969, p. 125
45) Thomas, K. (1971), pp. 778-9
46) Thomas, K. (1971), p. 779
47) Ewen, C. (1929), pp. xi-xii
48) Ewen, C. (1929), p. 115
49) Ewen, C. (1933), p. 10
50) Sharpe, J. (1996), p. 105
51) Ewen, C. (1929), p. 42
52) Sharpe, J. (2001), p. 39
53) Zilboorg, G. (1935), *The Medical Man and the Witch during the Renaissance*
54) Barstow, A. (1994), *Witchcraze*
55) Purkiss, D. (1996), *The Witch in History*
56) From 'Preface to the First Edition' in B. Levack (2006), p. xii
57) Briggs, R. (2002), p. 120
58) Ewen, C. (1933), p. 407
59) Goodcole, H. (1621), *The Wonderfull Discoverie of Elizabeth Sawyer a Witch*
60) Glanvill, J. (1681), *Saducismus Triumphatus,* p. 289
61) Ewen, E. (1929), p. 31
62) Stratton, J. (1969; 1978), pp. 44-5
63) Ewen, E. (1933), p. 457; reference to this supposed hunt was made in Dr Richard Burthogge's *Essay upon Reason* (1694)
64) Sharpe, J. (1996), p. 107
65) Ewen, E. (1933), p. 306
66) Ewen, E. (1933), p. 459
67) Ewen, E. (1933), p. 377
68) Ewen, E. (1933), p. 410
69) In Ewen, E. (1933), p. 455
70) Gaskill, M. (2005), p. 174

Bibliography

PRIMARY SOURCES

John Darrell (1562), *A true narration of the strange and grevous vexation by the Devil, of 7 persons in Lancashire, and William Somers of Nottingham..*

Anon. (1566), *The Examination of John Walsh.*

Anon. (1566), *The Examination and Confession of Certain Witches at Chelmsford in the County of Essex.*

Anon. (1579), *A Rehearsall both straung and true, of hainous and horrible actes committed by Elizabeth Stile, alias Rockingham, Mother Dutten, Mother Deuell, Mother Margaret, Fower notorious Witches, apprehended at Winsore.*

Anon. (1579), *A detection of damnable driftes, practized by three witches arraigned at Chelmifforde in Essex.*

W. W. (1582), *A true and just Recorde of the Information, Examination, and Confessions of all the Witches taken at St. Oses.*

Reginald Scot (1584), *The Discoverie of Witchcraft.*

Anon. (1584), *A true and most Dreadfull discourse of a woman possessed with the Devill.*

Anon. (1589), *The apprehension and confession of three notorious witches.*

Anon. (1593), *The most strange and admirable discoverie of the three witches of Warboys.*

King James I (1597), *Daemonologie.*

John Denison (1597), *The most wonderfull and true storie, of a certain Witch named Alse Geederige of Stapenhill.*

Anon. (1599), *The Triall of Maist. Dorrell, or a Collection of Defences against Allegations.*

Samuel Harsnett (1599), *A Discovery of the Fraudulent Practises of John Darrel, Bachelor of Arts.*

George More (1600), *A true discourse concerning the certaine possession and dispossession of 7 persons in one familie in Lancashire.*

Stephen Bradwell (1603), *Mary Glovers late woefull case together with her joyfull deliverance.*

John Swan (1603), *A True and Briefe Report of Mary Glover's Vexation.*

Anon. (1606), *The most cruell and bloody murther committed by an Inkeepers wife, called Annis Dell, and her sonne George Dell, foure yeeres since ... With the severall Witchcrafts, and most damnable practises of one Johane Harrison and her Daughter...*

William Perkins (1608), *A Discourse of the Damned Art of Witchcraft.*

Anon. (1612), *The Witches of Northampton-shire.*

Bibliography

217

Thomas Potts (1613), *The Wonderfull Discoverie of Witches in the Countie of Lancaster.*

Anon. (1613), *A most wonderfull and true storie of Witches Apprehended, Examined and Executed, for notable villanies by them committed both by land and water.*

Ben Johnson (1616), *The Divell is an Asse: a comedie acted in the yeare, 1616.*

Alexander Roberts (1616), *A Treatise of Witchcraft.*

John Cotta (1616), *The Tryall of Witch-craft shewing the true and right method of the Discovery: with a Confutation of erroneous ways.*

Thomas Cooper (1617), *The Mystery of Witchcraft.*

Anon. (1619), *The Wonderful Discoverie of the Witchcrafts of Margaret and Phillip Flower, daughters of Joan Flower neere Beuer Castle ... Together with the severall Examinations and Confessions of Anne Baker, Joan Willimot, and Eilen Greene, Witches in Leicestershire.*

Henry Goodcole (1621), *The wonderfull discoverie of Elizabeth Sawyer a Witch.*

William Rowley, Thomas Dekker, and John Ford (1621), *The Witch of Edmonton.*

Edward Fairfax (1622), *Daemonologia.*

William Drage (c. 1637), *Daimonomageia.*

Anon. (1638), *The Compost of Ptolomeus.*

Anon. (1643), *A most Certain Strange and True Discovery of a Witch, Being taken by some of the Parliament Forces, as she was standing on a small planck-board and sayling on it over the River of Newbury.*

Anon. (1645), *The Lawes against Witches, and Conjuration.*

Anon. (1645), *A True Relation of the Arraignment of Eighteen Witches.*

Anon. (1645), *The examination, confession, triall, and execution, of Joane Williford, Joan Cariden, and Jane Hott.*

Matthew Hopkins (1647), *The Discovery of Witches.*

John Stearne (1648), *A Confirmation and Discovery of Witch Craft.*

Anon. (1649), *The Divel's Delusions; or A faithful relation of John Palmer and Elizabeth Knott, two notorious Witches.*

Anon. (1649), *A Collection of Modern Relations of matter of Fact concerning Witches and Witchcraft upon the Persons of People.*

Mary Moore (1650), *Wonderfull News from the North, or, a True Relation of the Sad and Grievous Torments Inflicted upon the Bodies of three Children of Mr George Muschamp, late of the County of Northumberland, by Witch-craft.*

Anon. (1652), *The Witch of Wapping.*

E. G. (1652), *A Prodigious & Tragicall History of the Arraignment, Tryall, Confession, and Condemnation of six Witches at Maidstone, in Kent.*

Anon. (1659), *Strange and terrible newes from Cambridge.*

Thomas Ady (1656), *A Perfect Discovery of Witches.*

Anon. (1659), *Strange and terrible newes from Cambridge.*

M. Y. (London, 1669), *The Hartford-shire Wonder, or Strange News from Ware.*

Anon. (1674), *A Full and True Relation of the Tryal, Condemnation, and Execution of Ann Foster.*

Thomas Overbury (1676), *A True and perfect Account of the Examination, Confession, Tryal, Condemnation and Execution of Joan Perry and her two sons ... for the supposed murder of William Harrison, Gent..*

John Webster (1677), *The Displaying of Supposed Witchcraft.*

Richard Head (1677), *The Life and Death of Mother Shipton.*

Joseph Glanvill (1681), *Saducismus Triumphatus.*

Anon. (1681), *Strange and Wonderful News from Yowell in Surrey.*

Anon. (1682), *An Account of the Trial and Examination of Joan Buts.*

Anon. (1682), *A Trial of Witches ... at Bury St. Edmunds.*

Anon. (1682), *A True and Impartial Relation of the Informations against Three Witches*.

Richard Head (1684), *Life of Mother Shipton*.

Anon. (1686), *A True Account of a Strange and Wonderful Relation of one John Tonken of Pensans in Cornwall*.

Nathaniel Crouch (1688), *Kingdom of Darkness*.

Anon. (1689), *Great News from the West of England*.

Anon. (1690), *The full tryals, examination, and condemnation of four notorious witches at the assizes held at Worcester*.

Richard Baxter (1691), *The Certainty of the Worlds of Spirits*.

Matthew Hale (1693), *A Collection of Modern Relations of Matter of Fact concerning Witches and Witchcraft upon the persons of People*.

Samuel Petto (1693), *A Faithful Narrative of the Wonderful and Extraordinary Fits which Mr Thos. Spatchet ... was under by witchcraft*.

Anon. (1702), *A Full and True Account of the Apprehending and Taking of Mrs. Sarah Moordike, Who is accused for a Witch*.

Anon. (1705), *An account of the Tryals, Examination and Condemnation of Elinor Shaw, and Mary Phillips, &c. by Ralph Davis*.

SECONDARY SOURCES REFERENCED IN THE TEXT

Robin Briggs (2002), *Witches and Neighbours: the social and cultural context of witchcraft*, Blackwell.

Norman Cohn (1974), *Europe's Inner Demons*, Paladin.

E. L'Estrange Ewen (1929), *Witch Hunting and Witch Trials*, The Dial Press.

E. L'Estrange Ewen (1933), *Witchcraft and Demonism*, Heath Cranton.

Malcolm Gaskill (2005), *Witchfinders: A Seventeenth-Century Tragedy*, John Murray.

Marion Gibson (2000), *Witchcraft Cases in Contemporary Writings*, Routledge.

G. L. Kittredge (1929), *Witchcraft in Old and New England*.

Anne Llewellyn Barstow (1994), *Witchcraze*, Harper Collins.

Brian Levack (2006), *The Witch-Hunt in Early Modern Europe*, Pearson.

Alan Macfarlane (1970), *Witchcraft in Tudor and Stuart England*, Routledge.

Wallace Notestein (1911), *History of Witchcraft in England from 1558 to 1718*, The American Historical Association.

Darren Oldridge (2002), *The Witchcraft Reader*, Routledge.

Barabara Rosen (1991), *Witchcraft in England, 1558-1618*, University of Massachusetts.

James Sharpe (1996), *Instruments of Darkness*, Hamish Hamilton.

James Sharpe (2001), *Witchcraft in Early Modern England*, Pearson.

Lawrence Stone, 'Literacy and Education in England, 1640-1900', Past and Present, xlii, 1969.

J. M. Stratton (1978), *Agricultural Records; A.D. 220-1977*, John Baker.

Keith Thomas (1971), *Religion and the Decline of Magic*, Penguin.

Index